Exploring Books with Gifted Children

Exploring Books
with Gifted Children

By
Nancy Polette and Marjorie Hamlin

Libraries Unlimited, Inc.   1980
Littleton, Colorado

LIBRARIES UNLIMITED, INC.
P.O. Box 263
Littleton, Colorado 80160

Library of Congress Cataloging in Publication Data

Polette, Nancy.
    Exploring books with gifted children.

    Includes index.
    1. Gifted children--Books and reading. I. Hamlin,
Marjorie, joint author. II. Title.
Z1039.G55P64   371.95'6   80-23721
ISBN 0-87287-216-5

Libraries Unlimited books are bound with Type II nonwoven material that
meets and exceeds National Association of State Textbook Administrators'
Type II nonwoven material specifications Class A through E.

PREFACE

Over the past ten years, educators in the United States have undergone a radical change in thinking concerning programs in gifted education. Until 1965, the gifted child was considered a rare being and was identified either by exceptionally high IQ scores or by demonstrated superior academic achievement. Fortunately, this narrow view of giftedness has expanded in recent years to include those children who have demonstrated, or who have potential for demonstrating, exceptional leadership capabilities or dramatic, artistic, musical, or literary creativity. This wider view of giftedness has brought about an increased demand for programs that will assist these children in developing their abilities.

Often, the child who is an avid reader is left to his or her own devices in the selection and interpretation of books, and the teacher's energies are spent with those learning disabled children who "can't get it on their own." Few would argue with the need to provide special programs for learning disabled students, but more and more educators are beginning to see the need to provide special programs of another kind for gifted students. The realization has slowly emerged that unless we nurture the minds of our young, gifted children, their giftedness may be lost in a sea of academic regularity.

Exploring Books with Gifted Children is an attempt to answer the cry for help this author has heard in ten years of traveling the United States and Canada to provide teacher training for school districts in methods and materials for bringing fine books into the hands and hearts of children. Throughout the country, school librarians are becoming involved in gifted education and classroom teachers are discovering that the traditional teacher's manual and basal reader were not designed for the gifted child.

The basic premise of this book is that the creativity that is such a powerful part of the gifted child, no matter what the specific area of his or her giftedness, must be brought to the reading experience. The educator who guides these children must *know* literature and be able to help in extending their choices (and their minds) to ever greater literature challenges. This book details the two ways in which this can be done.

First, strategies and techniques are suggested to build excitement and anticipation for the reading experience. The units, the areas of concentration, and the specific titles recommended were chosen to help children become sensitive to the personal and social as well as the technological problems of mankind—to realize that many problems do require creative solutions and that creative thinkers may be the hope of mankind. The questions that are included for many suggested titles *are not* test questions nor even comprehension questions. They are provided as a *guide* for the teacher or librarian in stimulating creative thinking—in helping children to analyze that which they read and to use the insights gained in creating new solutions for problems. The child whose reading horizons are expanded through the enthusiastic suggestions and support of a teacher or librarian who really cares, will have an ever-widening area of experience for problem solving, for decision making, and for bringing his or her creativity not only to the reading experience but to life.

Second, *Exploring Books with Gifted Children* attempts to help educators provide those conditions in which the child can *act upon* what he or she has read. Suggestions are given for creative reproduction, elaboration, rearrangement, and for transformation or going entirely beyond the author's premises to the child's experiences. This book is intended as a beginning. In any program of gifted education there must first be an identified need for going beyond the usual curriculum. However, as the curriculum changes to meet this need, the effects of the change should be felt by every child in the school. For example, as bright underachievers begin to see the genuine excitement of others in exploring books, they, too, may want to peel the words off the page to get to the ideas underneath.

Although we cannot be in tune with all of the mental wanderings and the discoveries that our gifted children are experiencing, we can lure gifted children to meet gifted writers. We can introduce them to those who through the centuries have spoken to the greatness lying within those who are listening. They speak through the pages of literature; we only need to get the books into the children's hands to bring together the lively, creative minds of reader and writer.

And that is what this book is all about.

N.P.

ACKNOWLEDGMENTS

The authors are indebted to the writers and educators who have contributed their work to this book. The basic content of the many unit models included is the work of practicing educators with additions by the authors of divergent questioning models where appropriate. Appreciation for the use of their work is extended to:

Cora Borgmier for the unit on The Books of Lois Lenski; Lloyd A. Hauge for the author unit on Judith Viorst; Beverly Hopkins for the case study, "A Dramatization of *First Crop*"; Virginia Mealy, Editor of *The Bookland Times*; Elizabeth Meyerhoff for the unit, "Character Encounters of the Gifted Kind"; Peggy Rinegar for the unit on Lloyd Alexander; Marigene Sullentrop for the unit, "Basic Needs of Primary Children"; Roger Taylor for "Characteristics of the Gifted and Academically Talented Child"; Mary Vishy for the unit on Zilpha Keatley Snyder; Janice Williams, Cindy Saum, Teddy Hindes, Susan Strinni for their dramatic adaptation of *First Crop*; author Gertrude Bell, and Independence Press Publishers for allowing the reprinting of the adaptation of *First Crop* as a play; authors William O. Steele, Donald J. Sobol, and Lloyd Alexander, for quotations from their letters.

TABLE OF CONTENTS

1   LITERATURE FOR THE GIFTED —
A Gateway to Greatness

Each second we live is a new and unique moment of the universe, a moment that never was before and never will be again. And what do we teach our children in school? We teach them that 2 + 2 are 4 and that Paris is the capital of France. When will we also teach them what they are? We should say to each of them: Do you know what you are? You are a marvel. You are unique. In all the world there is no other child exactly like you. In the millions of years that have passed, there has never been a child like you. And look at your body — what a wonder it is! You may become a Shakespeare, a Michelangelo, a Beethoven. You have the capacity for anything. Yes, you are a marvel. And when you grow up, can you then harm another who is, like you, a marvel? You must cherish one another. You must work — we must all work — to make this world worthy of its children.

— Pablo Casals

Every child is a potential genius. That spark of individuality and original-ity, like a thumbprint or a leaf, has never had its exact duplicate on this earth. Each second of his life is new and irreplaceable. We who have control over the use of those moments, who hold these priceless children captive in our classrooms, have a cherished responsibility to the future. The visionaries, the problem-solvers for the next generation of humankind on this planet, are right now scattered about our nation — tucked away, often obscured in crowded classrooms.

"We must all work to make this world worthy of its children," the great humanitarian and cellist, Pablo Casals tells us. Are we willing to expend the effort to make this world a more secure and beautiful place in which to live? As teachers, librarians, administrators, and parents, we have a continual obligation to posterity through the children who pass through our lives. Are we recognizing those with special academic gifts, those with unusual intellec-tual promise? What are we offering them? More and more of less and less? Busywork to keep their minds focused on their hands? If we continue to feed them pap, meaningless exercises, and ordinary reading materials, these poten-tial solvers of the world's problems may slump into mediocrity.

A small child was asking his mother question after question. She, busy with her own concerns, ignored his pleas or passed them off as inconsequential for the moment. Suddenly he planted himself in front of her, looked up into her face and admonished her, "Mother, you are wasting me!" Let us never be guilty of wasting the genius of young minds bristling to explore and examine the intricacies of human life. The raw material of genius naps through the commonplace and routine; when recognized, cherished and nurtured, it will skyrocket into meaningful arenas where mental skills can be exercised.

We cannot all be like Flynn, in *Mr. God, This Is Anna*, who spent endless hours responding to the mental probings of that brilliant and lively little Anna. His challenges met hers as they continued examining the wonders of existence together. This kind of time is rarely available to most of us.

But we are not helpless; for writers with profound messages and artistic brilliance are focusing their creative talents in books for gifted children. Although we cannot, however dedicated we are and no matter how hard we try, be in tune with *all* of the active mental meanderings and discoveries which our gifted students are experiencing, we can lure gifted children to meet gifted writers. We can introduce them to those who through the centuries have spoken through the pages of literature to the greatness within those who are listening. Lively, creative minds are writing today as well, and we need but to get their works into the children's hands.

And that is what this book is all about.

Do the gifted really need a literature program? Surely, children who started reading early and are already fluent in written language can find their own way. The slow learners take so much time and attention; those who are struggling to achieve need constant supervision. For some, failure is a way of life, and motivation has expired. It seems to many that we should expend our major efforts to reawaken and encourage.

Indeed, we must care for the needs of students at each end of the spectrum; we cannot afford to neglect either extreme. Let us continually look beyond the stereotypes which label by age, or IQ, race, or environment. Gifts often come in surprising wrappings. So we must be continuously aware that the budding Einstein, Schweitzer, or Madame Curie could be lurking behind the freckles in the third row. And let us not lose sight of the desperate need in the world for deeper thinkers, more creative solution seekers.

Yesterday's bright children of technology have taken us outward to the moon — but have we traveled inward far enough to find our own hearts? Yesterday's young intellectuals have built nuclear power plants, a continual threat to life — but have we found the power which reinforces all life? Yesterday's quiz kids have constructed bridges spanning the waters between nations — but have we bridged the chasms which prejudice and bigotry have dug amongst the family of man?

After the Japanese surrender in 1945, General MacArthur, in his historic speech on the battleship Missouri, said,

> Military alliances, balances of power, League of Nations, all in turn have failed. We have had our last chance. The problem basically is theological and involves a spiritual recrudescence and improvement of human character, that will synchronize with our almost matchless advance in science.

How can we help? Do we have time for yet another program in our busy days? Yet can we afford *not* to take the time to share literature which will reach the spirit of a potentially great thinker?

In the little country of Togo, West Africa, an American Peace Corps teacher was having trouble understanding African "time." A young Togolese student was helping her to learn the tribal language of Moba, and she made a fascinating discovery. The word "won" means both yesterday *and* tomorrow. This explained the confusion to her. It symbolized the importance of *today* in African society. "Now" exists, and there also exists everything that is not "now." What matter if it is yesterday or tomorrow? Neither of them is today, so in effect they are really the same thing. What is of primary importance is this present moment. The Peace Corps teacher, a recent college graduate, writes: "The contact I am having with students at this moment is immensely more important than what I was doing before, or what I am going to do later. The fullness of this moment together must be savored and completely enjoyed without imposing confining time limits." And she has over 200 students, none of whom can yet speak the English she is attempting to teach them.

It is no accident that this recent college graduate has been an eager reader all of her life. Fine literature enriched her childhood so that she is able to appreciate fresh concepts and accept new practices, and has the imagination and flexibility to keep growing. Inspired teachers and family recognized the importance of "now" in her growth. They kept feeding her hungry intellect with books which not only permitted her to explore other worlds and ways of being human, but shaped her values and character so that she is now using her gifts for the betterment of mankind.

What do bright young readers today feel about the books they are reading? One wrote that Bette Green's, *"The Summer of My German Soldier* [New York: Dial, 1973] was real and alive to me. How sad that the father had to beat his daughter to take out his own frustrations. The friendship between a Jewish child and a German POW was beautiful. But the strong message of the book got me to thinking of the harsh things we Americans use to threaten, even in play. Why do we project such violence?"

A college student recognized a current need in Betty Baker's *Killer-of-Death* (New York: Harper and Row, 1963). She writes,

> Betty Baker, the author, portrayed the main characters, Apache Indians, as real people, individuals, with honest fears, thoughts and desires. The typical stereotyping is virtually eliminated by taking the Indian out of a mass concept. Not all Indians fall into certain modes of behavior. For me, this concept helped to break through, to a degree, a prejudice I have held since childhood. Growing up near an Indian reservation in Arizona, my feelings about Indians were often negative and definitely circumscribed in a mass concept. Indians were lumped together in my thought. This book has made me check myself more carefully on how I am thinking about people. It brought to life a human struggle against new and sometimes devastating changes that would threaten the familiar, traditional ways of life. Not just Indians, but many groups, have had and are having these same struggles. Individuals need to deal with this concept almost daily. *Killer-of-Death* assures us that we are not alone.

Would that this book had been placed in her hands earlier! Perhaps she will yet help to resolve one of the sticky problems which have plagued mankind since the beginning of time.

A literature program can do much to enrich the lives of gifted children who would otherwise have no stimulus to strive for excellence. Competition in an average classroom can be suffocating ... or demanding to the sleeping intellectual.

A librarian was working with two groups of young people in a Junior Great Books program. One group was from an upper-middle class suburban junior high school. The other group was from the honors program in an all-black inner-city high school. The black ninth graders were readers. The suburban ninth graders were active intellectually and involved with innumerable extra-curricular activities. When discussing the book, *William Tell*, by Schiller, the questioning led to considering whether William Tell had the right to kill the tyrant, Gessler, from ambush. The suburban students agreed unanimously. "The bad guy must be eliminated. He endangers everyone. *Any* way to get rid of him is justified." The inner-city students responded, "No man has the right to take away another's life. Life is too precious. The Bible says 'Thou shalt not kill' ... it does not say 'thou shalt not BE killed'."

The next week, while discussing *Population Bomb* by Paul Erlich, they considered whether the United States should follow the triage system of aiding other countries. (Giving no aid to countries who are already doomed by their population growth and inability to feed themselves.) The suburban students felt this was the only intelligent solution. "Why jeopardize our own future, when these other countries are doomed anyway?" The inner-city students responded "Would we want to live in a world where people could watch their neighbors die of starvation while they themselves had enough to eat?"

There are no easy answers to these questions, but the contrast of approaches interested the librarian. She asked an inner-city fourteen year old where he had received most of his education. (She was aware of the poverty and illiteracy of his background.) His eyes lit up as he quickly answered "Through books! I had a teacher who kept giving me classics to read — and several librarians have been helping me since then." When asked why he continued to read, he thought a moment, then answered, "I hope to become a better man, and if I am a better person perhaps I can help to make a better world." He was an exceptional student, graduating at the top of his high school class before getting a full scholarship to Cornell University. One teacher had seen the spark and put a classic into his hands. She provided the meeting ground; the authors and the child communicated.

Great books do help to shape great minds. Understanding real humanity, nobility of character, and the vitality of love through books of quality, rather than through counterfeit, superficial, remote, and plastic mannikins of the TV world, helps one to live life deeply. Real writers know that love and life are inseparable. Isaac Bashevis Singer, the talented Yiddish storyteller admits, "Kindness, I've discovered, is everything in life." Humor and subtlety, as well as kindness, radiate from his rich tales for children.

Through inspired books, our children have the opportunity to know those who live their lives with skill. A single masterpiece can teach more than a lifetime of mediocre books. A masterpiece plays upon the finest feelings, awakening the unspoken and the unseen, and impels the reader to respond.

A teenage reader who had never been directed to Madeleine L'Engle's *A Wrinkle in Time* (New York: Farrar, Straus & Giroux, 1962) in grade school, upon finishing the book commented,

> Madeleine L'Engle challenges thoughts and behavior I had never thought of challenging — such as time, space and genius. These concepts are intriguing, and broadening in dimension. Everyone can relate to the discouragement, cowardice, and hopelessness which had to be met and mastered. The desire to love one another brought the power to destroy evil. Oh! Such an impact in this book! I have learned to unlimit certain traditional beliefs, behaviors, or activities. The emphasis on challenging wrong and persisting with right is so applicable to me. The 'transforming' experience in this book made me wonder if a misfit might just be a true genius who understands worlds beyond ours.

It made her wonder; all children should have the opportunity to wonder. They are so easily catapulted into a world of pure academia, a world of facts and figures and reason. But without the wonder, the human-ness of compassion, charity, and empathy, where is the link to bind all people together? We must keep on the alert not to bypass those sharp perceivers who will help the world to find answers for living together in harmony. Enlightened authors with lucid minds and fresh styles of communicating ideas will help us.

A six-year old who was reading at ninth grade level entered a private school. He was unable to tie his shoes, skip, or to relate to the other children. His teachers were conscious of his need for growth in awareness of others, but his parents were dedicated to his intellect, feeding him a steady and heavy diet of fact books — astronomy, biology, and paleontology. Will he grow into an adult recluse, or will someone reach him with mythology and folklore to help his humanity keep stride with his academic genius? It will take dedicated teachers to help balance his exploding intellect with an understanding of the needs of his neighbors. A literature program will help his heart to sing along with his mind.

John Dewey has written "All science is already poetry; we pull against the firmly entrenched nostalgic music of myth and magic. When science shall have cooperated with the course of events and made clear and coherent the meaning of the daily detail, then science and emotion will inter-penetrate, practice and imagination will embrace, poetry and religious feeling will be the unforced flowers of life." Our gifted deserve this balance!

There are diversities of gifts, but for the purposes of the chapters that follow, the focus is upon those children whose talents currently lie in the intellectual. How many geniuses have drifted through school unrecognized, or been failures? The list goes beyond Einstein and Edison. It includes Isaac Newton, Leo Tolstoy, Louis Pasteur, Winston Churchill. How many others left their talents lying dormant? The invasion of mediocrity into classrooms produces an incalculable loss; the tyranny of modern thought sets limits on mental powers and obscures potential excellence.

Gifted literature can lure it to the surface. Literature can help us to identify those with a quickened heart and mind. Watch for the child who bursts with sudden laughter at subtle humor or irony when you are reading aloud in a classroom. Watch for the brimming of tears when a deep source of compassion for the human condition is unleashed. Be alert to notice the spark of recognition of an underlying profound truth beneath a simple tale. We can use literature to control, guide, discipline, and to keep joy bubbling in every classroom—and the gifted children will soon become apparent.

Not all children see life alike. Yet the sensitivity of perceptions will often reveal a child's gifts. A good piece of literature is not one-way communication. It is a catalyst to facilitate the reader's own source of unfolding thought. Reading is only incidentally visual or aural; the print has no power in itself. It is the power of the gifted reader's deep personal intuition, knowledge, and understanding, that activates the message.

Our gifted children do not need more and more words bombarding them from all sides. They need deeper, more beautiful, more heart-stretching and mind-stretching ideas to confront. They need to be offered books with a variety of levels of meaning to free their minds for the gymnastics of which they are capable.

Books such as *The Chestry Oak* (New York: Viking, 1948), by Kate Seredy, can reinforce an awareness of the indomitable human spirit. Hope, loyalty, love, and courage surmount all obstacles which war and homelessness create. "Sir Gibbie" [in *The Complete Fairy Tales of George MacDonald* (New York: Schocken Books, 1977)], by the classic fairy-tale master of the nineteenth century, George MacDonald, alerts discerning readers to the imperishable goodness anchored in humanity. *Tuck Everlasting* (New York: Farrar, Straus & Giroux), by Natalie Babbitt, leaves one pondering the meaning of temporal life. Would physical immortality be a blessing? *Hakon of Rogen's Saga* (Boston: Houghton Mifflin, 1963), by Eric Haugaard, can impel a reader to contemplate the meaning of freedom, to recognize courage and resourcefulness, and to feel the subtle power of a timeless saga. Holling's brilliant books help to expand literary awareness for children who are committed only to facts. The facts are there aplenty—but along with the sweep of history, geography, biology, oceanography, ecology, and anthropology, the thread of a tale grows and blooms into realistic suspense.

There are innumerable books to pump the bloodstreams of our talented children with feeling. And how many biographies inspire the reader to set his goals high? More than can be tallied here. By the largeness of one's dreams does one truly live! Books initiate and enhance those dreams. They tell us that nothing is impossible, that love heals, that different is not bad.

Humanity is inching along a tightrope. Who are we sending out into the world to lead us across the chasm of mindless consumption and greed, pollution and proliferation of mediocrity, pornography and distrust of one's fellow man? The problems become increasingly complex as we hang in the balance. There do not appear to be instantaneous solutions in our generation. Will the children of tomorrow have the vision, the moral stamina, the dedication and conviction to pursue achievable solutions? Are we helping the children in our classrooms and in our homes to develop the clearest thinking, the most perceptive minds, the most creative discernment to cut through the entangled mess which less inspired thought has permitted to occur?

We need not feel inadequate to the task, for the gifted writers of yesterday and today still proclaim eternal truths. Our challenge is but to direct wisely.

2 WELCOME, GIFTED TEACHER!

"The whole art of teaching is only the art of awakening
the natural curiosity of young minds for the purpose of
satisfying them afterwards."

— Anatole France

Introduction

During the seventies many school districts throughout the United States concluded that the art of teaching as defined by Anatole France could not be fully explored with gifted children as long as the status quo in school organization and instruction was maintained. Intellectually gifted children *do* differ from others in learning ability. Their learning rate and rate of retention are much greater than those of other children and they tend to think much more deeply about what they learn. It is extremely difficult, if not impossible, to provide for the needs of these children within the regular school curriculum. Thus, educators have turned to alternative programs and strategies designed to meet the demands of gifted learners.

Among these new structures are entire schools devoted exclusively to the needs of gifted children; gifted classes within one school; groups of gifted children together for the major part of a school day, but assigned to a regular class as well; students removed from their regular classrooms on a part-time basis to work with a special teacher; and students grouped by ability to meet before or after the regular school day. The selection of teachers for any of these programs is sometimes an involved screening process and at other times, a matter of "who's available when?" In establishing a literature program for gifted students, the school librarian is often the prime candidate to serve as "gifted teacher," and this choice is often an excellent one.

Aidan Chambers, writing in the December 1975 *Horn Book*, defines the basic problem in establishing a literature program of any kind in the elementary school:

Despite the lip-service paid to the unique importance of
literacy, most people involved in education, including a great many
teachers, do not actually believe in the importance of literature.
Most of them — including, sadly, many English specialists — are not
in love with literature, do not read for their own pleasure, and are
ignorant of children's books and reading interests. Meanwhile, ever
more investigations confirm again and again that nonreading
children are made by non-reading adults.

The good school library provides a far less restrictive environment than does the classroom library. Using a rich and diverse collection of materials the child can, if given proper guidance, discover and interact with the great minds of the past and present who have left their legacy to us through the pages of a book, and ultimately, enrich his or her own life and the lives of others.

It matters not whether the child's guide into the world of literature is the creative teacher or school librarian. What is important is that the teacher of the gifted enjoy interacting with these students, respecting their ideas and learning from them as well as teaching them. The gifted teacher must have enormous self-confidence which incorporates risk-taking and the ability to admit mistakes and to learn from them.

In the literature program specifically, the teacher must *know*, as differentiated from "knowing about," books and have a genuine enthusiasm for tackling new literary adventures with eager young minds. *Enthusiasm*, not knowledge per se, is the key. Teachers and pupils can explore together unfamiliar authors or new avenues of thought if the exploration is looked upon as a glorious adventure to be tackled together and if the teacher assumes the role of guide rather than sage.

This is not to infer that the newly assigned teacher of gifted students does not need preparation for this highly demanding, but rewarding task. In addition to knowing the children as individuals and knowing and loving children's literature, the teacher must be aware of those characteristics which set the gifted, or academically talented child apart from his or her peers, and be able to utilize those teaching strategies which lie primarily in the domain of gifted education.

First: it is important to examine the characteristics of the gifted, academically talented child. Roger Taylor, consultant on gifted education for Educational Consulting Associates, has compiled the following list of characteristics for his nationally known workshops on the gifted and talented [from *The Gifted and the Talented* (ECA, n.d.)]:

CHARACTERISTICS OF THE GIFTED CHILD

I.   Grasps and retains knowledge

    1.   comprehends meanings

    2.   responds quickly and accurately

    3.   questions critically

    4.   transfers learnings to new situations

II.   Conveys ideas effectively

    1.   follows logical sequence and order

    2.   has extensive vocabulary and uses it appropriately

    3.   is selective

    4.   is critical

    5.   is fluent

III.   Shows skill in abstract thinking
   1.   makes generalizations
   2.   senses cause and effect
   3.   recognizes relationships
   4.   can understand and apply rules
   5.   foresees new possibilities

IV.   Uses wide variety of resources
   1.   is versatile
   2.   is self-reliant when meeting problems
   3.   is ingenious in knowing when, where, and how to seek help

V.   Has creative and inventive power
   1.   shows curiosity and originality
   2.   is alert to possibilities
   3.   enjoys experimentation
   4.   uses trial and error method
   5.   finds ways to extend his ideas

VI.   Exhibits power to work independently
   1.   shows ability to plan
   2.   shows ability to organize
   3.   shows ability to execute
   4.   shows ability to judge

VII.   Assumes and discharges responsibility
   1.   shows perseverance
   2.   shows desire to forge ahead
   3.   shows will to succeed

VIII.   Adjusts easily to new situations
   1.   understands and accepts reasons for change
   2.   anticipates outcomes
   3.   maintains optimistic attitude toward new adventures
   4.   is challenged by new ideas

IX.   Has physical competence
1.   is alert
2.   is active
3.   is energetic
4.   is free of nervous tension
5.   is generally healthy

X.   Appreciates social values
1.   senses right and wrong
2.   respects the rights of others
3.   is willing to share
4.   contributes constructively to group activities
5.   maintains spurts of growth and changes in attitudes and behavior
6.   is conscientious and truthful

XI.   Establishes favorable relationships
1.   has self-respect
2.   has permanence of mood
3.   has sense of humor
4.   is friendly, helpful and cooperative

While the intellectually gifted child can be, and often is academically talented, it does not always follow that this is true. Note in the list of "Characteristics of the Academically Talented Student" below that each of these characteristics lies well within the accepted school definition of *conformity*, a definition which stresses the importance of being in step with society to achieving the ultimate goal of human efficiency. On any continuum conformity and creativity would occupy opposite poles. Thus, the creative, gifted individual can only develop his or her gifts to the fullest by *not* conforming, by creating a totally new approach, method, or idea foreign to society at large. Many academically talented pupils, on the other hand, would be uncomfortable in the type of program necessary for the intellectually gifted. Those students who normally do quite well on achievements are most comfortable working in the Cognitive Domain, with well-structured, sequential instruction and with few surprises in the curriculum or in the approach to the curriculum. These students learned the system well in the first grade and would, in many cases, be frustrated with unfamiliar structures or approaches to learning.

CHARACTERISTICS OF ACADEMICALLY
TALENTED STUDENTS

1. Superior physique as demonstrated by above-average height, weight, and coordination endurance, and general health

2. Longer attention span

3. Learns rapidly, easily, and with less repetition

4. Learns to read sooner and continues to read at a consistently more advanced level

5. More mature in the ability to express himself or herself through the various communicative skills

6. Reaches higher levels of attentiveness to the environment

7. Asks more questions and really wants to know the causes and reasons for things

8. Likes to study some subjects that are difficult because he or she enjoys the learning

9. Spends time beyond the ordinary assignments or schedule on things that are of interest to him or her

10. Knows about many things of which other children are unaware

11. Is able to adapt learning to various situations somewhat unrelated in orientation

12. Reasons out more problems since he or she recognizes relationships and comprehends meanings

13. Analyzes quickly mechanical problems, puzzles, and trick questions

14. Evaluates facts and arguments critically

Most truly gifted children ARE aware of their giftedness. The gifted achiever has decided to play the school game, to subdue his or her creativity in the school setting and to disguise boredom. The gifted underachiever is rarely identified as gifted by the classroom teacher. This child, through his or her choice not to conform in any way, is often the problem child of the class. These are the children who particularly need a large portion of their work in the Affective Domain, the area in which a literature program excells. When gifted writers reach out to touch hearts and minds, cognitive and affective learning can not help but be integrated. The imparting of knowledge gives way to opportunities for students to assess how characters relate to each other and to society and to the knowledge that they as individuals have choices to make in all types of relationships. Through appropriate role models provided by its young protagonists, literature can free students to become self-aware and self-accepting, to share strengths, weaknesses, feelings, needs, and values, and to learn that all of us have the right to fail but should become stronger by using our failures as starting points for building anew.

Whether gifted students have decided to accept or buck the traditional educational system, the initial task of the teacher is to break the attitudes toward learning that many of the children have acquired and to gain the trust and confidence of these children so that they will allow themselves to be led to the mind-stretching experiences which await those willing to peel the words off a page to get to the IDEAS underneath.

Teachers of the gifted must realize that these children are, first of all, CHILDREN, who have the same desire as other children to be accepted by their peers. Many of these children have gained fluent reading skills as a means of escape from drill, repetition, and a lack of challenging experiences in the traditional classroom. Their escape reading has for the most part been self-directed and self-selected, which often results in perspectives that need to be stretched and imaginations that must be allowed to soar. As adults they will remain similarly advanced beyond the average and will assume distinctive social roles as leaders in the reconstruction and advancement of whatever lines of activity they engage in. In *Reading Guidance in a Media Age* (Scarecrow, 1975) we wrote that, "We could liken the consciousness of each child to a giant jigsaw puzzle, with pieces missing here and there. Each literary experience can perhaps fit a missing piece of understanding into the whole, until a world view is achieved which is solid and beautiful."

The challenge is great; for before one can touch the consciousness of these children both their respect and their trust must be gained. By the time they have reached the middle grades many have had their accomplishments minimized by parents, teachers, and peers. Occasionally, in offering unique responses so typical of the gifted, many of these students have at best been ignored and at worst ridiculed. Conversely, the teacher must be aware that in any given group of gifted students, some will have a tendency to overlook their own limitations and often to be less than understanding when dealing with slower-learning pupils. Since as adults these students will be in contact more often than not with minds less gifted than their own, it is essential that life adjustment skills be an integral part of any program designed for them.

Basic Guidelines for Working with Gifted Children

1. Understand that these children will not always want to conform to school routines and social situations and are easily bored. Children must be helped to understand that conformity at times is a price paid for being a member of a civilized society, but at the same time, the teacher must allow for deviation from routine when necessary and must vary the style of teaching and methods of presentation.

2. There are many times when the gifted child will be alone in an opinion or belief. Encourage the child to support or deny the concepts held through the use of a wide variety of materials. At the same time, work patiently with the child in helping him or her cope with differing opinions.

3.   Gifted children often want to explore areas that society says are not within normal expectations because of age or because of sex. Such exploration should not be discouraged if resources are available or can be found.

4.   Encourage creative thought. The great minds of the ages are those that would not accept the idea that a thing could not be done. Science fiction of fifty years ago is science fact today. Do not dismiss an idea simply because it does not seem possible given the limits of our present knowledge.

5.   Allow these children, within the limits of safety, to experience the consequences of their behavior, both acceptable and unacceptable behavior. Help children to examine consequences *before* behavior choices are made.

6.   Let children test their ideas without threat of evaluation. Assign grades only when absolutely necessary. Parent/child/teacher conferences are far more valuable than a letter grade.

7.   Encourage the child to *read, read, read*! As author Scott Corbett says, "Reading gives one an entire second life and two lives are certainly better than one."

Summary

The structure of programs for gifted students varies from total "pull-out" programs in which the gifted are completely isolated to "mainstream" programs in which the teacher attempts to provide for these children within the regular classroom. There are many variations between these two extremes.

The major requirements of the teacher of the gifted in a literature program include knowledge, creativity, a love of books and of reading, a respect for children and their ideas, and a high risk-taking potential. The teacher must know both the positive characteristics and the prevailing negative attitudes of the students with whom he or she will work, being able to capitalize on the positive and deal effectively with the negative. Finally, the teacher must know precisely the teaching strategies that are more suited to gifted students than to the average or below average student.

The principal guideline of gifted education simply stated is, "If all children can do it, it *isn't* gifted education."

3 PROGRAM MODELS AND MATERIALS

As was noted in the listing of characteristics of the gifted child (page 18), these children need the challenges of leadership roles, group interaction, and the individual pursuit of knowledge. Therefore, a program model for the study and enjoyment of literature should provide opportunity for each of these learning styles to be utilized. Literature program models for individual schools will be based on the structure of the gifted program itself. In any program where gifted students are together all day, considerably more experimenting can be done to perfect a model which will fully meet student needs. In pull-out programs, or after-school programs where time is limited, the program model will need to be more highly structured to make the best use of every minute available.

The two models presented in this chapter can be adapted to individual programs. The models themselves provide both for group interaction and independent study. Model I outlines a plan for the Literature Learning Center where the student may work independently to acquire literature skills and understanding. The structured learning center approach is often used in programs where the gifted are mainstreamed in the regular classroom. However, many gifted students do not work well in a highly structured program unless they have a specific interest in the topic or the author being studied. As much freedom of choice as possible should be allowed these students in the materials used and the activities pursued. Model II allows for considerable group interaction and suggests a topic or thematic approach to literature study. Under this model, a modified group plan may be desirable for primary students. Groups may meet only once a week to discuss books which have been read. For variety, the teacher may introduce author units sharing the books of one author with the entire gifted class and directing follow-up activities.

Model I: Literature Learning Centers

The Literature Learning Center is a place in either the classroom or library where a student has available equipment and materials to pursue a particular topic independently. The materials available can include teacher- and student-produced materials and commercial materials. Normally, a variety of activities using both print and nonprint materials is available. Among these might be:

1. Programmed materials and/or activity booklets on a variety of topics in children's literature
2. Practice exercises in creative writing
3. Recordings and sound filmstrips of children's books

4.   Manipulative materials

5.   Literature games

6.   Tape directed activities

Whatever the specific activity, it should allow the student to acquire literature skills and understanding independently.

Because gifted children often do work well independently, and, indeed, often prefer independent study to group interaction, these children can be very successful in utilizing learning centers fully. Success, however, presupposes that the student is given specific guidelines. Teacher guidance *is* necessary, particularly in the field of literature where interchange of ideas assists the child in gaining full comprehension of an author's work. Learning center activities should be carefully monitored. Pupils working independently should be assigned to a teacher who will have an initial conference with the student to determine goals and activities and to make sure that all necessary materials are available to allow the student to meet the stated goals and to carry out the activities.

PROCEDURE

Learning centers should allow for pupil choices but at the same time should require that a specific amount of material be covered within a stated time span. Thus, the pupil and teacher know what is expected and the approximate amount of time the study should take. The procedure might operate as follows:

1.   The student reports to the teacher upon entering the center or beginning the independent study work.

2.   Attendance is checked; guidance is given; procedural problems are solved through teacher-pupil conference.

3.   A written unit guide is given the student containing the content areas of the unit to be studied and all other parts of the program including a listing and location of books and audiovisual materials to be used.

4.   The pupil decides which content area he will begin and the order in which subsequent portions of the overall assignment will be done. When the total assignment is completed (this may be a period of a week or longer) the student completes a schedule card indicating that all components of the study are completed.

5.   The pupil is required to complete one entire unit study before being free to go on to another.

6.   A daily record is kept in a student folder of what has been accomplished, work unfinished, and reactions to the day's work. At the end of each day this record is filed with any completed written material in the student's folder.

EVALUATION OF LEARNING CENTER PROGRESS

Evaluation of completed work is usually done by the base teacher through weekly pupil-teacher conferences. The record of work done is studied and the work itself is evaluated 1) to check understanding, progress, and areas needing special attention or possible concentration of effort, and 2) to recognize effort and achievement.

For primary-aged children learning center tasks should be of short duration and a variety of tasks should be available for pupil choice.

COMMERCIAL MATERIALS AVAILABLE FOR USE BY GIFTED STUDENTS IN THE LITERATURE LEARNING CENTER

Literature for Children. Pied Piper Productions. P.O. Box 4, Glendale, CA 92109.

Sixteen sound filmstrips covering basic types of children's literature and including visual booktalks and instructions on locating the literature in the library. A student activity sheet follows the viewing of each filmstrip.

Newbery Literature Activities Packs. Miller-Brody Productions. 342 Madison Ave., New York, NY 10017.

Twelve literature packages based on thematic units which provide a wide range of activities to follow the reading of Newbery Award or Newbery Honor books. Activities, which include word scrambles, riddles, puzzles, sketching, rhyming, inventing, writing and research projects are designed to engage the child creatively in gaining literature skills and understanding. Among packages available are "Worlds of Adventure," "Other Times, Other Places," "The Lure of Nature," "Growing with America," "A Variety of Families," "Unforgettable Characters," and others.

Literature Activity Booklets for Student Use. Book Lures, Inc. P.O. Box 9450, O'Fallon, MO 63366.

A variety of student activity books designed to introduce children to meaningful and exciting literature experiences. Booklets available include "Activities with Folktales and Fairy Tales" (grades 3-7), "The Book Report Book for Primary Grades" (grades K-3), "Book Encounters of the Best Kind" (grades 4-8), "Pick a Pattern for Creative Writing" (grades K-6), "Building Research Skills with Folk Music" (book and tape, grades 4-8), "Dear Reader: Letters to Young Readers from Favorite Authors."

Model II: Gifted Group Program for Literature Study

ADVANTAGES

1. Easily administered

2. Provides for student selection of material read

3. Promotes leadership skills, self reliance, and group interaction

4. Allows teacher time to observe and give student assistance when needed

5. Requires active participation of all students in learning process

PROCEDURE

I

The class is divided into literature study groups of four to seven students per group. If a group reaches eight pupils it should be divided into two groups. Groups are formed according to the topic chosen by each student. If one or two students select a topic area different from those of their classmates they should explore the theme independently in the Literature Learning Center area.

Each group should elect a chairman and secretary. Guidelines for these jobs are decided upon early in the school year including the qualities needed in each. Chairing a study group should be looked upon both as a responsibility and a privilege.

Each group is provided with the books for the topic unit. Multiple (paperback) copies of the books should be available to allow for freedom of choice of group members in selecting their personal reading. Reading should not be confined to literature time, but if students want to take books home this should be allowed. Students should be encouraged to read as many books in the unit as they wish. They should be required, however, to read a minimum of two books during the unit study time. A theme unit should be concluded within three weeks.

II

A. Following the reading of the first book selected, each student should write a brief summary of the book. Summarizing improves the ability to separate main ideas from details, the significant from the less significant, and to identify basic story elements.

B. Each student should compose six questions for the book he has read. It may be necessary initially to provide students with a list of divergent questions to be completed. For example:

1. List all of the events you can think of that lead directly to the climax of the story.

2. Suppose the main character had taken a different action at a crucial point in the story. How would the story be changed? Explain.

3. The main character in your story has been given the power to _____. How would he or she use this power?

4. How would the main character's problem look to a _____?
   your choice

5. How would you feel if *you* were the main character of this story?

6. How is this book like _____?
   name another title

   How is it different?

Primary-aged students may develop two or three questions for the book which has been read. These need not be divergent questions. Primary-aged students will omit listing examples of literary style as required in the next item.

C. Each student should list examples of literary style found in the reading. If possible, one example of each should be listed: similes, metaphors, puns, personification, hyperbole, symbolism and examples of irony, satire, parody and particularly descriptive language. (All elements will not, often, be found in a single book.) Students should list those they do find.

III

A. Silent reading should be allowed during the first week. The first book should be read and questions completed by that time. Group meetings are held the last half of the period. The teacher moves from group to group. The chairman conducts the meetings. Each group need not meet every day. Meetings are delayed until everyone has read at least one book. Following several days' discussion, reading time should then be allowed for additional books before new discussions take place.

B. Group discussions should begin with each student reading his or her summary. The group decides which story summary is most successful and why.

C. The chairman then asks members of the group to read and answer one or more of the questions composed. Comment is invited from any other member of the group who has read the book.

D. Each member presents one or more examples of literary style he or she has found. Examples may be compared.

E. The secretary collects the papers, checks them off against the name in a notebook making sure that each paper has a summary, questions, and examples of literary style.

F. Papers are given to the teacher and are handled as written composition. Standards of handwriting, spelling, grammar, sentence structure and language usage are maintained. Errors are noted and used as the basis for individual or group help.

G. Any student who is disruptive in the group is removed from the group. The student is still responsible for the assignment but not allowed to attend group meetings for a specified time.

H. Occasionally group meetings are devoted to oral reading in which members take turns interpreting passages which are favorites.

I. When new theme units are begun the composition of groups will change. It is desirable that the jobs of chairman and secretary be rotated so that each child has an opportunity to serve in this capacity.

Conclusion

Whether the model selected for gifted instruction is a group or individualized model or a variation of either, certain basic tenets should apply. In working with gifted students much of the study material should be in the Affective Domain. In the material which follows, when specific authors are studied, authors were selected whose ability to evoke genuine reader response is unquestioned. At least one-half of the literature program should be devoted to allowing students to discover, to savor, and to digest numerous literary morsels. Reading in itself implies individualization in which drill and repetition have no part. If the child lacks particular reading skills these can be taught, *but not at reading time.* This is the time to allow authors and children to communicate with each other, and to discuss (not question) with students the insights, the joys, and the disappointments this experience has brought.

The numerous models which follow are designed to assist the teacher in sharing to the fullest the works of gifted authors and to use the literature and the student's understanding of it as a spring to release the child's own creative talents in reading and writing.

4 APPROACHES TO INSTRUCTION

Once the decision has been made as to whether the model for instruction of the gifted shall be individualized learning, group interaction or a combination of the two, the actual approach to instruction must be carefully considered. It was stated earlier that much of the activity should be in the Affective Domain, requiring the student not only to receive and respond to ideas and concepts but to attach value to them, to bring together different values, to resolve conflicts among values, and to develop his or her own value system. With elementary students, the exploration of literature must involve basic cognitive skills in order to lead to that highest level of the Cognitive Domain which IS evaluation. Fortunately, little time need be spent with these children in repetitious drill, in phonics, or in word attack skills, but considerable time must be spent in the areas of analysis, synthesis and evaluation—areas in which the interests of gifted children are most easily captured and in which assistance and training is needed.

The sequential development of language moves from EXPERIENCE, to LISTENING, ORAL EXPRESSION, READING, and WRITTEN EXPRESSION. In all of these areas the learner must first REMEMBER what has been seen or heard, come to UNDERSTAND it, and then APPLY the knowledge or skill. Repeated research indicates that a child cannot easily read what has not been heard and that a minimum of seventeen exposures to a word is necessary before the child can internalize the word in order to read it and write it.

The gifted child often begins school with quite advanced reading skills. While this child has certainly been able to internalize language patterns more rapidly than his or her peers, an additional, very essential factor has been identified among the great majority of these precocious readers. These children were fortunate enough to spend their early childhood surrounded by books. Their parents are readers in the full sense of the word and books are a cherished and valued part of family life. In being read to from the cradle these children were given the opportunity to internalize written language patterns long before their less fortunate peers, and, because the sharing of books in the home was a pleasurable experience, both the right and left sides of the child's brain were operating in the learning experience to enhance the number of language skills acquired.

Contrast this with the experiences of many children in the primary grades. Repetitious drill in recognizing written symbols for oral sounds is a left brain activity. When stress occurs as it often does when the child struggles to decode the squiggles on a page, the right brain (the feeling or emotional part of the mind) shuts down in protest and the child is left to learn with only one-half of his mental ability. Thus many children never become readers.

Many gifted children read in spite of the boredom of drills and exercises. In fact, reading often becomes an escape from the tedium of education. Yet, these children who are so often ignored because they "can get it without help" often do need help to extend reading horizons beyond the level on which they can travel alone. Selectivity, then, is one major goal of any literature program for gifted children. It can only be achieved when the child gains a full knowledge of literature skills and understanding as differentiated from basic reading skills.

These skills include an understanding of plot construction, development of setting, characterization, theme and mood; recognizing point of view; and appreciating literary style and language. While all of these skills can be taught (but often are not) in the normal classroom, it is the *level* of the material used and the *approach* taken which set the gifted literature program apart. Gifted students are not necessarily required to read *more* than normal students, but their approach to the literature must be not from lower to higher levels of cognitive thinking; rather, they must begin at the higher levels where the Cognitive and Affective Domains blend.

To understand this approach, a review of the categories of thinking processes is necessary.

Stating Behavioral Objectives for Classroom Instruction

The following are the major categories in the Cognitive Domain as delimited in *Taxonomy of Educational Objectives: The Classification of Educational Goals: Handbook 1: Cognitive Domain*, edited by B. S. Bloom, et al. (©1956 by Longman Inc.). They are reprinted here with permission of Longman.

Descriptions of the Major Categories in the Cognitive Domain

---

1. KNOWLEDGE. Knowledge is defined as the remembering of previously learned material. This may involve the recall of a wide range of material, from specific facts to complete theories, but all that is required is the bringing to mind of the appropriate information. Knowledge represents the lowest level of learning outcomes in the cognitive domain.

---

2. COMPREHENSION. Comprehension is defined as the ability to grasp the meaning of material. This may be shown by translating material from one form to another (words to numbers), by interpreting material (explaining or summarizing), and by estimating future trends (predicting consequences or effects). These learning outcomes go one step beyond the simple remembering of material, and represent the lowest level of understanding.

---

3. APPLICATION. Application refers to the ability to use learned material in new and concrete situations. This may include the application of such things as rules, methods, concepts, principles, laws, and theories. Learning outcomes in this area require a higher level of understanding than those under comprehension.

---

4. ANALYSIS. Analysis refers to the ability to break down material into its component parts so that its organizational structure may be understood. This may

include the identification of the parts, analysis of the relationships between parts, and recognition of the organizational principles involved. Learning outcomes here represent a higher intellectual level than comprehension and application because they require an understanding of both the content and the structural form of the material.

5.   SYNTHESIS. Synthesis refers to the ability to put parts together to form a new whole. This may involve the production of a unique communication (theme or speech), a plan of operations (research proposal) or set of abstract relations (scheme for classifying information). Learning outcomes in this area stress creative behaviors with major emphasis on the formulation of new patterns or structures.

6.   EVALUATION. Evaluation is concerned with the ability to judge the value of material (statement, novel, poem, research report) for a given purpose. The judgments are to be based on definite criteria. These may be internal (organization) or external criteria (relevant to the purpose) and the student may determine the criteria or be given them. Learning outcomes in this area are highest in the cognitive hierarchy because they contain elements of all of the other categories, plus conscious value judgments based on clearly defined criteria.

Examples of General Instructional Objectives and Behavioral Terms for the Cognitive Domain of the Taxonomy

	Illustrative General Instructional Objectives	Illustrative Behavioral Terms Stating Specific Learning Outcomes
K N O W L E D G E	Knows common terms Knows specific facts Knows methods and procedures Knows basic concepts Knows principles	Defines, describes, identifies, labels, lists, matches, names, outlines, reproduces, selects, states.

C
O
M
P
R
E
H
E
N
S
I
O
N
	Understands facts and principles
	Interprets verbal material
	Interprets charts and graphs
	Translates verbal material to
	    mathematical formulas
	Estimates future consequences
	    implied in data
	Justifies methods and procedures
		Converts, defends, distinguishes, estimates, explains, extends, generalizes, gives examples, infers, paraphrases, predicts, rewrites, summarizes

A P P L I C A T I O N	Applies concepts and principles to new situations Applies laws and theories to practical situations Solves mathematical problems Constructs charts and graphs Demonstrates correct usage of a method or procedure	Changes, computes, demonstrates, discovers, manipulates, modifies, operates, predicts, prepares, produces, relates, shows, solves, uses.
A N A L Y S I S	Recognizes unstated assumptions Recognizes logical fallacies in reasoning Distinguishes between facts and inferences Evaluates the relevancy of data Analyzes the organizational structure of a work (art, music, writing)	Breaks down, diagrams, differentiates, discriminates, distinguishes, identifies, illustrates, infers, outlines, points out, relates, selects, separates, subdivides.
S Y N T H E S I S	Writes a well organized theme Gives a well organized speech Writes a creative short story (or poem, or music) Proposes a plan for an experiment Integrates learning from different areas into a plan for solving a problem Formulates a new scheme for classifying objects (or events, or ideas)	Categorizes, combines, compiles, composes, creates, devises, designs, explains, generates, modifies, organizes, plans, rearranges, reconstructs, relates, reorganizes, revises, rewrites, summarizes, tells, writes.
E V A L U A T I O N	Judges the logical consistency of written material Judges the adequacy with which conclusions are supported by data Judges the value of a work (art, music, writing) by use of internal criteria Judges the value of a work (art, music, writing) by use of external standards of excellence	Appraises, compares, concludes, contrasts, criticizes, describes, discriminates, explains, justifies, interprets, relates, summarizes, supports.

   In the normal classroom, 70% of instruction is geared to areas one, two, and three; 30% of instruction is geared to areas four, five, and six. In working with gifted students the reverse must be true. Seventy percent of the time must be spent with the higher thinking processes of analysis, synthesis and evaluation. The procedure *begins* with EVALUATION and *progresses* to SYNTHESIS AND ANALYSIS. Obviously these higher thinking processes cannot be called into play unless the student remembers and understands, and can apply particular knowledge, precisely the three areas that gifted students do get on their own.

   The application of a knowledge of these cognitive levels is illustrated in the two questioning models below. The first is based on *Little Red Riding Hood*, and the second on Lloyd Alexander's *The Truthful Harp* (New York: Holt, Rinehart & Winston, 1967).

Example One

Question Model for *Little Red Riding Hood*

Evaluation — Authors develop their characters by showing what the character does and says and by what others say or think about the character or how other characters act toward the character. How is the character of Red Riding Hood developed? Is it a well developed characterization? Why or why not?

Synthesis — Suppose the hunter had arrived at the cottage before Red Riding Hood? How would the story change?

Analysis — When were you first aware that Red Riding Hood might not heed her mother's advice and stop along the way? Does the author imply this at any point before the actual event?

Application — Briefly dramatize the scene from the story when Red Riding Hood meets the wolf in the forest.

Comprehension — Why did Red Riding Hood's mother send a basket of food to the Grandmother?

Knowledge — Name the characters in the story.

Example Two

Question Model for Lloyd Alexander's *The Truthful Harp*

Evaluation — Compare the plot structure of *The Truthful Harp* with the plot structure of Lloyd Alexander's *Coll and His White Pig*. Which is the more complex plot? Why?

Synthesis—Write a sequel to *The Truthful Harp* explaining what happens when Fflewddur returns to his kingdom. Will the harp be important to him in ruling his kingdom? In what way?

Analysis—When the Chief Bard told Fflewddur "May you ever be as grateful as you are right now," what do you think he meant?

Application—Develop a storyboard for a roll movie of *The Truthful Harp*. Illustrate each segment of your storyboard and show the movie to the class.

Comprehension—Briefly retell the story in your own words.

Knowledge—List all of the things Fflewddur did to prepare for his first appearance before the Chief Bard.

A Critical Reading Unit

The following unit on propaganda techniques in picture books emphasizes the analysis, synthesis, and evaluation of literature. The unit introduces students to the wide variety of propaganda techniques and then requires an analysis of literature to find these same techniques. A culminating activity requires the student to write an original story to promote a particular cause in which the student believes, incorporating as many of the propaganda techniques as possible. (From *Approaches to Literature with Gifted Children*, Book Lures, Inc., 1979 with permission.)

Propaganda Techniques

A Critical Reading Unit for Gifted Students (Gr 4-6)

Subject Area: Literature

Objectives:
1. Students will recognize the techniques, types of reasoning and choice of words used by individuals or groups to promote special interests or particular ideologies and understand that writing for such purposes is known as propaganda.
2. Students will be able to analyze children's books for devices, wording and faulty types of reasoning often used by propagandists.
3. The students will be able to recognize and carry out the six levels of cognitive thinking in Bloom's taxonomy.

Introduction:
In studying children's literature for the purpose of identifying propaganda techniques it is important to differentiate the author who uses these techniques to promote a personal viewpoint and the author who is writing to promote the purposes of an organized group. Careful attention should be paid to the jacket blurb, the publisher of the book (is it a recognized children's publisher with no

particular ax to grind, or an organization whose purpose is to promote one viewpoint), and any reviews of the book which can be located. Students may want to write directly to the author and inquire about his or her purpose in writing the book or story. If the book is not a work published by an organized group, then students must walk the fine line between deciding whether the book is pure propaganda or whether the author, in promoting a personal viewpoint has employed *some* propaganda techniques.

Activities:

1. Given a collection of children's books (selected by the teacher) students will analyze the contents for:
   (a) propaganda based on faulty types of reasoning
   (b) typically used propaganda devices
   (c) propaganda based on choice of words
   (d) trick selection of alleged facts

2. Using the "Propaganda Road" scoring sheet included in this unit on page 40, the student will assign scores or numerical value to each element of propaganda discovered. Scores will be totalled for each book and compared. Students will determine which of the selections are HIGH on the propaganda weight score and which authors have used only a few propaganda devices to make a point.

3. When the initial collection of books has been analyzed, students should be allowed ample browsing time to locate additional titles for analysis.

4. Note: Often an author may use satire or irony to make a particular point. Students should be cautioned to analyze whether or not an author really means exactly what his or her words say, or whether the author is using satire or irony to make a point (which can be in itself a propaganda technique).

To Begin:

Before students can analyze any piece of writing for propaganda techniques the student must have a clear definition of propaganda and an understanding of the techniques that are used.

True propaganda is nearly always promoted by ORGANIZED groups which may range from political or social organizations to manufacturers and merchants. The purpose of propaganda is to sway the thinking of the public toward a certain cause, ideology, or product. Whether used to promote a product or a cause, the appeal is to the emotions and can be done both verbally and visually. The most obvious use of propaganda is in advertising. Students who are aware of the techniques used by advertisers will be able to analyze these techniques not only in regard to a particular product, but in determining any author's point of view.

Activity One:

Students will examine advertisements in newspapers and magazines with a critical eye as to language and veracity of statements and bring to class advertisements or articles which, in their opinion, are good examples of propaganda. The following are good examples:

Absolutely free! No obligation whatsoever!
For the lift of a lifetime!

Guaranteed sale of your mobile home ... if we don't sell it,
 we'll but it!
Super Sale
Save on Utility Bills
The Best Tire Deals to Fit Your Wheels
Introducing the Inflation Fighter
First Time Offer

Activity Two:
 Analyzing methods used by propagandists in advertisements.

 1.   **Analogy:** This car is a one owner car so it has to be better than any other used car you could buy.

 2.   **Superstition:** During the downtown renewal project you don't have to walk under any ladders to find the bargains in our store.

 3.   **Faulty Arguments:** Buy now while interest rates are low.

 4.   **Generalizations:** Everyone is hurrying to XYZ car dealers to get in on the bargains.

 5.   **Appeal to Ignorance:** Tried other Doctors? Now try Doctor X. I can cure heart trouble, cancer, headaches, and nervous conditions through adjustment of the spine which controls all body functions.

 6.   **Ego Trip:** It costs a little more, but YOU'RE worth it!

 7.   **Argument in a Circle:** Our computer dating service has matched hundreds of happy couples many of whom are now happily married, so you, too, should join up now.

 8.   **Emotional Appeal:** Prowlers are on the loose in our town. Keep YOUR family safe, call ABC burglar alarms today.

 9.   **Faulty Use of Statistics:** Mary B. lost 30 pounds in 24 days; or our weight loss graduates lose more weight than graduates of any other program.

 10.   **Vagueness:** Everyone is talking about the new Edsel!

 11.   **Choice of Words:**
  Super, great, best ever, wild sale. Astonishing new product.

  It's a Communist plot.

 12.   **Repetition:** (Slogans) How many can your students identify?
  Reach out, reach out and touch someone. (Bell Telephone)
  The Wings of Man (Eastern Airlines)
  When it rains, it pours. (Mortons Salt)
  Babies are our business, our only business. (Gerbers)
  It's the real thing (Coca Cola)
  Better things through better living — through chemistry (DuPont)

 13.   **Exaggeration:** Come in today, don't miss the Sale of a Lifetime!

 14.   **Quoting Out of Context:**
  From a book review: "Not worth reading, the bigger than life characters have appeal only when well handled by a competent author ... this author certainly is not competent." *Pattonville Times.*

  Book ad says: PATTONVILLE TIMES REVIEWER SAYS BIGGER THAN LIFE CHARACTERS HAVE APPEAL ..."

15. **Half Truths:**
"She was treated in a mental hospital."

The "she" in question was injured in an automobile accident and taken to the nearest emergency room which happened to be in a hospital most noted for its treatment of mental patients.

16. **Omitting Pertinent Facts:** In a recent nuclear power accident the news media were instructed to omit facts which would have indicated the true extent of the danger to nearby residents.

17. **The Bandwagon Approach:** Don't miss this big event. EVERYONE will be there.

18. **"Just Like One of the Boys":** Vote for Mr. X. He's born and raised in this town and knows the folks and their problems.

19. **Transfer:** Long Distance is the next best thing to being there.

20. **Snob Appeal:** For those who want the very best! Where the great meet to eat.

21. **Name Dropping or Name Calling:**
Miss Blank (a famous movie star) uses this brand.

    or

Governor X promised no tax increase before he was elected; now look what's happened. Vote for Mr. Y instead.

22. **Testimonials:** Hospital tested! Recommended by more doctors than any other brand.

Activity Three:
Introduce *The Forbidden Forest*, by William Pene DuBois (New York: Harper & Row, 1978), to the class. Read the book aloud and invite discussion on possible propaganda techniques used by the author to promote his anti-war point of view. Stress that it is not the point of view that is being analyzed. Whether a student agrees with the author or not is not in question. The analysis is of the TECHNIQUES used to promote the point of view. Read the book a second time. Distribute to students a list of propaganda techniques. Have them find specific examples from the book to match points on their lists. Some examples are given below:

Propaganda Techniques Used in
The Forbidden Forest **by William Pene DuBois**

Technique	Example
Analogy: Because A = B, C should equal D.	The German shot the dog, therefore all Germans are cruel to animals.
Argument Beside the Point	Men with red moustaches are mean.
Superstition	Red hair means a fiery temper.

Technique	Example
Overhasty Generalization	All Germans eat sauerkraut and sausages and drink beer. All Germans (except one) are cruel.
Appeal to Ignorance	"The greatest honor a war hero can receive is to be returned home by special warship."
Argument in a Circle	"Wars at best are stupid struggles. They are easy to start, easier to keep going but hard to stop." Thus, wars at best are stupid struggles.
Emotionalism	Germans printed death warnings on the backs of menus. They shot the dog and condemned Lady Adelaide to death.
Use of Statistics	Big Bertha was the biggest cannon in history, used to bombard Paris 80 miles away with 275 lb. shells.
Bandwagon Approach	People admire war heroes so much that they name songs and dances after them.
Transfer	"Keep turning that spit, you lazy Kaiser dog!"
Name Dropping	This book is dedicated to Jane Fonda.
Half Truths or Omissions	In the dogfight, Baron Von Wilheim was machine gunning the wingtips off of British Captain Seagraves' plane. (What was Captain Seagraves doing?)

Duplicate (or construct your own) "Propaganda Road" scoring sheet like the one on page 40. Distribute to students. As they begin reading the books selected for the unit, have them score each book for the number of different techniques used. On a separate sheet the student should cite specific examples of techniques he or she has found.

PROPAGANDA ROAD

TOTAL
SCORE

Speed
Travelled

Use of Purr
or Snarl
Words
5MPH

Slogans
5MPH

Half Truths
or Important
Omissions
15MPH

Exaggeration
10MPH

Quoting
out of
Context

Vagueness
10MPH

SPEED LIMIT
55MPH

Snob
Appeal
10MPH

Testimonials
5MPH

Transfer
10MPH

Card
Stacking
5MPH

Just
Plain
Folks
5MPH

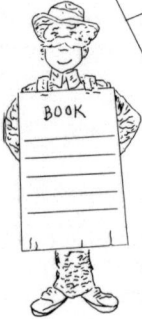

BOOK

Name
Calling
10MPH

DIRECTIONS
Circle the speed limits
in each box which apply to the
book you have read. Total the speeds.
This book gets a ticket for going over the
propaganda limit _____YES _____NO

Bandwagon
Device
5MPH

Argument
beside
the
Point
5MPH

Wide
Generalization
15MPH

Appeal
to
Ignorance
15MPH

Faulty
Use of
Statistics
10MPH

Superstition
10MPH

Emotionalism
20MPH

False
Analogy
5MPH

Begging
the
Question
5MPH

Argument
in a
Circle
5MPH

BIBLIOGRAPHY

The annotated bibliography below is intended as a starting point for selecting books to be used in this unit. Some of the titles are out of print but are included in the hope that many school or public libraries will have copies of them.

Bemmelmans, Ludwig. *Parsley*. (New York: Harper & Row, 1955). (Gr. 5-up).

This sometimes beautiful and sometimes brutal book makes a strong plea against the stripping of our nation's forests and the killing of wildlife. The reader follows the life of a crooked and twisted pine tree which continues to grow and is left to stand in the forest because of its deformity. Deer and other wildlife find shelter near the tree and see the forest stripped of its beauty. As the tree approaches its death a hunter appears on the scene and aims at a deer with his rifle. At that moment a violent storm arises and the branches of the tree break in the wind, knocking the hunter into a deep ravine where he is killed. The hunter's binoculars, which have caught on the tree, serve as a warning for the deer when future hunters come into the forest.

Bolognese, Don. *A New Day* (New York: Delacorte, 1970). (ps-2).

Mexican migrant workers, following the crops, arrive in the South searching for a place to stay. They find shelter in the garage of a gas station and are joined by a group of travelling musicians. The woman gives birth during the night and the poor people of the town bring gifts. Because of the crowds and excitement the sheriff orders the arrest of the couple, who are warned and are able to leave in time to avoid trouble.

Cowley, Joy. *The Duck in the Gun*. Illustrated by Edward Sorel. (New York: Doubleday, 1969).

In this anti-war story, a duck takes up residence in the invading army's only cannon. Since she is about to hatch her family, the soldiers ponder a number of ways of getting her out of the gun, but none are successful. Leaders on both sides of the conflict meet and decide to postpone the war for three weeks until the eggs hatch. The idle soldiers are put to work painting houses in the enemy town. When the duck finally leaves the gun both sides see the foolishness of continuing the war.

Dahl, Roald. *The Magic Finger*. (New York: Harper & Row, 1966). Illustrated by William Pene DuBois. (Gr. 1-5).

This is the story of what happens to a family when they are turned into wild ducks for a night. The wild ducks, in turn, take over their home which includes duck-hunting guns. The family learns an obvious lesson through the fear they feel when their guns are turned towards themselves. The one responsible for this strange turn of events is the narrator, who has a magic finger which she points, with extraordinary results, at all those she feels are unfair.

Darrow, Whitney, Jr. *I'm Glad I'm a Boy– I'm Glad I'm a Girl!* (New York: Windmill Books, 1970). (ps-3).

He's glad he's a boy, she's glad she's a girl. He tells her why he's glad, she tells him why she's glad. Examples: "Boys have trucks. Girls have dolls. Boys are doctors, girls are nurses. Boys fix things. Girls need things fixed."

Haley, Gail E. *Noah's Ark.* (New York: Atheneum, 1971). (ps-3).

A modern-day Noah has a dream in which the animals of the earth disappear. Humans had destroyed them for their pelts, furs, feathers and trophies. Pollution and the encroachment of civilization on animal habitats completed the destruction. Believing in his dream, and having his warning ignored by others, Noah builds a most unusual ark and gathers pairs of animals from many continents. finally the animals on the ark become the only animals left in the world and only after many years when the land is ready to receive them are the animals returned to Earth.

Kantrowitz, Mildred. *Maxie.* (New York: Parents Magazine Press, 1970). Illustrated by Emily McCully. (Gr. K-3).

Maxie was an old woman who lived alone on the top floor of a brownstone house. Her days were exactly the same. "At 7:10 the orange cat leaped onto the middle window sill; at 7:20 Maxie raised the shade; at 8:15 she opened her door with a squeak and at 8:45 her tea kettle began to whistle." Only on the morning when Maxie stays in bed does she discover how much she is needed by the other families in the house.

Merrill, Jean. *The Toothpaste Millionaire.* (Boston: Houghton Mifflin, 1972). Illustrated by Jan Palmer. (Gr. 2-5).

The message concerning the roles of big business and government in the lives of citizens come through as clearly in this book as in Merrill's earlier *Pushcart War* (New York: Grosset and Dunlap, 1964). Twelve-year-old Rufus Mayflower did not start out to make a million dollars; it just happened. It began when Rufus got upset over the cost of toothpaste and came up with his own formula for a good-tasting, cheaper toothpaste. His rise to fame took him from his original idea to head of a million dollar corporation with all the headaches inbetween, including a few brushes with government agencies.

Mendoza, George. *The Hunter, the Tick and the Gumberoo.* (New York: Cowles, 1971).

In this allegory a hunter sets out to find the Gumberoo, killing every small animal he sees on the way. His search seems fruitless although his gamebag is full when a tick bite begins to grow on his face ... and grow and grow. The hunter begs for relief from the monstrous growth but finds none. In the end he raises his gun, points it at the growth on his face and pulls the trigger. "Some time later, two hunters happened to cross the ground where the body of a man lay, clutching a rifle in his hand. He had two rabbits and a quail tied to his belt, a bullet hole in the center of his head, and on the side of his face was a speck-like brown wood tick." Thus ends the tale.

Miles, Miska. *Wharf Rat.* (Boston: Little, Brown, 1972). Illustrated by John Schoenherr. (Gr. 1-3).

This is a story of survival. Despised by man, the wharf rat manages to exist through stealth, courage, and instinct. An oil spill from a damaged freighter leaves hundreds of helpless killdeer and gulls floundering on the sand. People come to help the injured birds, but upon seeing the rat, try to destroy it. The rat escapes only to continue its percarious existence for another day.

Peet, Bill. *Farewell to Shady Glade.* (Boston: Houghton Mifflin, 1966).
(Gr. K-3).
Sixteen animals live in Shady Glade: six rabbits, a pair of possums, one
skunk, an old raccoon, five green frogs, and a bullfrog. The plight which they
face is that of progress as bulldozers enter the glade to build roads and
buildings. The animals' trip to find a new home takes them from tree limb to
train top, through cities, into stations and finally through a deep woods where
the sudden stop of the train throws them to the ground into a new "Shady
Glade."

Peet, Bill. *The Wump World.* (Boston: Houghton Mifflin, 1970). (Gr. 3-5).
The Wump World was grassy meadows with green trees and small lakes
and was perfect for the Wumps who had no enemies. Then the Wump World
was turned upside-down by steel monsters that arrived bringing "Pollutians"
who worked night and day to improve the Wump World by building cities and
factories. The Wumps retreated to an underground world and did not emerge
until the Pollutians had so polluted their world that they could no longer live in
it and so got in their spaceships and left. The world the Wumps beheld was
very different from the one they had known.

Stone, A. Harris. *The Last Free Bird.* (Englewood Cliffs, NJ: Prentice-Hall,
1967). Illustrated by Sheila Heins. (ps-3).
"Once there were many—living in quiet valleys and green fields" and "I
am the last free bird," are the opening and closing lines of this dramatic book.
The opening scenes of bubbling brooks, forests and marshlands gradually give
way to towns, cities and monstrous factories with smoke stacks which "spilled
and spewed and changed the world."

Timmermans, Gommaar. *The Little White Hen and the Emperor of France.*
(Reading, MA: Addison-Wesley, 1976). (Gr. K-up).
Farmer John Sprout and his hen, Blanche, plant, cultivate, and harvest
the crops together. They are very happy living on the quiet farm. But fate
intervenes. The Emperor of France declares war on the Czar of Russia and
Blanche is drafted into the Emperor's army as a beast of burden. Since Blanche
must go off to war John Sprout goes with her. Naturally Blanche saves the day
and prevents the great war after making her way around rules, regulations and
bureaucratic nonsense.

Divergent Questioning Models

When gifted students are given the opportunity to discuss these or any
books they have read, young minds will be stretched if divergent questions (no
one right answer) are stressed rather than the typical convergent (one right
answer) questions found in many basal readers. The Divergent Questioning
Models which follow demonstrate how basic literature skills and understanding might be developed with gifted students.

Divergent Questioning Model

Primary Grades

Book: *Star Mother's Youngest Child,* by Louise Moeri
(Boston: Houghton Mifflin, 1975).
Illustrated by Trina S. Hyman. (ps-2).

Quantity Questions:
1. List all the ways you can think of to celebrate Christmas.

2. How many different ways can you imagine that youngest child might have used to travel from the sky to Earth?

Reorganization Questions:
1. What would happen if the old woman had refused to open her door?

2. How would the story change if youngest child hadn't looked so disappointed each time the woman refused to do something?

Supposition Questions:
1. Suppose before leaving the sky, youngest child had been given magical powers to make wishes come true. Would the story be different? Why or why not?

2. Suppose youngest child could visit the old woman every Christmas. Might he find things changed? How?

Viewpoint Questions:
1. How would the Old Woman's cottage look to a king?

2. If you were a millionaire and found an old silver buckle under your Christmas tree what would you think or do?

Involvement Questions:
1. If you could travel to youngest child's home in the sky, what would you see there?

2. If you found a stranger on your doorstep looking for something what would you do?

Forced Association Questions:
1. How are the stories *Star Mother's Youngest Child* and *A Christmas Carol* (television version) alike?

2. What ideas did you get from the story to use in your own holiday celebration?

Divergent Questioning Model

Middle Grades

Book: *Summer of the Swans*, **by Betsy Byars.**
(New York: Viking, 1970).
Illustrated by Ted Colonis. (Gr. 7-up).

Quantity Questions:
1. List all of the ways you can think of that Sara might employ to enter-
   tain herself during a "boring" summer.

2. While Charlie slept in the woods, a number of animals might have
   been curious about his presence there. List the animals that might
   have seen Charlie.

Reorganization Questions:
1. In what way would the story change if Sara had not taken Charlie to
   see the swans?

2. Do you think Sara's relationship with her father would have changed
   if he had come immediately when notified that Charlie was missing?
   Why or why not?

Supposition Questions:
1. Suppose Sara had been beautiful. Would this have solved all her
   problems?

2. Suppose Joe Melby HAD taken Charlie's watch. Would Sara have
   eventually become friends with him again?

Viewpoint Questions:
1. If Aunt Willie were telling the story, in what way might it be
   different?

2. Would you expect the local police to be as concerned about Charlie's
   disappearance as Sara was? Why or why not?

Involvement Questions:
1. How would you feel if you had most of the responsibility for looking
   after a younger child?

2. You are a swan. Describe how it feels.

Forced Association Questions:
1. Compare *Summer of the Swans* with *Me, Too*, by Bill and Vera
   Cleaver (Philadelphia: Lippincott, 1973), and *Don't Take Teddy*, by
   Babbis Triis Baastad (New York: Scribner's, 1967). How do the
   children in these books handle the problem of a retarded brother or
   sister?

2. In what ways are Charlie in *Summer of the Swans* and Andy in
   Patricia Wrightson's *A Racecourse for Andy* (New York: Harcourt,
   Brace & World, 1968) alike? How are they different?

Recommended Titles

When gifted children have many choices in their reading and opportunity to discuss freely what they have read, a talented, knowledgeable teacher can help these children to gain literature skills and understanding without resorting to worksheets which require a simple regurgitation of information. As authors' works are discussed and compared, guidelines should emerge which the student can apply to his or her own creative work. Gifted students will respond more effectively if allowed to develop their own guidelines rather than studying extensive taxonomies of literature skills and understanding. (For teacher reference Charlotte Huck's "Taxonomy of Literature Skills and Understandings" is useful.) As analysis begins, emphasis can initially be placed on one element of the literature until the student becomes familiar with the techniques involved in developing plot, or characterization, or setting, theme, mood and style. The following titles are suggested as a starting point for analysis in each area. Students will want to add many other favorites.

PLOTS WITH A TWIST

Against Time. Roderick Jefferies. (New York: Harper & Row, 1973). (Gr. 5-6).

Among the Dolls. William Sleator. (New York: Dutton, 1975). (Gr. 5-6).

The Best Christmas Pageant Ever. Barbara Robinson. (New York: Harper & Row, 1972). (Gr. 3-6).

Captain Grey. Avi. (New York: Pantheon, 1977). (Gr. 4-6).

Eighteenth Emergency. Betsy Byars. (New York: Viking, 1973). (Gr. 4-6).

Flight of the Doves. Walter Macken. (New York: Macmillan, 1970). (Gr. 4-6).

The Hero from Otherwhere. Jay Williams. (New York: Walck, 1972). (Gr. 5-7).

James and the Giant Peach. Roald Dahl. (New York: Knopf, 1961). (Gr. 2-4).

Mrs. Frisby and the Rats of Nimh. Robert C. O'Brien. (New York: Atheneum, 1975). (Gr. 4-6).

CHARACTERS TOO GOOD TO MISS

Call It Courage. Armstrong Sperry. (New York: Macmillan, 1971). (Gr. 4-6).

The Foxman. Gary Paulsen. (Nashville, TN: Nelson, 1977). (Gr. 5-7).

Grandmother Orphan. Phyllis Green. (Nashville, TN: Nelson, 1977). (Gr. 5-6).

Island of the Blue Dolphins. Scott O'Dell. (Boston: Houghton Mifflin, 1960). (Gr. 5-7).

Louie's Lot. E. W. Hildick. (New York: David White, 1968). (Gr. 4-6).

Me and Caleb. Franklin Meyer. (Chicago: Follett, 1962). (Gr. 4-6).

Our John Willie. Catherine Cookson. (New York: New American Library, 1975). (Gr. 4-6).

Queenie Peavey. Robert Burch. (New York: Viking, 1966). (Gr. 4-6).

Shoeshine Girl. Clyde Bulla. (New York: T. Y. Crowell, 1975). (Gr. 3-4).

Where the Lilies Bloom. Bill and Vera Cleaver. (Philadelphia: Lippincott, 1969). (Gr. 4-6).

A TIME AND A PLACE

Bakers Hawk. Jack Bickham. (New York: Doubleday, 1974). (Gr. 5-7).

Cricket in Times Square. George Seldon. (New York: Farrar, Straus & Giroux, 1960). (Gr. 2-3).

Down the Long Hills. Louis L'Amour. (New York: Bantam, 1978). (Gr. 4-7).

Hurry-Up Harry Hanson. Mel Ellis. (New York: Four Winds, 1972). (Gr. 4-6).

Ironhead. Mel Ellis. (New York: Holt, Rinehart & Winston, 1968). (Gr. 5-7).

Julie of the Wolves. Jean George. (New York: Harper & Row, 1972). (Gr. 4-6).

The Shad Are Running. Judith St. George. (New York: Putnam, 1977). (Gr. 4-5).

The Three Toymakers. Ursula Williams. (Nashville, TN: Nelson, 1971). (Gr. 3-6).

Trouble River. Betsy Byars. (New York: Viking, 1969). (Gr. 3-5).

A Wrinkle in Time. Madeleine L'Engle. (New York: Farrar, Straus & Giroux, 1962). (Gr. 4-6).

THEMES LONG REMEMBERED

The Bears' House. Marilyn Sachs. (New York: Doubleday, 1971). (Gr. 4-6).

Bridge to Terabithia. Katherine Paterson. (New York: T. Y. Crowell, 1977). (Gr. 4-7).

The Cay. Theodore Taylor. (New York: Doubleday, 1969). (Gr. 4-6).

Certain Small Shepherd. Rebecca Caudill. (New York: Holt, Rinehart & Winston, 1965). (Gr. 2-4).

A Day No Pigs Would Die. Robert Newton Peck. (New York: Knopf, 1972). (Gr. 5-8).

Grandma Didn't Wave Back. Rose Blue. (New York: Watts, 1972). (Gr. 5-6).

The Hayburners. Gene Smith. (New York: Delacorte, 1974). (Gr. 4-6).

The Loner. Ester Wier. (New York: McKay, 1963). (Gr. 5-6).

Meaning Well. Sheila Cole. (New York: Watts, 1974). (Gr. 5-7).

Slakes Limbo. Felice Holman. (New York: Scribner's, 1974). (Gr. 5-7).

Summer of the Swans. Betsy Byars. (New York: Viking, 1970). (Gr. 4-6).

A Taste of Blackberries. Doris Smith. (New York: T. Y. Crowell, 1973). (Gr. 4-6).

Tuck Everlasting. Natalie Babbitt. (New York: Farrar, Straus & Giroux, 1975). (Gr. 4-6).

5 THE TELLING AND THE TALE

How often has one heard horror tales of friends or older students who were totally "turned off" to the world of literature by a teacher who insisted on analyzing every word and comma of a particular selection and then testing students to be sure that the pearls of wisdom which were dropped during the course were retrieved in the same order in which they were dispensed?

If our major concerns in working with gifted children are to center instruction in the areas of analysis, synthesis and evaluation, then the "spitting back" of facts or information has no part in instruction. The plot of a story, if it is fast-paced, may keep the reluctant reader reading to resolve the conflict, but plot has little appeal to the fluent, gifted reader. It is the author's style that captures the heart and the imagination even though most elementary children cannot define elements of style. One of the quickest ways to identify gifted readers in an elementary school is to read aloud a selection in which the author has used the pun as a literary device. Those children who thoroughly enjoy and understand the play on words will soon be trying their own puns on friends and therein lies the key. To help children gain an understanding of the elements of style they must use these elements in their own creative writing as tools to more effective expression. To understand the elements of plot children must develop plots and carry them through to a conclusion. The development of a believable character, the creation of a realistic setting, the exploration of a chosen theme or the changing of a mood must all be taught, first through enjoyment of the literature and then by encouraging students to be risk-takers and to develop their own literary works incorporating their understanding of the basic elements of literature. The term "risk-taker" is an appropriate one; for students who have learned the system in education are most comfortable with the workbook where a check in a particular space or a term underlined correctly leads to the "A" every time. To minimize the risk in requiring students first to understand the elements of literature *without being tested on them*, and then to incorporate them in their own work, the final product must not earn a grade. The student should be rewarded with recognition in some other way, including publication either within the school or without.

Pure enjoyment must be stressed in the initial reading of a book or selection. The analysis of those elements involved in the creation of a book or story can follow, but must evolve from the students themselves. Any discussion of a work must extend the enjoyment of the work.

While it is difficult to separate one element of literature from another since all must work in harmony to make the whole, it is possible to emphasize style, or plot or character or setting if the works which are read and enjoyed are selected with an author's particular strengths in mind. The authors cited and the sample units given in this chapter and in those that follow were chosen to emphasize a particular literature skill or understanding.

To Begin: Style

It is an author's style that sets his or her work apart, for in any great book, including children's books, style and story cannot be separated. In the concern with developing a particular feeling or mood, the writer carefully chooses words to lead the reader to that feeling or mood. This choice might be between literal or figurative language including the use of metaphors, similes, hyperbole, onomatopoeia, alliteration or understatement. In his classic, *Charlotte's Web*, E. B. White uses all of these devices and children do not have to go through hours of laborious definition of the elements of style in order to enjoy the author's facility with words. The parodies of George Mendoza and Raymond Briggs or the not-so-subtle use of satire in both the picture books and the junior novels of Jean Merrill are of equal delight to children. Since enjoyment of anything usually leads to wanting further contact with it, children can be led first to ENJOY, then to discover the source of that enjoyment, and finally to use their new discoveries in the CREATION of their own work.

The study of style can begin in the primary grades. The fluent reader reads not word by word, but through recognition of clues to language patterns. It is the rate of internalization of these patterns which determines the speed at which a child reads. The structure of language is absorbed through the ear, but unless the feeling of the language is absorbed in the heart it will rarely take.

Young children who delight in discovering language patterns are, in essence, discovering STYLE. Very young children do not have to be able to define every word in Kipling's *Just So Stories* in order to delight in his masterful use of rhyme and alliteration in moving his tales from one point to another. It is essential that children OF ALL AGES hear the written word read aloud in order to internalize language patterns. Primary teachers should begin with books which have obvious patterns and much repetition, taking care, however, to choose only the best, those in which the flow of the language will bring a sparkle to the listener's eye. Favorites that can be found in many school libraries include:

The Important Book, by Margaret Wise Brown (New York: Harper & Row, 1949).
"The important thing about an apple is that it is round, it is red, you bite it...."

May I Bring a Friend?, by Beatrice DeRegniers (New York: Atheneum, 1964).
All children have asked this question and will delight in hearing and repeating the pattern.

Bears, by Ruth Krauss (New York: Scholastic Books, 1968).
"Bears on the stairs, washing hairs...." A delightful rhyming pattern.

Do You Want to See Something?, by Eve Merriam (New York: Alfred Knopf, 1970).

"In the park there is snow, in the snow there is a...." A pattern on which elaboration can be endless.

Amelia Bedelia, by Peggy Parish (New York: Harper & Row, 1963).
Howls of laughter (and creative writing experiences) result from Amelia's attempts to interpret literally the instructions she receives from her employer.

My Mama Says ..., by Judith Viorst (New York: Atheneum, 1972).
After sharing what "my mama says" children delight in imitating the style with other characters: "My teacher says," "My coach says."

In sharing picture books which have an obvious style, or a discernible pattern the teacher should read them aloud several times. Children may begin to chime in as familiar parts of the pattern appear. When children have caught the pattern, the first few lines can be placed on the board and the students encouraged to expand on the pattern. Finally, and most important, the children should be allowed to share their work with others.

While most children, given enough exposure to a book, will internalize, analyze and be able to imitate the language patterns, the gifted child moves beyond imitation to CREATION, tapping his or her own experiences to expand the basic pattern and create new patterns. The following examples of student work show how the basic pattern of a picture book can serve as a guide to understanding style and as a catalyst for creative writing.

1. *Fortunately*, by Remy Charlip. (New York: Parents Magazine Press, 1964). (Gr. K-3).
   This easy story pattern can be used with any group of primary children.

   Fortunately one day Ned ... was invited to a birthday party.
   Unfortunately the party was in Florida and he was in New York City.

   Fortunately....

The tendency of most children with this pattern is to ramble on with a series of "Fortunately, Unfortunately" couplets. The gifted child, however, should identify the element of conflict in the story and introduce this element in his or her own writing. Note how the element of conflict appears in the first grader's story:

   Fortunately my Mom thought I was big enough to stay home alone at night. Unfortunately, I heard someone creeping up behind me.
   Fortunately, it was my Mom!

Other examples show how creative thought is stimulated when young gifted minds meet the works of gifted writers.

2. *Noel the Coward*, by Robert Kraus. (New York: Windmill Books, 1977). Illustrated by Jose Aruego and Ariane Dewey. (Gr. 3-7).
   Former New Yorker cartoonist, Kraus, famed for giving the cliche a funny twist, does it again in this book, a good study in cliches for older students, a fun story for the young.

Noel was a coward. So was his father. "Better a live coward than a dead hero," said Noel's mother. "Noel's coward powered," they (his friends) shouted throwing sticks and stones. So Noel and his father both went to Charlie's School of Self Defense. "The bigger they are the harder I fall," was pint-sized Charlie's motto...."

Chuck T., Grade 7 writes:

Julius Seizure—White House Reporter

Julius's office, home and pressroom were in the depths of an over-stuffed chair in the Gold Room below the Oval Office which, of course, placed him at the seat of government. Accuracy and brevity were Julius' style, for one of the earliest lessons learned at his mother's knee was that "Clarity begins at home...."

3. *Spoiled Tomatoes*, by Bill Martin, Jr. (New York: Holt, Rinehart & Winston, 1970).
   Martin provides an interesting pattern for older students: a round-robin ecology statement.

The tomatoes spoiled. We dumped the spoiled tomatoes into the river. The polluted river rose up and killed the fishes. The dying fishes rose up...."

Kent L., Grade 5 writes:

The belching smoke stacks shut down. The leftover smoke drifted away into the atmosphere. The cleansing atmosphere surrounded the people. The surrounded people gulped the clean air. The gulped air expanded their lungs. The expanded lungs made healthy bodies. The healthy bodies fought to keep the smoke stacks shut down.

4. *David Was Mad*, by Bill Martin, Jr. (New York: Holt, Rinehart & Winston, 1967).

David was made! Mad! Mad! Angry! He was so angry he kicked the wall as hard as he could. He felt hot—all red inside. Grandma knew David was mad. She knew because....

Darren Z., in Cathi Dame's 6th Grade class, writes:

The elephant was skinny. Skinny! Skinny! Thin! He was so skinny he could tie 3 knots in himself. He felt stringy, thin all around. The snake knew the elephant was skinny because he could wrap his tongue around his waist. The hummingbird knew the elephant was skinny. He knew because he outweighed him. The elephant doctor knew the elephant was skinny. He knew because he stayed on his diet too long.

5. *The Mountain*, by Peter Parnall. (New York: Doubleday, 1971). (Gr. 5).

Another ecology statement in parody form:

This is the mountain that stood in the West. These are the flowers that grew there. These are the moles that smelled the flowers that grew on the mountain that stood in the West. These are the birds....

Mary G., Grade 5, writes:

This is the ocean that touched the Alaskan Coast. These are the fishes that swam there. Here are the seals that ate the fishes that swam in the ocean that touched the Alaskan Coast. Here are the hunters who killed the seals that ate the fishes that swam in the ocean....

The use of picture books to introduce language patterns to very young children can serve a dual purpose. Children who have had few experiences with literature can enjoy language patterns not previously encountered and internalize the patterns by sharing the flow of language orally. At the same time, gifted students can savor an author's creative interpretation of familiar patterns and explore the many possibilities for bringing new approaches to the language experience.

Summaries and Adaptations

One of the best ways for children to analyze the work of an author is to summarize it as in a review or adapt it into another form such as a play or poem. In either of these activities, true analysis must occur so that the student can identify main ideas and separate the significant from the less significant. If summaries or adaptations are dull the student has lost those elements of style which make an author's work memorable.

Note how the style of the journalist has been recreated in these summaries of favorite titles taken from *The Bookland Times*, which was written and published by a class of gifted fifth-graders.

R. MAYFLOWER, TEN-YEAR OLD MILLIONAIRE

Ten year old Rufus Mayflower of Cleveland, Ohio, has become a millionaire practically overnight.

Rufus appeared on the Joe Smiley show and told of his experience.

"My toothpaste is made out of stuff any one can buy for a few cents and mix up at home in a few minutes. It tastes pretty good. And for about 2¢ you can make as much as you get in a 79¢ tube. My product is called "TOOTHPASTE.""

With help from a classmate, Kate MacKinstrey, his math teacher Mr. Conti, and other friends, Rufus now owns his own factory. He says he was just trying to prove something and instead became famous. Rufus now plans to retire.

A BLUE RIBBON FOR WILBUR

A now-famous pig named Wilbur has won a blue ribbon this week at the county fair.

This pig came to our attention last week when the word RADIANT was woven into a spider's web about the pig's pen. Scientists are baffled as to how it got there. Some think it was a freak of nature, but a few believe that maybe there is a spider that can spell!

The pig was named Wilbur by Fern Arable, a small girl of eight. Her father, Mr. Arable, said: "And to think I wanted to kill that pig. I'm so ashamed."

It seems that Wilbur was the runt of the litter. Fern persuaded her father to let her raise him and she nursed him with a baby bottle. "Now we're all glad she did," says Mr. Arable, "because she has turned our little town into a city almost. We owe a lot to this runt of a pig that was raised on a manure pile."

The little girl, Fern, claims that a spider Charlotte can spin anything in her web. She says that a rat named Templeton finds words for her to write in the trash pile. Fern also says that the other animals in the barn also talk!

Well, if a spider can weave words in its web, who's to say that the other animals in the barn can't talk!

FOR HIRE, RENT, SALE, OR TRADE

FOR HIRE: Detective experienced in kidnapping and robbery cases. Works cheap. Contact Malcolm (Mallard) Westerman.

FOR HIRE: Musicians to play at weddings, parties, bar mitzvahs, etc. Specializing in rock. Contact the Bremen Town Musicians: Donkey, Dog, Cat or Cock.

FOR RENT: If your child is selfish, cure this ill by renting Mrs. Piggle-Wiggle's Shelfishness Kit. $10 per week. Call Mrs. Piggle-Wiggle at Up-Side-Down House.

FOR SALE: Bright red hair, soft and fluffy. Could be used for mop or wig. Contact Mr. Barberoli, Mop Top's barber immediately.

TO TRADE: Mystery recipe for Dinglenut Puffs in exchange for one pound of dinglenuts. Contact Mrs. Graymalkin.

This student newspaper which contained book reviews disguised as news articles, recipes, sports events, advertisements and classified ads was sent to each author whose book was "reviewed." The author response was so overwhelming that a subsequent issue of *The Bookland Times* was published to share author letters with the entire school.

Imagine the excitement level in this particular class when this letter arrived from one of their favorite authors, Gary Paulsen, author of *The CB Radio Caper* and *The Curse of the Cobra*:

> Through great good fortune one of your excellent papers has been sent to me. I read it through twice, once for fun, and once because I frankly was so surprised by it. It is good, very good, and I have taken the liberty of forwarding it to my agent for a second critical comment. Thank you for sending it to me and keep up work like this — it is a rewarding thing to see such good quality work done by young people.
>
> P.S. I need some advice. I did not, unfortunately, have a brick wall when I tried the delicious squash recipe. On top of that my aim wasn't too swift. Two of the peaches managed to hit the wall all right, though they pretty well destroyed the print in the wallpaper. But the other three missed. One took out a window pane over the sink, another took my Great Dane right between the eyes and the third hit the cat in a strange place. In your next paper would you please include a handy hint column? I specifically need to know how to (A) clean wallpaper before my wife divorces me, (B) replace window panes because it's twelve below zero (Mr. Paulsen lives in Solway, Minnesota), (C) apologize to a Great Dane — *fast*, and (D) find a cat who is never coming back. Ever. Even if I promise never to do it again.
>> Thank you."

The books listed on pages 56-58 are only a small portion of the hundreds of delightful, creative, and imaginative picture books that can be enjoyed for the many elements of style used in their creation. Gifted students who are encouraged to explore the picture book collection to find those gems in which style is all important, will be as excited as any treasure hunter; for the child who delights in the clever use of words by others is ready to try his or her hand at playing with words to create a word picture, a poem, or a story. The creative writing examples which follow are by children who have gone beyond "patterning" to a study of specific elements of style and have used one or more of these elements in the creative writing process. (These pieces first appeared in *Running Off with the King* (Missouri Arts Council Anthology, 1976-77, St. Louis, MO).

Point of View, by Kim Tritsch, Grade 2

I was a girl giant and went through the woods
I saw a toy car,
the trees looked like tiny trees.
I came upon a town and it was an earthquake
when I walked.
The people looked like toys, too.
I looked funny and they were laughing
But then I started to like them
and they started to like me
and we became friends.

Recipe, by Brian W., Grade 4

Slug slobber, chopped up snails
twist of lemon and beached dead whales;
add some Japanese bettle legs
and then some wine from year old kegs.
Cover all in King Snake Venom
and add another twist of lemon.
Put to bake in graveyard light
and have a frightful dinner tonight!

The Bolivia of Chile, by Melissa Burke, Grade 5

One morning I thought I woke up in Chile
with hot sauce running out my ears.
Dancing girls were dancing on chilly beans
(which were shaky with coldness)
I tried to get up, but I fell into Bolivia.
Bolivia was shaped into a bowl.
I couldn't get out because of the sides.
Finally, I was awake, climbing the bedpost.
Boy, I shouldn't have eaten that Bowl of Chili.

Red As, by Ann McCammon, Grade 5

Red as
    the cherry lollipop stuck in your notebook
    the cracks between your fingers when you hold a flashlight to them
    apples, grapes, raspberries, and even Kool Aid
Stop, the end.

Recipe for Four Billion Counts of Murder, by Jeff Spitzer, Grade 6

4 super deep oil drills with oil
59,673,048 sticks of dynamite
1 truckload atomic bombs
unlimited amounts of arsenic, strychnine and curare
1 match   1 space shuttle
I pack chewing gum (optional)

Take oil drills and drill til you hit oil. Spread oil around world. Take poisons, mix well for taste. Spread evenly in water reservoirs around world. Mix bombs and dynamite GENTLY! Get into shuttle, drop match on oil. Take off quickly. Chew gum to prevent ears from popping.

As the preceding pages illustrate, one of the best means of introducing the elements of style to students of all ages is to examine the way in which many picture book authors have used these elements. Picture books which incorporate many elements of style and which can therefore be read and enjoyed on many levels include:

THE CLICHE WITH A TWIST

Robert Kraus. *Leo, the Late Bloomer* (New York: Dutton, 1973). (ps-2).

Robert Kraus. *Noel, the Coward* (New York: Dutton, 1977). (Gr. 3-7).

Robert Kraus. *Pinchpenny Mouse* (New York: Dutton, 1974). (ps-3).

HYPERBOLE

Sid Fleischman. *Longbeard the Wizard* (Boston: Atlantic — Little, Brown, 1970).

Sid Fleischman. *McBroom's Ghost* (New York: Grosset & Dunlap, 1971). (Gr. 3-5).

James Flora. *Grandpa's Farm* (New York: Harcourt, Brace, Jovanovich, 1965). (Gr. 1-4).

James Flora. *Stewed Goose* (New York: Atheneum, 1973). (Gr. K-4).

Glen Rounds. *Ol' Paul, the Mighty Logger* (New York: Holiday House, 1976). (Gr. 4-6).

FIGURATIVE LANGUAGE

Fred Gwynne. *A Chocolate Moose for Dinner* (New York: Dutton, 1976). (Gr. K-4).

Fred Gwynne. *King Who Rained* (New York: Dutton, 1970). (Gr. K-up).

Peggy Parish. *Amelia Bedelia Series* (New York: Harper & Row). (Gr. 2-3).

METAPHOR

Lloyd Alexander. *Coll & His White Pig* (New York: Holt, Rinehart & Winston, 1965). (Gr. K-3).

Lloyd Alexander. *The Truthful Harp* (New York: Holt, Rinehart & Winston, 1971). (ps-3).

ALLITERATION

Eric Carle. *All about Arthur* (New York: Watts, 1974).

Florence Heide. *Alphabet Zoop* (New York: Holiday House, 1971).

Cheli Ryan. *Hildilid's Night* (New York: Macmillan, 1971). (Gr. K-3).

PARODY

Raymond Briggs. *Jim and the Beanstalk* (New York: Coward, 1970). (Gr. K-3).

George Mendoza. *A Wart Snake in a Fig Tree* (New York: Dial, 1976). (ps-3).

PERSONIFICATION

Rebecca Caudill. *Certain Small Shepherd* (New York: Holt, Rinehart & Winston, 1965). (Gr. 2-6).

Rudyard Kipling. *Just So Stories* (New York: Doubleday, 1972). (Gr. 2-5).

Julian Scheer. *Rain Makes Applesauce* (New York: Holiday House, 1964). (Gr. K-3).

PUNS

Roy Doty. *Gunga, Your Din Din Is Ready* (New York: Doubleday, 1976). (Gr. 4).

Roy Doty. *Puns, Gags, Quips & Riddles* (New York: Doubleday, 1974). (Gr. 6-9).

Charles Keller. *Ballpoint Bananas* (Englewood Cliffs, NJ: Prentice-Hall, 1976). (Gr. 3-7).

Charles Keller. *Laugh Lines* (Englewood Cliffs, NJ: Prentice-Hall, 1974).

Jane Sarnoff. *The Giant Riddle Book* (New York: Scribner's, 1977). (Gr. 1-5).

SIMILE

Charles Keeping. *Through the Window* (New York: Watts, 1970).

Maxine Kumin and Anne Sexton. *The Wizard's Tears* (New York: McGraw-Hill, 1975). (Gr. 4-6).

SYMBOLISM

Little Burnt Face. In *Arbuthnot Anthology of Children's Literature*. Compiled by May H. Arbuthnot; revised by Zena Southerland. (New York: Lothrop, Lee & Shepard, 1976).

William Steig. *Sylvester and the Magic Pebble* (New York: Windmill Books, 1969). (Gr. 1-4).

ONOMATOPOEIA

Verna Aardema. *Who's in Rabbit's House?* (New York: Dial, 1977). (Gr. K-3).

Verna Aardema. *Why Mosquitos Buzz in People's Ears* (New York: Dial, 1975). (ps-3).

Peter Spier. *Crash Bang Boom* (New York: Doubleday, 1972). (ps-1).

SATIRE AND ALLEGORY

Barbara Emberley. *Drummer Hoff* (Englewood Cliffs, NJ: Prentice-Hall, 1967). (ps-1).

Florence Parry Heide. *Fables You Shouldn't Pay Any Attention To* (Philadelphia: Lippincott, 1978).

George Mendoza. *The Hunter, the Tick and the Gumberoo* (New York: Cowles, 1971).

George Mendoza. *The Inspector* (New York: Doubleday, 1970).

Jean Merrill and Ronni Solbert. *The Elephant Who Liked to Smash Small Cars* (New York: Pantheon Books, 1967).

Understanding Plot Construction

Far too many teacher's manuals cover the development of plot by requiring the student to recall events in a story in the order in which they happened. This activity not only bores most students but does little toward promoting an understanding of plot construction. Even very young children can acquire a basic knowledge of plot construction if examples are used that they readily understand. In considering the elements of plot children can be led to see that all stories must have characters and a setting, a conflict or problem, events to move the story along to the most exciting point (climax), and a way of solving the problem.

Students of all ages enjoy identifying these elements in well-known fairy and folk tales. For example: there will be no lack of correct responses if students are asked to identify the characters and setting of *Little Red Riding Hood* or *The Three Bears*, but even some high school students have trouble in identifying the basic conflict in these stories. When "conflict" is defined as "opposing forces," some students will quickly determine the conflict in *Little Red Riding Hood*, i.e., "The wolf wanted to eat Red Riding Hood, but she did not want to be eaten." Differentiating between the climactic event and those events that simply move the story from one point to another is also a problem for many students. The key question to ask is "What line in *Little Red Riding Hood* takes the reader (or listener) directly to the climax point? When students respond, "The better to eat you with!" they are showing an understanding of the element of climax. The resolution is usually clearly seen by students after the problem and climax point have been identified. The exercise can be expanded at that point to the literature most appropriate for each particular age group. For example, students in third grade can identify these same elements in *Charlie and the Chocolate Factory* (New York: Knopf, 1964) or *James and the Giant Peach* (New York: Knopf, 1961), by Roald Dahl. Fourth grade students might analyze *Kneeknock Rise* (New York: Farrar, Straus & Giroux, 1970), by Natalie Babbitt, or *Peter Graves* (New York: Viking, 1950) by William Pene DuBois. Let fifth graders try *Incident at Hawks Hill* (Boston: Little, Brown, 1971), by Alan Eckert, or *A Wrinkle in Time*, by Madeleine L'Engle. Sixth graders will have a challenge with Katherine Paterson's *Bridge to Terabithia* (New York: Crowell, 1977) or Ursula LeGuin's *Wizard of Earthsea* (New York: Penguin, 1971). The choices are endless.

If students are successfully to analyze the techniques an author uses to develop an exciting plot or memorable character they must be helped to see beyond the story details to specific structure or techniques and compare the plot or character development of one author with another.

For example, in analyzing a story for plot construction students should identify the *basic* conflict from the four basic conflicts on which authors build their works: 1) man against man, 2) man against nature, 3) man struggling against his own inner values, and 4) man against society.

An exercise for gifted students which allows them to get to the "bare bones" of a story is to summarize a story in general terms avoiding mention of specific characters or incidents. Here are summaries of well-known tales done by an enrichment class of eleven year olds:

"A young boy becomes a lucky contest winner and his family's fortunes change from rags to riches as he becomes a wealthy factory owner"—Lance B., *Charlie & the Chocolate Factory*

"A very strong man marries a wicked woman who betrays him and gives him to his enemies. Even though he's tortured, he eventually overcomes all his enemies before his own death"—Mike R., *Samson* from the *Old Testament*

"A young girl goes to visit her invalid grandmother only to find she has been battered and tied up and the mugger is still there. After screaming for help, the young girl and her invalid grandmother are rescued by a passing stranger"—Mike W., *Little Red Riding Hood*

"Two boys, best friends, live in the country and enjoy being mischievous—slinging apples at church windows, rolling down hills in barrels, tying up girls. When they grow up, one becomes a minister and the other an author"—Joe V., *Soup.*

"When two children learn they are to be taken away from their family because the father can't support them, they run away instead and stumble onto a deserted house, murder the old lady who lived there, and take her riches back home so they can be a family"—Kenny W., *Hansel & Gretel.*

"Coming back from the 'Y,' a boy finds a waif, breaks the law, gets picked up by the police and then goes home for dinner. Life continues in an ordinary fashion—for a boy"—Carla P., *Henry & Ribsy.*

"An English gang, led by a daring young outlaw who's always outsmarting the law, steals from the rich and gives generously to the poor. The leader, even though he's called a thief, always seems to be performing the best of deeds"—Patty S., *Robin Hood.*

"A prominent businessman ventures into many businesses, and because of his personal touch each one becomes very profitable. Even his daughter (because of her father's influence) becomes very wealthy"—Connie R., *King Midas & the Golden Touch.*

"A young girl is drugged and falls into a deep coma. Finally a handsome young man finds the cause and brings her back to consciousness. She is so grateful, she falls in love with her rescuer and marries him"—Mike W., *Sleeping Beauty.*

Creating a Story

Once an understanding of the basic elements of story or plot construction is achieved, children may use their mastery of the information to create stories of their own. At this point students should understand that a good story has characters, an interesting setting, a conflict to be resolved, events to move the story along, a climax, and a resolution. However, for students who have not been encouraged to write often and on themes which interest them there may still be roadblocks to creativity. Even the gifted child will claim a good case of "writer's block" from time to time by having nothing to write about. Once again, books can help.

Challenge students to write a sequel to a favorite book or story. Allow students to brainstorm with the writer's favorite question, "What IF???" Help them to become observers of the simple, everyday things around them, to become more adept at describing the things they see and in the use of sensory images; to incorporate a historical event or figure in a story. The possibilities for writing topics are everywhere.

At the same time, gifted children in particular need to understand that writing does not always flow easily from the mind to the pen. Writing IS hard work which requires not only inspiration but perspiration and perseverance. To keep children from becoming discouraged before the writing has barely started, it is wise to discuss the writer's task, including the difficulties involved. If possible, invite a writer to talk with the students concerning the problems a writer faces.

Teachers, too, sometimes become discouraged at the efforts of students who are gifted or academically talented, feeling that the work of these students in creative writing is not on a level with their work in other subject areas. Perhaps this is because of several of the myths that have been perpetuated, not by writers who know they are not true, but by other educators.

Among the myths which need closer examination are:

Myth 1) Every child can write a story about his or her own experiences.

If the words "a story" were removed from the statement it would probably be true. However, the definition of "story" assumes a plot with basic conflict, characters who struggle with the conflict, and a setting in time and place appropriate to the action; and finally, events which build upon earlier events to move the story along to a conclusion wherein the conflict is resolved. That all this is done in a specific style to create a mood which supports a theme is clear in any true definition of the concept of "story." Thus, few children but the gifted are capable of weaving all of these parts into the unified whole called a "story."

Myth 2) If a child is being "creative" one does not need to be concerned with grammar and spelling.

Gifted children particularly do not buy this myth. Writing is communication and those who ignore the writer's basic tools of spelling, grammar and good sentence construction will fail to communicate. Thus the major goal of any writing program must be communication; it must provide ample opportunity for the sharing of creative works in a variety of ways. These can include dramatizations, tape scripts, buckram bound student works, storyboards, news articles, letters and reports, all with careful attention to correct composition.

Myth 3) Writing is easy.

As the writing process moves along many students who expected the words to flow quickly and the plot to move easily along a predetermined course, find that writing can be, and often is, hard work. It is most helpful when gifted children can be brought together with gifted writers of children's books to discuss the joys and the problems involved in the writing process.

These writers in their letters to young readers discuss the problem:

William O. Steele

"Have no doubt about it—writing is work. One always hopes to sit at a typewriter, roll in a piece of paper and have words and sentences appear on the paper without any effort at all. Alas, it has never happened to me.

I have an idea for a book and I begin to write Chapter One. It is terrible. I save any good sentences and throw the rest away and set to work to rewrite Chapter One. By editing and re-writing I finally shape the chapter so that it builds up to a cliff-hanging ending. I'm quite pleased with it and I'm off writing another book."

Lloyd Alexander

"Writers, like readers, are real people. Books don't suddenly appear out of thin air! A real human being has to write them, word by word, day by day.

That's why each book is part of the writer's life. And for writers the greatest thing that can happen is for their books to become some part of a reader's life."

Donald J. Sobol

"The writing of books is always hard work. Each new book is a new beginning. The struggle to see it through does not get easier.

Yet it is this struggle that makes writing books exciting—the mind racing hotly, fighting to find a fresh way of describing a character, or a wave dashing whitely on a beach, or a single coconut palm swaying against a field of stars."

Knowing that the challenge which lies ahead for the writer is the same whether one is a successful author or a beginner in the field should prove to be reassuring to students.

Story Structure

Even bright and eager young minds welcome structure in initial writing experiences. This is a major reason for the popularity of the "pattern" books discussed earlier. However, gifted children should again be led in developing their own structure for particular types of tales. The following structure for the hero folk tale was developed in three stages by an enrichment literature class of sixth grade students culminating a study of folk literature.

Stage One: A comparison of characters in the film, *Star Wars*, and the books, *The High King*, by Lloyd Alexander, and *The Hobbit*, by J. R. R. Tolkien.

Stage Two: A listing of basic folk tale elements found in *Star Wars*, *The High King*, and *The Hobbit*.

Stage Three: A basic outline for the hero folk tale.

STAGE ONE
A comparison of folktale characters

From *Star Wars*	From *The High King* by Lloyd Alexander	From *The Hobbit* by J. R. R. Tolkien
LUKE SKYWALKER The noble hero who searches for adventure	TARAN WANDERER The orphan who seeks a chance for glory	BILBO BAGGINS Gentle, peace loving, a hero in spite of himself
BEN KENOBI Teaches Luke all he must know	DALLBEN Wise old man who teaches and guides Taran	GANDALF Persuades Bilbo to undertake a dangerous mission
PRINCESS LEIA Brave and beautiful; saved by Luke	PRINCESS EILONWY Loved and protected by Taran	GALADRIEL Beautiful enchantress
DARTH VADER Death Lord who vows to destroy rebels	ARAWN Death Lord who fights good in Prydain	SMAUG Evil reptile of the underworld
R2D2 and C3PO Droids who help the rebels	FFLEWDDER, COLL & HEN WEN Strange characters who help Taran	13 DWARFS Whom Bilbo leads on a dangerous mission
CHEWBACCA Half-human, half animal co-pilot of the space ship	GURGI Half-human, half-animal. Helps Taran	BEORN Hunter who can change into a bear. Helps Bilbo
HAN SOLO Captain of spaceship of rebel forces	PRINCE GWYDIAN Brave knight who battles evil forces	THORIN Brave leader of the dwarfs
STORM TROOPERS Darth Vader's evil forces	CAULDRON-BORN Walking dead of the Death Lord	LAKE PEOPLE, WOOD ELVES, GOBLINS, WARGS Underworld creatures whom Bilbo must battle

STAGE TWO
The Pattern of the Folk Hero Story

The following elements found in most folk hero tales are present in: *Star Wars*; *The Prydain Series*, by Lloyd Alexander; *The Hobbit*, by J. R. R. Tolkien; *The Narnia Series*, by C. S. Lewis; and countless other hero tales.

THE FOLKHERO:
1) Is alone; does not have, or loses his or her family
2) Longs for adventure or glory
3) Is taught by wise and powerful older person
4) Travels through barren or desolate land
5) Has 3 to 7 tasks to perform
6) Meets those who have enchanted powers for good
7) Has companions that are not always human
8) Rescues and/or wins the love of a beautiful woman or man
9) Makes a trip to or confronts the dark world of evil forces
10) Battles strange creatures
11) Wins out against evil in the end
12) Receives honor of some kind
13) Proves that pain or sorrow must come before joy

STAGE THREE
Story Outline: The Hero Folk Tale

I.   Hero or Heroine's Origin
    a) Origin of birth_____
    b) Origin of name_____
II. Elements of Setting
    a) Time_____
    b) Place_____
III. Deed or tasks to be performed_____
IV. Wise older person who helps_____
V.   Obstacles to overcome
    a)
    b)
VI. Companions—name and describe
    a)
    b)
VII. Evil Forces—name and describe
    a)
    b)
VIII. Steps in achieving the task
    a)
    b)
    c)
    d)
    e)
IX. Honors received
    a)
    b)

Similar plot and character comparisons can be done for many other types of fiction, including "formula fiction," mysteries, science fiction, and realistic stories.

6 A TIME, A PLACE, AND A FEELING: The Study of Setting and Mood

Introduction

In his book, *Sounder* (New York: Harper & Row, 1969), William Armstrong is faced with the problem of depicting a fairly long passage of time as the boy in the story seeks his imprisoned father. The book is very short, and because it is modeled on the Greek tragedies, the text is spare. To solve the problem, the author does what he does best. He shows the passing of time through the changing seasons using a simple line or two to describe an element of nature undergoing change.

As the seasons change so changes the mood of the story. The desolation of winter and the hope of spring are reflected in the degree of despair or hope the boy experiences in his search. Thus, the author uses setting not only to move the story along, but to set the mood and, finally, to emphasize the theme as the boy surveys the new growth of spring and recalls the words of the philosopher which assure him that death is not the end of life.

From their earliest literature experiences children should be able to recognize those elements which depict setting, including the time in history, the time of year, the time of day. But they must be led, too, to understand the *importance* of setting, its effect on characters, plot, and mood, and the significance of changes in setting.

In historical or regional novels authenticity of setting is all important. Not only must the author be accurate in selection of details, but authenticity must extend to an accurate representation of the *spirit* of the time or place.

These elements can be introduced early in the gifted literature program through the enjoyment by second or third grade students of the regional books of Lois Lenski. Because she has lived with the people in her books, the author has truly been able to capture the spirit of the setting. As Lenski says:

> I am trying to introduce the children of one region to another, thus widening their horizons. I want to tell how they live and why, to point out details in backgrounds, occupations and customs peculiar to each region. But along with these differences, I show also the inward likenesses—the same universal struggle for the things we all hold dear—truth, security and happiness. My stories emphasize not the things that hold us apart, but all those things that bring and hold us together in the one great human family.[1]

The questioning models and activities which follow are designed to involve students in a very personal way. Most of the questions are based on the forced involvement model given earlier to help children feel the mood generated by a particular setting, to identify elements which create the mood and to understand how cultural and social attitudes are largely determined by setting.

This involvement of the reader extends through the activities suggested to sensory involvement as well. Certainly all children can, with help, bake a shoo-fly pie in the classroom, but what better way to recreate the smells of baking in an Amish kitchen than to have a classroom filled with the same delicious aroma! Then, too, in our search for ways to stretch young minds, we must not forget that our gifted children are, indeed, children, and enjoy sensory and manipulative experiences as much as their less gifted classmates.

Fortunately, books by Lois Lenski can be found in most school libraries and the reading and enjoyment of these books will not only clarify a gifted author's unique use of setting but will give children a broader, more understanding view of the country and the world in which they live.

The Regional Books of Lois Lenski
by Cora Borgmier

Bayou Suzette (New York and Philadelphia: J. B. Lippincott Company, 1943).

Small, thin, wiry, ten-year-old Suzette Durand faces two loyalties in this typical picture of Louisiana bayou life. One of six children, Suzette loyally defends her father's seemingly shiftless character. She brings a homeless, Houma Indian girl, Marteel, to their home, facing strong family resistance. The father subtly counters the mother's resistance as he rallies to Suzette's attempt to make a place for Marteel. Marteel comes and goes through the story as she meets with continual rebuffs due to different cultures. Suzette maintains her loyalty as Marteel, with her Indian wisdom and native ingenuity, wins her place in the family circle. Woven into the bayou story are the legends of Jean Laffite, and the great flood when the Mississippi River broke the levee. The setting is in the Barataria country near the mouth of the river. Lenski's black and white drawings, simple but realistic, are in total harmony with the story. Especially notable is the authentic map of the Barataria country to which she has added pictures of indigenous wildlife in their specific area. To help her in achieving full authenticity, Lois Lenski lived with these people.

Springboards

Compare living in your region with the Louisiana bayou. Imagine you have been abandoned in a store as Marteel was. If you are a boy, change the character of Marteel to a boy. What thoughts might you be thinking?

If you lived in that area, what things would appeal to you? What might be frightening? What might be beautiful?

Would you be willing to stay in an attic of a house during a flood? Have you ever been a victim of similar circumstances?

Have you ever been tempted to catch a wild animal and keep it caged?

What might you expect to find in an Indian Mound?

What holiday did you think of while reading about the Mardi Gras celebration?

If you lived near a place where treasure was supposed to have been buried, might you be tempted to hunt for it? What would you do if you found it?

Creative Ideas

Check the card catalog for information on Jean Laffite. Try to find/locate on a map any of the places mentioned in *Bayou Suzette.*

Can you find any information on medicinal plants or plants used for dyes? Are there recipes for making dyes and directions for dying thread or cloth? Would you like to try some? Are any of these materials seasonal?

Choose one of the animals mentioned. Find information about it. Is it one of the endangered species? If so, assume that the Department of the Interior has hired you to develop a plan to save this animal. What would be the major points in your plan?

As a group, list the French words and find their English translations. Divide in two groups. Which group can find all of them first?

The phonograph is a clue to the time of the story. Try to find the time of this particular type of phonograph. Suzette described it as looking like a big morning glory.

Draw pictures of their Christmas customs compared to ours. Create a skit showing their Santa Claus and the family's reactions.

Compare the Indian's thought of migration to the white man's (page 173). Which reveals the beauty of nature?

Set Suzette's song to music (pages 135-365). Using it as a pattern, add additional verses. The first two lines are different. The next two are repeated in each verse.

Strawberry Girl (New York and Philadelphia: J. B. Lippincott Company, 1945). (Gr. 4-7).
Awarded Newbery Medal, 1946

This is an authentic piece of regionalism depicting Florida life at a time when old Florida ways were changing to new. Birdie Boyer dreams of an education that would include playing the organ. Her industrious family's struggle to make a living from their strawberry patch is a marked contrast to their adjoining shiftless neighbors, the Slaters. The Boyer's neighborliness and industry overcomes the Slater's hostility which leads to influencing work habits.

Springboards

How did the name "Florida Cracker" originate? Are there similar regional names for people in other states?

If you were a newcomer in a neighborhood and your neighbors were unfriendly, how might you become friends?

Are neighbors as important now as in years past? Why?

Does distance play a part in neighborliness?

What do you think was the bravest thing Birdie did? Why?

Does a person's environment affect the way he or she lives and speaks? Cite examples to support your conclusions.

Creative Activities

Laugh Lines: Choose a favorite humorous incident in the story. Draw a cartoon illustration for it, or use this incident as the first entry in a collection of anecdotes from favorite books.

Creature feature: Write about, or illustrate, the scariest animal incident in the story.

Research the effect of hibernation on animals.

Use the first two lines of the Cattlemen's song (page 93), and add two last lines to finish the verse.

1. Sittin' on a Cowhorse - - -
2. The whole day long - - -
3. (Make a tune for a sing-a-long.)

For another, try Pa's song as a pattern for writing a verse.

What natural catastrophes occurred in the story? Research the years in which one or more of these have occurred and find the year with the greatest financial loss.

Blue Ridge Billy (New York: J. B. Lippincott Company, 1946). (Gr. 4-6).

The material for *Blue Ridge Billy* was gathered largely in Ashe County, North Carolina. The author presents a typical picture of farm life in the Blue Ridge Mountains before the coming of the auto. All experiences are true.

Ten year old Billy Honeycutt's love of music and his nagging vision of an instrument that plays dance music, is threaded through the rugged, simple life of the Blue Ridge Mountain people. Even Sary Sue is "cravin' " for a "calikur" dress. Billy's hope is almost defeated by his harsh, hard-working father. Coupled with his despondence is the question of his father's possible involvement with the law. Billy knows he's "gotta walk that lonesome valley all by himself." This characteristic determination is a simple, dramatic picture of the rich spirit of the mountain people. Receiving the name of "Blue Ridge

Billy" is the culmination of Billy's highest hope and his friend Sary Sue's, dreams. (A glossary of mountain words and phrases is a special enrichment noting many words used in the Southern Highlands which are pure "Old English," Anglo-Saxon forms. These are words used by Chaucer and Shakespeare, a rarity of preservation by the "ignorant" mountain people.)

Springboards

Do you like to explore new and unknown words?

How could you be rich and poor at the same time?

Have you ever wished for something that you felt you needed to make you "heart-happy"? What did you do to earn it?

Do things you have worked for bring greater pleasure than things given to you? Why?

What was Granny's philosophy?

Are the Blue Ridge people really different from us? Would our speech seem odd to them?

Creative Ideas

There was beautiful description in this story. Re-read the first two pages.

Now try to complete these descriptions. (If you don't recall, use your own words.)

1. Mountains were _____.

2. Still as _____.

3. So still _____.

4. He felt a deep content, as if he _____.

Game: *Climb the Mountain* — Use Taste — Touch — Smell — Sound

1. Divide into two groups as in a Spelling Bee.

2. The first person tries to think of a "Taste" word, the second a "Touch" word, the third, "Smell," the fourth, "Sound." Then the pattern is repeated.

3. Anyone missing goes to the Valley (center of floor). That player may regain his or her place by thinking of a fitting word before his opponent does.

4. The group with larger number of players still on the mountain when the end of the line is reached, has reached the summit. They are the winners.

Research

Locate the range of mountains to which the Blue Ridge Mountains belong. Are they considered "old" or "new" mountains today? Why?

Sketch your favorite scene in the story, or sketch one that was pictured by words. Add a new character or element to the scene. Describe how this might change the story.

Continue collecting folk songs, singing them, and composing melodies if you have only the words. Add new verses using the pattern of the song.

Go "a' yarbing" in reference books. Look for Granny's "yarbs." Do any of these have value in modern medicine today? Find out through interviews with pharmacists in your area.

Make a collection of "folk-proverbs" from Lois Lenski's books, using a similar style, create proverbs relevant for society today.

Judy's Journey (New York and Philadelphia: J. B. Lippincott Company, 1947). (Gr. 4-6).

With deep insight the author portrays the migrant workers as they follow the crops in 1947. Conditions were so bad for Judy's sharecropper family that they had to sell some of their possessions and begin following the crops. Her father spends the money as he makes it. He does not want to work inside a factory. He dreams of the right to own a little piece of land. As the family works in Florida and up the coast, they face the harsh realities of few opportunities for the migrant. Their pride precludes help from the Salvation Army or the women's Welfare Society as they struggle on. The difficulty of migrant children's getting an education is paramount throughout the story. The parents' need for the money that their children can make in the fields usually overcomes their desire for an education for their children. They need that money to stay alive.

Spunky Judy has to deal with her temper as she is confronted at school with the town kids. Against all odds, she does learn to read and to care for the cuts and bruises of others. Judy comes to two profound conclusions: I am a part of all that I have met, and people are fundamentally good—I will be kind to others first.

Springboards

Have you ever had to move to a different home? To what did you look forward? What did you leave that you thought you could not part with?

What does migrant mean? Is there more than one meaning to the word?

Have you ever been a new pupil in a classroom? When a new pupil is enrolled in your room what do you notice about that person?

What could you always give a newcomer?

Have you never had a book of your own or in your home? How might a book help you in making friends?

Do people influence others? How?

Creative Ideas

Choose one of family problems. Assign characters.

Using the author's map of "Judy's Journey" — duplicate it mural size with the opaque projector. Research the route she travelled. Find additional information about a contrasting style of life in that particular region.

Using this sentence from the story, "Nothing so important had ever happened to Judy" as a start, complete the paragraph as you recall the story. Do not be concerned that it is not exact. Use your words if necessary.

Locate and read another story of migrant life. What similarities do you find as different authors write about these people. What, if any, inconsistencies?

Find newspaper articles or pictures about migrant life, including articles about individuals who are striving for improvement in the migrant's life.

Look through old magazines for pictures of foods that might have been produced from some of those Judy's family picked or other migrant families picked.

Find pictures of machines that have replaced some of the pickers.

Try to find the song "You Are My Sunshine." You might find an old recording. Listen to it and sing along. Why do you think the song is not popular today?

Cotton in My Sack (Philadelphia and New York: J. B. Lippincott Company, 1949). (Gr. 3-7).

Set in Mississippi County, Arkansas, the story of the cotton sharecroppers and their families is seen through the eyes of ten-year-old Joanda Hutley. Joanda knows cotton in their sacks means money which is the fragile thread that is the tie to their existence. Human character is seen in action, as controlled by an environment — children having already acquired a superimposed courage, stoicism, and fortitude through endured hardships, sorrow, and meanness. Uncle Shine returns to Arkansas. Seeing the family falling into the old sharecropper pattern, he adroitly assists in shifting their sights to a more substantial future.

Springboards

What does "adventure" mean? Can adventures occur in everyday life?
What is meant by the "magic of words"?
What is a home? How is it different from a house?
What is the most important day of your week? Why?

Creative Activities

Lois Lenski, the author, wrote the words to the song "Cotton in My Sack," and hoped that the use of it would be an incentive to the making of dramatizations of the story. Review the story for a possible dramatization, using the song.

Find and learn: "Pick a Bale of Cotton."

Draw a picture map of Arkansas. This story was written in 1949; locate books on this period. What other things might be added to Lois Lenski's map?

Make a glossary of unusual words and phrases.

Texas Tomboy (Philadelphia: J. B. Lippincott Company, 1950).

Rebelling against her sex role, Charlotte is an irrepressible tomboy, demanding to be called "Charlie Boy." Her aim is to be a ranchwoman. In old overalls and her father's old hat, she rides over the plains with her father learning the lore of ranching. Her strength and fearlessness coupled with her imagination and energy, often result in problems. Charlie Boy brings the reader close to disliking her with her display of thoughtlessness, disobedience, and sometimes cruelty. But through the conflicting demands of society and the individual, and the demands of ranch life and nature, Charlie Boy gains new insights toward the relationships of others and, most importantly herself.

Springboards

The setting of this story is the 1920s when the expectations of society were quite different from those of today concerning the role of girls Charlotte's age. Do you believe the changing attitude today is good or bad? Justify your answer.

Could a terrible disaster help bring people together in real friendship — people whose ways had been so different they had felt they could never be reconciled?

How can defeat be turned into an opportunity?

Why must man respect nature's laws?

Have modern advances changed the Texas ranch way of life? In what way?

Creative Ideas

1. Change in laws of the Texan range
2. Range wars
3. Sodbusters
4. Railroads; effect on this region
5. Automobiles; effect on this region

Look for stories that picture problems of this time.

Make a simple diary for Charlie Boy. One day might need only one sentence. Other days may require a page or more. Would Charlie's diary be more a diary of events or of feeling?

Try an imaginary diary for yourself using the time and setting of this story.

For two weeks, or longer if you wish, keep a personal diary. After completion, re-read to see if you had any problems or adventures. Did they help you? How do you feel now? (Not to be shared unless you wish.)

Classroom Diary Box: Box with slit opening. Children may drop in unsigned sentences of something they did or thought. This, too, remains between teacher and individual.

Find some songs that cowboys sang to tell of their feelings, or to add a spark of fun to their lives. From these choose some to sing.

Dramatize some of the funny situations in the story.

Draw a picture of an unusual creature in a bathtub.

Make a mobile for the story.

Research methods of conservation of soil and water for this region.

Classroom Activities

Make two maps of Texas. Use the author's map for the first. For the second, update the map to the present.

Using a Texas roadmap — list unusual names. Make riddles with some of these names as the answer (e.g., Muleshoe).

Prairie School (Philadelphia and New York: J. B. Lippincott Company, 1951). (Gr. 3-7).

"Born of the Wind" is a realistic description of the children who crossed the windswept South Dakota plains to go to school. How they met this basic terror is realistically pictured by the author as the Great Blizzard of 1949 swept down upon "Teacher," Miss Martin, beloved by Darell, Delores and their schoolmates. Dramatic rescues, a hay drop and Miss Martin's heroic effort to get Delores through the storm for an appendectomy depict the arduous life of the prairie and the hardy people who have ridden the prairie storms. Lois Lenski says, "this is no synthetic, manufactured adventure."

Springboards

Why do you think "Born of the Wind" would be a song of the prairie children?

What are tumbleweeds?

What is a "mirage"?

Would farmers be leasing lands from Indians?

Why would anyone prefer artificial flowers to real ones?

What are immigrants?

Find the definition of "sesame." Can you recall a magical term using this word?

Did the Indians have a natural sense of the conservation of nature?

What is a "black blizzard"?

Creative Ideas

Detective work:

Find recipes for Kuger, casenipfla, wurst and halvah. Together try one of the simpler recipes. Find their origin. Find the reason for not drinking alkaline water.

Someone said, "Neign, neign." Skim the story for clues to the nationality of the speaker. Find the English word for "neign."

See how many descriptions you can add to these sentence starters:

1.   The wind sounds like _____.
2.   The snow looks just like _____.

Play the game "New Orleans." Choose sides. Try to think of things in the story to pantomime.

In the story Darrell tried to repair the dead radio storage battery. He took a nail and made some holes in one end and then poured some vinegar in and set it on the back of the stove to soak. Check scientific facts on chemical composition of vinegar. Look for information on a storage battery. Try making a simple demonstration of one.

Learn the song "Born of the Wind, Song of the Prairie Children." Select part of the story for dramatization.

Sketch some snow scenes. Try whipped soap flakes, cotton, Dacron® pillow filler, or other white materials to represent snow in your scenes.

Draw your version of a "Galloping Goose."

Reproduce Lenski's picture map of South Dakota. What changes are needed to make the map accurate for today?

Find more information about Standing Rock Indian Reservation.

Mama Hattie's Girl (Philadelphia and New York: J. B. Lippincott Company, 1953). (Gr. 4-6).

Ten-year-old Lula Bell portrays real life experiences which a Negro girl might have in her adjustment to North and South. Hattie's struggles as a human being with the faults and virtues common to all races are simply stated.

Mama Hattie is a dominant figure as Lula Bell's grandmother. Mama Hattie represents the "ol' ways" in contrast to her family's struggle for the new.

Springboards

Did you ever brag about something and add things that were not true to impress a friend?

Did you ever hate the place in which you lived?

Did you change your mind?

Were you ever refused entry to an eating establishment?

Why did some of the Negroes wish to move to the North?

Can prejudice be wiped out by the making of laws? Why or why not?

Creative Ideas

Use chapter 8, "First Prize," in creating a play depicting Lula Bell's reaction to her big city school.

These statements come from Lois Lenski's story of *Cotton in My Sack*, but are fitting for this story. (If you disagree, state your disagreement in your writing.)

1. "We're all the same color when the lights are out."

2. "The rain is God's fertilizer. It falls on rich and poor alike."

3. "If you want a friend, first show yourself friendly."

Use these statements as a starter for a paragraph. Finish the paragraph with your own thoughts.

Accept the author's generous offer to use her "Farewell Song, Song of the Negro Children." The words offer a suggestion for a pantomime. Try it. The song presents a picture, too. Try illustrating it.

Corn-Farm Boy (Philadelphia and New York: J. B. Lippincott Company, 1954).

This is another book in the series of the author's regional books written in answer to American children writing her "to come and see where we live and what we do ... write about us."

Ten-year-old Dick Hoffman returns from school on the pretense of sickness — even facing castor oil — to catch a glimpse of the machine, a new green tractor! Through Dick and his family the reader lives the corn-farm life. Presented in the story is the transition to the mechanized farm, which in itself is a personal type of heartbreak. All aspects of raising a crop of corn, from preparation of the seed bed to the final harvesting, are factually presented, coupled with the constant concern about weather elements, insects and crop diseases. The reader also becomes acquainted with the joys and humor of the people, and a very important factor in farm life, neighborliness.

Springboards

What does "hybrid" mean?
What part does nature play in raising a crop of corn?
What state leads in the production of corn? (1980)
What is meant by contouring land?
What else is raised on a corn farm?
How has mechanization changed the pattern of corn farming?
How does a good neighbor play a part in our lives?
How does one become a good neighbor?

Creative Ideas

Compare Dick's attitude toward wildlife with that of his friend's, Elmer Ruden. Role play one of their differences.

Careers: Dick decides to become a small animal veterinarian. Find information he will need in becoming one.

Green cockleburs are mentioned in the story as being poisonous. Refer to reference books for the type of poison. What other wild plants are poisonous?

Make a time-line drawing of the progress of the methods of corn farming (26 years have elapsed since this book was written). You should find many changes.

Research: Hybrid corn—who discovered it? How was it discovered? How did it affect the corn industry? How is the seed produced? What is its cost?

Create a mobile for the story, or, choose a main character in the story and create a mobile for him or her. Write a paragraph sketch of the character chosen.

Pretend you are on a detassling truck. Compose a fun song you might sing as you ride.

Laugh Lines: Use the story situation—riding the sow; the black kitten with a white stripe down its back; or, write a joke using an original funny, farm-story situation.

If possible interview some of your community's older citizens. Ask them to share one of their growing-up experiences. Tape their story.

Learn the author's song, "Listen to the Tall Corn Grow, Song of the Corn-Farm Children" (music by Clyde Robert Bulla). Try adding verses to it.

Flood Friday (Philadelphia and New York: J. B. Lippincott Company, 1956).

The flood tragedy struck Connecticut on "Flood Friday," August 19, 1955. Eleven-year-old Sally's family and their neighbors' experiences are simply told. A major flood needs no dramatic telling—it is terrifying, tragic, raw drama! Its surging waters reveal the true character of the people in its path. The author's simplistic black and white drawings supplement the storm. A foreword, a map of the area, and a song fitted to the story are included.

Springboards

Were you ever in a flood?

What is a refugee?

How is a flood a "test"?

What is a U.S. Army "duck"?

How could you survive in an emergency if all conveniences were cut off?

Do you think it would be more difficult to survive in a disaster now than in pioneer days?

Creative Ideas

Draw a picture of how the children looked to the National Guard soldier.

If you have not been personally involved in a flood, interview and tape the story of someone who has.

What medical advances made since 1955 could have aided in the 1955 flood.

Coal-Camp Girl (Philadelphia and New York: J. B. Lippincott Company, 1959).

The strong influence of a region upon its character is exemplified in *Coal-Camp Girl*. A West Virginia family experiences hunger during a winter when there is no food. The specter of a "cave-in" is always present. They know the agony of waiting for news of the rescue of loved ones trapped in a mine. The harsh experience of being paid in scrip and forced to buy in the high-cost company store is an economic lesson life forces them to learn — to endure. Even the air they breathe takes its toll.

Springboards

Why is coal not used for heating homes as much today as 30 years ago?

Have you ever seen a coal-mine town? Would it differ in any way from your city or town?

Have you ever heard of a mine cave-in with men entrapped? When? Where?

The "black-lung" disease is still a danger to miners today. Can anything be done to eliminate this threat to health?

What is "strip mining"? Why do you suppose many cattle ranchers in the West are opposed to strip mining?

Has the energy crisis placed coal mining in the public eye? In what way?

Creative Ideas

Try to find pictures of coal mining and miners. Use these in making a booklet. Make a caption for the picture; add other comments of your own.

Using resource books, find information about the use of coal and its by-products.

Search for information on health hazards in coal mining and on its effect on the community.

Check newspapers, magazines, or television for problems of the coal miners. Watch for governments' and big business' reactions to their problems.

Make a duo-mural showing a coal-camp town of 1959 in contrast to one of 1978.

Shoo-Fly Girl (Philadelphia and New York: J. B. Lippincott Company, 1963).

The story depicts authentically the customs of the Amish in one district of Lancaster County, Pennsylvania, as there are many variations in Amish customs. That such a life style has been preserved is just short of a miracle. Suzannah, nicknamed Shoo-Fly, lives a confined, controlled life, yet a happy one. Her encounters with the outside world, particularly with her non-Amish neighbors, bring confusion. Her curiosity and questions are reconciled with her Great-Grossommy's answer: "... To keep humble, to avoid false pride. We are the plain people. We eat plain, we live plain, we dress plain, to show that our hearts are not set on the things of this world, but above. We are Amish. These things we have always done. So we will always do." The foreword is an important part of this book and should be read by the teacher or librarian to the children. The author includes her picture map of the state designating the setting of the story.

Springboards

Can you imagine having four sewing machines in your home and each one being used? How is this different from homes today with three or four television sets?

Would you be happy to live in a community of people who believed in using only things you could make with your hands? Before answering, think of things you have made yourself. How did you feel when the item was completed?

The life of the Amish people is very much the same today as it was when this book was written. What aspects of this life style would appeal to you?

Are there differences in Amish and Mennonite beliefs, or are they the same sect?

Creative Ideas

Make a picture dictionary of the Amish words used in the story. Add the English definitions.

Trace the settling of the Amish people in the United States.

Group Project: Make Amish figures representing the main characters of the family in *Shoo-Fly Girl*. Use liquid soap bottles filled with sand as the basic figure.

If you do not play a harmonica, see if you can find someone who does. Ask that person to play a song. Tape it and share it with your classmates.

Have a "schnitzing" party. Determine the amount of apples needed. Purchase apples best for drying. Cut ("schnitz") them, and place them on a clean cloth on top of a car (covered with a plastic drop cloth). Bring the apples in at the close of the school day. This step may have to be repeated until the apples are dry. (This method has been very successful — of course you have to watch for apple snitchers.) Use your dried apples to make "Fried Apple" pies.

Make a Shoo-Fly pie. Assemble the necessary ingredients. This is the author's authentic recipe. She stated in her foreword that the making of a good one is an art, but one easily acquired by quite young Amish girls.

Shoo-Fly Pie

Mix 1 cup flour, ⅔ cup brown sugar, 1 tablespoon butter into crumbs. Set aside half the mixture. Mix 1 cup dark molasses, ¾ cup boiling water, 1 teaspoon soda, 1 beaten egg. Then mix with half the crumbs, *but do not beat*. Put in pie shell and cover with the remaining crumbs. Bake 11 minutes at 375°.

Peanuts for Billy Ben (Philadelphia: J. B. Lippincott Company, 1952).

From Norfolk, Virginia, to Edenton, North Carolina, in late October in the early fifties, the author uses verse and prose to draw a verbal, realistic picture of Billy Ben's family life on a peanut farm. Billy Ben lives on a half-shares farm; his father works the land. After all the bills were paid, Billy Ben's father got half of the profits and the owner got the other half.

Nature versus hard work is the same story in harvesting a crop and in a family's survival, regardless of the region or the people. Growing peanuts is a family affair.

Springboards

Have you or your family tried to grow peanuts?
What kind of soil and climate are best for their growth?
Would you like to learn how peanuts were grown 36 years ago?
Do you think it would be hard work to make your living in this manner?
Is a peanut really a nut?
What are some things made from peanuts?

Creative Ideas

Plant some peanuts in a flower pot in your classroom. You will need to find what kind of seed to use and what conditions are needed.

Find pictures of peanut products. Read about George Washington Carver. What uses did he discover for peanuts?

Using resource books, see which student can find the longest list of the uses of peanuts.

What are some other names for peanuts?

Find a simple recipe using peanuts. Try it.

Bring records that have banjo music. Listen to them. Try to fit some of the verses to the music. Pantomime shelling peanuts while singing these songs.

Find information about modern methods of raising and harvesting peanuts.

Little Sioux Girl (Philadelphia: J. B. Lippincott Company, 1958).

The author's foreword:

A tiny village on a plateau by a river bank—a church, a school, a house for the teacher and a dozen log cabins. That was all. It was in the Standing Rock Indian reservation in the Dakotas, and here Sioux Indian children lived.

Wind and dust and hot sun were their daily companions. Cut off from the world by a rough, at times impassable road, they ran and played and were happy. I visited them in 1950, talked to them and loved them.

Since then, the school has been closed, the Indian families have moved away and the cabins are empty.

This is the factual basis for the story of Eva White Bird and her family. One particular custom stands out: Unless the gift was something you treasured yourself, unless the gift was a sacrifice, it was not a gift at all. The Sioux people made themselves poor giving gifts they could not afford. They experienced the same floods that the characters of *Flood Friday* did learning the harsh lesson: When you see the river rolling it's no time to think of worldly goods.

Springboards

Locate filmstrips or pictures which show the Dakota Badlands. How could one make a living in this part of the United States?

If a government forced you and your family to leave your home and settle in a desolate place, how would you feel? What would you do?

Creative Ideas

Using brown craft paper make a "Prairie Rose" doll, or a Sioux Indian figure in native dress.

Play "Andy Over" using a low structure where the ball will not be lost or break anything. In the school gym you might use a volley ball net; teams turn backs to each other — use a bean bag instead of a ball. When "Andy Over" is called, the person catching the ball runs around and tries to tag one of the opponents. The victor is the team tagging all opponents.

Blueberry Corners (Philadelphia and New York: J. B. Lippincott Company, 1940).

(The dedication page reads: "To the Town of Harwinton, Connecticut where the biggest blueberries grow in 1940 just as they did one hundred years ago in 1840.")

Becky, the second daughter of Parson Griswold's family of eight, carries the story of the family's fundamental beliefs at odds with changing times and attitudes. The wealth and beauty of a newcomer her age are a marked contrast to their clean, but hand-me-down, dull clothing. Becky's pride and courage and sense of duty helps her to retain her faith in the beautiful, and likewise to meet the sternness of reality. She works out her own philosophy, that nice things do not come of themselves; you have to bring it yourself. She sets out to perform a miracle.

Springboards

What does the expression, "Fine feathers don't make fine birds," mean?
Compare the daily activities of the characters in the book with your daily activities. Which are similar? Which are different? Why?

Creative Ideas

Use the Apple Fable as a dramatization.
Have a Blueberry Party: Make blueberry cookies for refreshments.

Recipe for Blueberry Cookies:

1 box of Blueberry Muffin mix and any other ingredients the mix calls for (see recipe on box). Other items needed for baking them in your classroom: electric skillet, mixing bowl, mixing spoon, measuring cup and spoons, waxed paper, powdered sugar, vegetable oil, spatula.

1. Grease pan.
2. Set electric skillet at about 350° (this temperature may need adjusting as utensils vary). Place lid on skillet for oven effect.
3. Prepare mix. Have children help mix and measure. Each child will get in a "few beats."
4. Have children work in groups of four in overseeing the baking. (This will have to be closely supervised.)
5. Each child will do one cookie—drop one tablespoonful into skillet. Do not crowd cookies ... allow for rising. You may have to peek. If batter has bubbled up it is time to turn cookie over. Replace lid. Count to 10 slowly. Cookie should be done. Remove cookies from pan to waxed paper sprinkled with powdered sugar.
6. Let next group bake theirs, continuing until all have participated. (One box of mix may not be sufficient ... depends on the number of children.)

Teacher's Note

A third grade field trip resulted from the use of the word "treacle" in one of the children's stories, and finding its definition. We found it was another word for molasses. One of the children told of her grandather's making molasses from his sugar cane. (I had mentioned it was almost a lost art.) This was an opportunity too good to miss. Knowing we would not be able to see the product from start to finish, I recruited the child's mother to take pictures of the cane before cutting and of the cutting itself. On our trip, the mother told of the first steps in the process, showing the pictures and explaining the process that was in progress. (I continued taking pictures.) The children tasted the raw sugar cane and were given a piece to take with them. We all got a yummy lick from some cooled molasses before boarding the bus for our return. We received a jar of the molasses the next day. I suggested using it for molasses cookies. You guessed! A Molasses Cookie Party! We used the method described above to make Wagon Wheel Cookies. They were yummy, too. The delicious aroma arising from their baking pervaded the hall. Our secret was out! We had to share with other rooms—and of course with the Principal!

Fortunately, all the pictures were good. Slides were made of them. We taped a story to go with the slides describing the process and told about the Molasses Cookie Party.

This recipe is taken from *Betty Crocker's Picture Cook Book*, 2nd ed. (McGraw Hill, 1956).

Wagon Wheels

Mix well	½ cup soft shortening
	1 cup sugar
Stir in	1 cup dark molasses
	½ cut water
Sift together and stir in	4 cups sifted flour
	1 Tsp. soda
	1½ tsp. salt
	1½ tsp. ginger
	½ tsp. cloves
	½ tsp. nutmeg
	¼ tsp. allspice

Chill dough several hours or overnight. Roll out ¼" thick. Cut into 3" circles. Sprinkle with sugar. Place on well greased baking sheet. Press a large raisin into center of each. Bake until, when touched lightly with finger, almost no imprint remains. Leave on baking sheet a few minutes before removing to prevent breaking. If desired, make "spokes" of icing radiating out from centers of cooled cookies.

Temperature: 375° (quick moderate oven).

Time: Bake 10 to 12 minutes.

Amount: 2½ dozen 3" cookies.

Indian Captive: The Story of Mary Jemison (Philadelphia: J. B. Lippincott Company, 1941). (Gr. 7-9).

A biographical account of a real, twelve-year-old girl who is captured by the Seneca Indians and taken to live with them. The basic conflict of Indian and white culture is the principal theme. Unconsciously, Mary absorbs the Indian way of life as she struggles to keep fresh in her memory the white ways. Adopted into their tribe, she is treated kindly. She comes to understand and appreciate the Indians as a people rather than as a wild enemy. With her understanding comes her love for them. An agonizing decision confronts her upon her discovery by the white man; she chooses to stay.

This story is more fictionalized than the greater part of the author's works.

Springboards

Could this story have happened during any other period of our country's history? Why or why not?

What do you think your reaction would be if you were captured by an Indian?

Reverse the roles — an Indian captured by the white man.

Would it be difficult to return to your own people?

Would it be harder for the Indian captive or the white captive? Why?

Creative Ideas

Imagine you are captured by Indians. Choose a particular tribe. Compose a diary you might keep while captive. Use resource books for their way of life. Finally, you are discovered. Note your reactions and your decisions.

Reverse the role. The Indian is a captive of the white man. Make an English diary for him. If he is freed, what will be his people's reactions? Note these in the diary, including his reactions and decisions.

Role Play:

1. White captive's return to home.
2. Indian captive's return to home.

Footnotes

[1]Charles Adams, ed. *Lois Lenski: In Appreciation* (Durham, NC: Christian Printing Company, 1963), pp. 40-41.

7 CHARACTER ENCOUNTERS OF THE GIFTED KIND

A study of character development is, of course, an integral part of any literature program. In responding to selections students are expected to describe the characters in fairly standard terms. These include identifying particular traits, actions, or speech, showing how the character relates to others and how others feel or react toward the character. Two additional factors must be considered, however, in beginning character study with the gifted child.

This child, who can read before coming to school, whose interests expand so much more rapidly as he or she approaches adolescence, who questions everything more deeply and profoundly than his or her peers, who seems different because so much more an adult—this child lacks the role models which other children find so easily in their peers. Thus, the gifted child often must choose an adult as a role model at a time when the peer group is most important to the child's development.

A study of characterization with gifted children must, then, go beyond standard responses. It must deal heavily in the areas of emotions and values and must present characters who can serve as role models. Fortunately, a number of authors are writing today who do use a gifted child as the protagonist. In reading and discussing these books with each other gifted children can evaluate the actions, emotions, and values of the characters in light of their own actions, emotions, and values. In what way, for example, does the protagonist deal with the values of society: responsibility, respect for others, loyalty, self-satisfaction, self-control, knowledge, courage, honesty, self-respect, obedience, self-discipline, freedom, justice, equality? When are the values of society flaunted and why? What point of view does the author choose to tell the story? Is the point of view true and honest with respect to the main character and the persons with whom he or she interacts?

In order to evaluate the way in which an author has drawn a character, a second factor must come into play. Students must be well-grounded in techniques of literary criticism; they must be able to identify the factors which separate a convincing character from a stereotype, to evaluate character development or change and to recognize inconsistencies in character or plot development. Most important, they must be able to evaluate the worthiness of the characters themselves.

The emphasis in the junior novel studies that follow is on character development. However, in any literature study all elements that determine literary quality must be considered. In addition to the study of characterization, the student should be able to view the theme as the ultimate outcome of the story and its relationship to the gifted protagonist *and* to the reader. The student should also be able to analyze the setting for validity of time and place, and to examine plot development for the sequence of events in relation to characters, setting, theme, and resolution of the conflict as it pertains to the protagonist. In addition to the literary study, the student should be able to evaluate why he or she does or does not empathize with the protagonist, feel as the character feels, act as the character acts. Finally, the student should be able to determine whether the book is unified, whether it is an integral entity.

Introduction to the Unit

Four junior novels, one by each of four authors, have been chosen for this unit. A biographical sketch of the author and a summary of the story are provided for each. The teacher should introduce both the author and the story to the students or perhaps should even read all or part of the book aloud before the discussion. The list of discussion questions can be given before the book is read, after it is read, or at any point the teacher believes is desirable. It must be emphasized that there are no right or wrong answers to these questions; the purpose is to give the gifted child an opportunity to express his or her beliefs and thoughts after reading about another gifted person. Each group of gifted readers will be different, and the individual differences in the group should be taken into consideration. It may be most effective to meet with the group every day, once or twice a week, or at whatever interval of time is in the students' best interests. In any case, it should be pointed out to the children that they are going to be reading books by very special authors who have written about very special people.

Character Development in the Junior Novel

I.   *Father's Arcane Daughter*, by E. L. Konigsburg (New York: Atheneum, 1976). (Ages 11-15).

E. L. Konigsburg is a relatively short, dark-haired, dark-eyed lady who is very much aware of the foolishness and fun in the world. She was born in New York City and did most of her growing up in the small towns of Pennsylvania. Elaine Konigsburg is a chemist and taught science at a small girls' school. After her three children began school, she began writing. It always seemed she could not find the time to do the writing she wanted to do until then. She would write in the morning, read what she had written to her children when they came home for lunch, and do her housework in the afternoon.

Her children have been her best critics and they have helped her research some of her books. Konigsburg has received many awards for her dozen or so books, among them the Newbery Award for *From the Mixed-up Files of Mrs. Basil E. Frankweiler* (New York: Atheneum, 1967). Konigsburg fans soon discover that most of her books are about gifted children and are written for gifted children. One of the main traits of her protagonists is a sense of humor, which makes her works highly amusing.

Father's Arcane Daughter is the story of Winston Carmichael and his family: Charles, his father; Grace, his mother; Heidi, his sister; and Caroline, his half-sister. Winston was a bright boy who agonized over his little sister Heidi because she was a golliwog. Mrs. Carmichael simply spoiled her; Mr. Carmichael did not seem to notice anything. Caroline, kidnapped seventeen years earlier, suddenly arrives home. What she does for her half-siblings is a story of love and reality. But is Caroline real?

Discussion Questions

1. Read again just the italicized part at the beginning of the first eleven chapters and near the end of chapter eleven. Could these parts combined be a chapter? Where would you put it? Why did the author structure the story in this way? Does this structure add to the suspense?

2. Do you agree with Heidi when she says, "Life's like that. A little knowing. A lot of not knowing"?

3. What did you sense when Winston said that losing the full use of one of his senses made him Heidi's equal?

4. What is the significance of Thursday?

5. What does Winston mean when he says, "I had been busy being Columbus, discovering a new world."

6. Do you think the inheritance plot is real enough for the complete story effect?

7. What sort of adult did Winston think Caroline was?

8. How do you feel about the suspense? Does the way Konigsburg write make you want to keep reading? Why or why not?

9. How do you interpret the title of this book?

10. Does Winston's attitude toward money make him even more spoiled than Heidi?

11. Evaluate Winston's description of his mother, Caroline, and Heidi at the Christmas party.

12. Why do you think Winston gave the book he bought for Caroline to Heidi?

13. Was Winston jealous of Heidi or Caroline or both?

14. Would you write letters like Winston's? Do you think he shows imagination and creativity or do you think he is a smart-aleck?

15. Do you think that an ordinary brother would have felt the way Winston did about Heidi?

16. What does Martha Sedgewick mean when she says that money had bought too wide a margin for Winston and Heidi?

17.   Do you think that Heidi develops the most as a person throughout the book? What do you think of her feelings about her mother?

18.   Why do Winston and Heidi use the expression, "funny papers," at the end? Before they had said comic strips.

19.   Would you have buried Caroline and Martha Sedgewick the way Winston and Hilary did?

20.   Compare Winston and Hilary at the beginning and then at the end of the story.

21.   Some critics believe this story is unfinished. Do you? If so write an ending.

Other Books by E. L. Konigsburg

About the B'nai Bagels (New York: Atheneum, 1969). (Gr. 3-7).

Altogether, One at a Time (New York: Atheneum, 1971). (Gr. 3-7).

The Dragon in the Ghetto Caper (New York: Atheneum, 1974). (Gr. 4-6).

From the Mixed-up Files of Mrs. Basil E. Frankweiler (New York: Atheneum, 1967). (Gr. 3-7).

George (New York: Atheneum, 1970). (Gr. 4-9).

Jennifer, Hecate, Macbeth, William McKinley, and Me, Elizabeth (New York: Atheneum, 1969). (Gr. 3-8).

A Proud Taste for Scarlet and Miniver (New York: Atheneum, 1973). (Gr. 6-9).

The Second Mrs. Giaconda (New York: Atheneum, 1975). (Gr. 5-9).

II.   *Arilla Sun Down*, by Virginia Hamilton (New York: Greenwillow Books, 1976). (Gr. 7-10).

Writing about one single theme of the black experience and presenting it as clearly as possible is Virginia Hamilton's purpose. She claims to write of her past experiences, bringing them to the present with an eye on the future. Many of her protagonists experience an isolation of the spirit, and she knows that sometimes people do not know what she is pursuing. But Virginia Hamilton wants to make reading an extraordinary experience for children. Painting new worlds of darkness and light for children to discover is part of her aim. She believes that she learned to write in the best way — by living — and she often says she writes for herself.

Virginia Hamilton was born on March 12, 1933, in Yellow springs, Ohio. Her home life was happy and she loved school. She attended Antioch College on a full scholarship and after three years went to Ohio State University. Writing courses and literature classes made her happy. Many of her teachers believed that publishers would love her. After going to New York City it took her ten years of more writing courses and more study to have a book published. She has won several awards for her books.

Arilla Sun Down is the story of a twelve-year-old black girl who cannot come to terms with her family. She is ashamed of herself and her family. Her father is part black, part Indian. He has never accepted his dual heritage. Arilla's mother, a light-skinned black person, is a dancer and dance teacher who does not sufficiently understand her daughter. Jack Sun Run, Arilla's brother, in a sense causes her the most hurt and yet also loves her the most. The story is about a year in Arilla's life during which she grows tremendously because of her family and the many circumstances surrounding their lives together. Hamilton means the book to be partly autobiographical—her grandmother claimed Cherokee blood.

Explain to the children that this book may be difficult to read at first. It is written in the first person, and many of Arilla's thoughts are expressed in half sentences. It makes one feel as if one is suspended in mid-air.

Discussion Questions

1. From the tone of the first chapter, do you get the impression that Arilla always knew down deep that her parents and brother loved her and thought she was quite unique in spite of her thoughts through the rest of the story?

2. What does Arilla mean when she says, "But thinking back always makes me feel like I'm coming down with something incurable"?

3. Do you feel about school the way Arilla does? She says, "I don't hate the school here; but if I want to be cool, I can't say that out loud. I really like it." Why is it so important to her to be "cool"?

4. Would you let your brother (or sister) tell you who to invite to your party as Arilla did? Why do you think Arilla did this?

5. In spite of the fact that Arilla calls her family "peculiar," does she like being a part of it?

6. Why does Arilla seem ashamed of herself? Is it because she is, or because of her family?

7. Why did Arilla's dad keep going back to Cliffville? At the beginning of the story did Arilla understand why?

8. Is Arilla as different as she feels she is? Do you feel as she does sometimes?

9. Do you think many children have the notion they have been secretly adopted as Arilla did?

10. Is there any point in the story at which the first chapter makes a complete circle?

11. Does Arilla's brother surround her life as she says, or does she just imagine it?

12. Arilla says that Jack Sun Run is gifted like her father. What is Arilla's gift?

13. Do you think Arilla and her brother hate each other, or is their relationship natural with brothers and sisters?

14. What is your total impression of Arilla's birthday party?

15. What does James False Face mean by, "Life goes round and round. I am drawn within the circle."

16. Does Jack Sun Run want Arilla dead?

17. Think about this passage: "Never even noticed it before, but Mom is as strange and different as everybody else in this house. Or maybe I'm just strange and different." Who is strange and different? Anyone?

18. Is it natural for Arilla to wish she were a little brother and her brother were a big sister taking care of her? Why does she feel this way?

19. Can you explain Arilla's jealousy of her brother? Does she have a reason for being jealous?

20. What does Arilla mean when she says, "... Dad and Sun and Mom and me, are always the outsiders at other times"?

21. Arilla has the feeling that Sun Run has three layers. To what is she referring?

22. Arilla's father believes his children are different. Does this make Arilla happy?

23. Explain the trunk and the skate rink.

24. Discuss what Sun Run does to show he appreciates Arilla as a sister.

25. Why does Arilla always seem to be running to or from something?

26. What is your impression of Arilla as she listens to her father speak about Korea ignoring her brother the whole time?

27. How would you describe Arilla as a person?

28. Explain, "The summer comes and goes. A man enters, bringing a lifetime of riches. Goes, leaving you poorer."

29. What was the real effect upon Arilla of Sun's accident?

30. What is your interpretation of the last two lines of chapter 11, "Now his power is gone for us both forever. And that sure is some kind of sad"?

31. Can you evaluate Arilla's father as a person?

32. What is Arilla referring to when she thinks, "So it's gone, isn't it, whatever it is, so why feel it?"

33. Imagine that you are Arilla at the end of the story. What is your view of life?

34. Write another chapter for this book predicting what will happen when Arilla's mother finds out about the roller-skating and the trunk.

Other Books by Virginia Hamilton

The House of Dies Drear (New York: Macmillan, 1970). (Gr. 5-9).

M. C. Higgins, the Great (Boston: G. K. Hall, 1976). (Gr. 7-up).

Paul Robeson: The Life and Times of a Free Black Man (New York: Harper and Row, 1974). (Gr. 7-12).

The Planet of Junior Brown (New York: Macmillan, 1974). (Gr. 7-up).

Time-Ago Lost: More Tales of Jahdu (New York: Macmillan, 1973). (Gr. 2-5).

The Time-Ago Tales of Jahdu (New York: Macmillan, 1969). (Gr. 2-5).

W. E. B. DuBois: A Biography (New York: Thomas Y. Crowell, 1972). (Gr. 5-8).

The Writings of W. E. B. DuBois (New York: Thomas Y. Crowell, 1975). (Gr. 5-up).

Zeely (New York: Macmillan, 1967). (Gr. 5-7).

III. *The Great Gilly Hopkins*, by Katherine Paterson (New York: Thomas Y. Crowell, 1978). (Gr. 5-up).

  Katherine Paterson has won the National Book Award twice: in 1977 for *The Master Puppeteer* and in 1979 for *The Great Gilly Hopkins*. She also won the Newbery Medal for *Bridge to Terabithia* in 1978. In a television interview she said that if you want to write all you have to do is write.

  Born on October 21, 1932, in Tsing-Tsiang pu, China, Katherine Paterson has lead an unusual life. Her childhood was spent in China but she received her A.B. degree from King College in 1954 and her M.A. from Presbyterian School of Christian Education in 1957. She studied at the Naganuma School of the Japanese Language in Kobe, Japan, and received an M.R.E. from Union Theological Seminary, New York, in 1962. She has been a public school teacher, a missionary in Japan, and a teacher of sacred studies and English.

  Because she lived in Japan she has written three novels set in feudal Japan. Her love for this country is deep.

  Katherine Paterson's two daughters are adopted. The girls and her two sons often read her manuscripts and criticize them. She states that her children do influence her writing. *the Great Gilly Hopkins*, about a foster child, is dedicated to her adopted daughter Mary.

  Galadriel Hopkins is an eleven-year-old foster child. Her only hope is to be able to live with her beautiful mother, Courtney Rutherford Hopkins, from whom she hears very infrequently. Her brilliance and unmanageability keep her going from one foster home to another until she goes to live with Maime Trotter. Mrs. Trotter, a seven-year-old foster boy, and the blind black man next door teach Gilly the lessons she needs to learn in both a moving and a comic way that only the "gutsy Gilly" can fully appreciate.

Discussion Questions

1. What is your first impression of Gilly Hopkins?
2. And what does Gilly think of herself?

3. What was it about Maime Trotter that kept Gilly from getting the upper hand her first evening there?

4. Which name did she really prefer: Gilly or Galadriel?

5. If Mr. Randolph, Miss Harris, and some of the pupils had not been black do you think Gilly would have been different?

6. What does the statement, "It bothered her to have everything in a muddle," tell you about Gilly?

7. When did Gilly first realize that Trotter loved her and she loved Trotter?

8. What was it about Miss Harris that confused gilly?

9. How would you interpret the greeting card incident?

10. Why did Gilly make the mistake of using W.E. and Agnes? Was this typical of her? Does Gilly begin to change here?

11. Would you call Gilly a moody person? Give some examples if you think she is moody.

12. Do you believe that Gilly was perhaps too intelligent for her own good? If so, give an example of her intelligence leading her to be intolerant.

13. In spite of her apparent contempt for everyone and everything, why does Gilly keep remembering her former foster mother, Mrs. Nevins?

14. If you had been Gilly would you have "frozen" at the bus station? Why do you think that happened to her?

15. How would Gilly's bus station episode be reported on TV news? Write the script the reporter would read.

16. Why do you suppose Gilly wanted to teach W.E. to stand up for himself?

17. Compare Gilly in the chapter entitled "The Visitor" and the Gilly of the first chapter.

18. What did Miss Ellis mean when she said, "God help the children of the flower children"?

19. In "The Going" Gilly shows her love for a particular poem. Discuss what you think this says about her.

20. Why do you think Gilly felt Courtney's picture did not fit in Chadwell's room?

21. Characterize Courtney Rutherford Hopkins.

22. Gilly would not think of herself as good, but what would you say are Gilly's good characteristics?

23. What would you theorize is the great lesson that Gilly learned?

24. If you liked reading this book and would like others to read it also, give a sales pitch about *The Great Gilly Hopkins*.

25. Can you anticipate what kind of Christmas Gilly had and what her first year living with her grandmother was like?

26. Write the sort of letter Gilly will write to W.E. after being with her grandmother one year.

Other Books by Katherine Paterson

Bridge to Terabithia (New York: Thomas Y. Crowell, 1977). Illustrated by Donna Diamond. (Gr. 5-up).

The Master Puppeteer (New York: Thomas Y. Crowell, 1976). Illustrated by Hara Wells. (Gr. 7-up).

Of Nightingales That Weep (New York: Thomas Y. Crowell, 1974). (Gr. 5-up).

The Sign of the Chrysanthemum (New York: Thomas Y. Crowell, 1973). Illustrated by Peter Landa. (Gr. 5-9).

IV.   *A Wrinkle in Time*, by Madeleine L'Engle (New York: Farrar, Straus, and Giroux, 1962). (Gr. 7-up).

Madeleine L'Engle writes half of her books for children because she believes they are open-minded and still excited by new ideas. Fantasy keeps the windows of imagination open, and she thinks that when an idea is too difficult for adults she can write about it for children.

Born in New York City on November 29, 1918, Madeleine L'Engle lived there until she was twelve-years-old. Her family moved to Europe, living mainly in France and Switzerland, and she attended a Swiss boarding school. She returned to the United States and graduated from Smith College in 1941. Then she moved to Greenwich Village with three other girls who were aspiring actresses. L'Engle worked in the theater which she thought was an excellent school for writers. She met her actor-husband Hugh Franklin at this time.

After both she and her husband retired from the theater in 1952, they moved to Connecticut. While running a general store, managing an old farmhouse, being an active community member, and raising three children, L'Engle managed to write at night. Writing is an essential function of her life like sleeping and breathing.

The Newbery Award was given for *A Wrinkle in Time* in 1962. It was proclaimed the first juvenile science fiction novel. The utilization of a futuristic world of space travel, the speculation about life elsewhere in the universe, the portrayal of teenagers Meg Murry and Calvin O'Keefe as typical young people in search of identity, and the non-sexist view of females makes this an historically important book. Young people should be able to empathize with the characters as they become anxious over physical appearance; fret about relationships with parents, peers, and siblings; and confront the problems of good and evil. The characterizations of Charles Wallace and the good witches are so appealing that most young readers will want to keep reading for the sheer pleasure of discovering what they will do next.

Discussion Questions

1. If a teacher said to you, "... I don't understand how a child with parents as brilliant as yours are supposed to be can be such a poor student," how would you react?

2. What is your first impression of Charles Wallace?

3. Analyze Mrs. Murry's statement, "... you don't have to understand things for them to *be*."

4. Do you agree with Meg that facts are a lot easier to face than people?

5. Evaluate Charles Wallace's statement, "I think it will be better if people go on thinking I'm not very bright. They won't hate me quite so much."

6. Analyze the first encounter of Calvin O'Keefe and Charles Wallace.

7. Do you understand what Calvin means when he speaks of his family and love?

8. What does Calvin mean when he says, "I'm not alone any more"?

9. "Charles Wallace's difference isn't physical. It's in essence." Do you comprehend what this means?

10. Do you agree with Mrs. Which, "Thee onnlly wway ttoo ccope withh ssometthingg ddeadly sserious iss ttoo ttry ttoo trreatt itt a llittlle lligghtly"? Explain the true meaning of this statement.

11. Compare the relationship between Meg and Charles Wallace with that between Meg and her twin brothers.

12. What is your interpretation of "The Black Thing"?

13. How would you explain Mrs. Whatsit's statement that, "Only a fool is not afraid"?

14. What was your impression of all the children playing in rhythm? How did you feel when you read this? Read it again and explain your feelings.

15. Would you like to live in such an "oriented city"?

16. Why did Calvin say, "There is nothing to fear except fear itself," in chapter 7, "The Man with the Red Eyes"?

17. Can you interpret what Charles Wallace means when he tells the man with the red eyes, "Because you aren't you"?

18. Is Charles Wallace a believable character?

19. How would you explain the Prime Coordinator?

20. What is your interpretation of the planet, Camazotz?

21. "Maybe I don't like being different," Meg said, "but I don't want to be like everybody else, either." Do you believe very many people feel this way?

22. What is Charles Wallace trying to do when he tells Meg and Calvin, "IT sometimes calls ITself the Happiest Sadist"?

23. Can you deduce what Meg says when she says, "Maybe if you aren't unhappy sometimes you don't know how to be happy"?

24. Would you like to live on the planet, Camazotz? Why or why not?

25. Would you have felt the way Meg did if you ever encountered IT?

26. *"Like and equal are two entirely different things."* Discuss this statement.

27. "She teetered on the see-saw of love and hate...." What was happening to Meg?

28. Can you analyze the lesson Meg learns when she finds her father but he cannot make everything alright? Is this a difficult lesson for one to learn?

29. Describe Meg and her faults and give her some advice about how she can overcome them.

30. Can you explain to the beast the difference between what things *look* like and what things *are* like?

31. Try to explain artificial lights as Meg was going to do for Aunt Beast.

32. Help Meg, Calvin, and Mr. Murry tell the beasts about Mrs. Whatsit, Mrs. Who, and Mrs. Which without physically describing them.

33. Do you agree with Mrs. Whatsit that our lives are like a sonnet; we are given the form, but we have to write it?

34. Is there a special meaning in Mr. Murry's use of the names Megatron and Megaparsec when speaking to his daughter? Do you agree with this use?

35. What is the theme of *A Wrinkle in Time*?

36. Do you believe with Meg that love can overcome hate?

37. Is the use of Scripture too preachy or is it a good device, and does it have a place in the story?

38. Would you characterize Meg as strong or weak? Is there anything about her that makes her typical?

39. What lesson or lessons for use in ordinary life can you learn from *A Wrinkle in Time*?

40. Would *A Wrinkle in Time* make a good movie? Write a movie script for a chapter of your choice. Suggestions: chapter 6, "The Happy Medium," or chapter 11, "Aunt Beast."

Other Books by Madeleine L'Engle

And Both Were Young (New York: Lothrop, 1949).

The Arm of the Starfish (New York: Farrar, Straus, Giroux, 1965). (Gr. 7-up).

Camilla Dickinson (New York: Simon and Schuster, 1951).

Dance in the Desert (New York: Farrar, Straus, Giroux, 1969). (Gr. 4-up).

Dragons in the Waters (New York: Farrar, Straus, Giroux, 1976). (Gr. 7-up).

The Journey with Jonah (New York: Farrar, Straus, Giroux, 1968).

Meet the Austins (New York: Vanguard Press, 1960).

The Moon by Night (New York: Farrar, Straus, Giroux, 1963). (Gr. 7-up).

Prelude (New York: Vanguard Press, 1969). (Gr. 7-up).

The Twenty-Four Days before Christmas (New York: Farrar, Straus, Giroux, 1964).

A Wind in the Door (New York: Farrar, Straus, Giroux, 1973). (Gr. 7-up).

The Young Unicorns (New York: Farrar, Straus, Giroux, 1968). (Gr. 7-up).

V.   Culminating Activity

After the four books have been read and discussed students should be directed to compare and contrast them in the following ways:

1.   Can you see any similarities in the personalities of Arilla Adams and Meg Murry?

2.   Would Calvin O'Keefe and Winston Carmichael make a good intellectual match? Why or why not?

3.   In each book a good deal was said about the protagonist's mother. How would you compare Mrs. Murry, Mrs. Adams, Mrs. Carmichael, and Courtney Rutherford Hopkins?

4.   Which would you prefer: a little brother like Charles Wallace or a little sister like Heidi Carmichael?

5.   Of the four books which one did you like best? Why?

6.   Who was your favorite character? Discuss that character's personality.

8　EXPLORING THEMES AND VALUES

A major delight in working with gifted children is in discovering the total irrelevance of grade-level materials. The older student delights in savoring the real genius of the picture book author or illustrator; for it is here that theme is explored through a highly structured and disciplined blend of pictures and words. The younger child, too, is free to learn apart from the usual curriculum and in so doing may follow interests which lead from the picture book to the junior novel. Whatever the age of the child, it is in the area of theme exploration that the gifted literature program is truly set apart from regular or advanced literature programs.

With a high interest in the exploration of values, the gifted child needs careful direction in theme exploration, beginning at an early age; for even bright students often have difficulty in interpreting an author's theme. Yet that which goes beyond the literal meaning of a work separates truly great literature from books that are forgotten as soon as the last page is read. Every fine author has something important to say and it is an essential role of every teacher to create the kind of trusting environment which will allow children to be divergent in their search for truth, to question generalizations, to express ideas and reactions, to do critical evaluative thinking, to have his or her intelligence responded to.

In our lock-step, one-right-answer educational setting it is not surprising that students confuse plot and theme. Plot can be easily identified ... the child has little fear of making a mistake enumerating events in sequential order. The discussion of theme, however, requires an atmosphere which encourages open response, thoughtful discussion, and opportunities for observing believable situations in which the author's theme is evident.

The units included in this chapter are designed for these purposes. The questions are those which the children themselves might ask. The observations of life situations which are suggested in Unit Two should lead to further discussion and assist these children in using their powers of abstraction; to point out cause and effect relationships.

Unit One
Judith Viorst: An Author Study Unit
Compiled by Lloyd Hauge

There is no better way to begin literature study with primary students than with the humorous, poignant, enlightening, thought-provoking, and immensely entertaining books of Judith Viorst. The characters, settings, and plots of her books are based on her experiences as a mother of three boys which are recounted with humor, insight, and compassion. Her down-to-earth style of writing makes the curious world of parent-child interaction seem interestingly real to the young reader.

Students identify very closely with her characters. They feel, breathe, cry, and live with the joys and heartaches of Rosie, Michael, Alexander, Anthony, Nicholas, Annie, and Jodi. Viorst has a special way of touching the hearts of not only children, but adults as well.

When sharing the books of this talented author, both teacher and students become thoroughly involved in the action, the humor, the pathos. What better way to begin the sharing of literature with kindergarten and first grade children than with these books which elicit the student response, "Yes! It's just like that at our house, too"?

The Tenth Good Thing about Barney (New York: Atheneum, 1971). Illustrated by Eric Bleguad. (Gr. K-4).

"My cat Barney died last Friday. I was very sad." These are the first two lines of the book. They set the stage for a compassionate and tender exploration of death and dying, but mostly of life and living. Loving parents comfort their little boy in the loss of his pet cat and tell him they will have a nice funeral for Barney the next day. His mother asks him to think of ten good things to say about Barney at the funeral. The boy can think of only nine. The tenth good thing about Barney occurs to the boy while he is helping his father plant their garden after the funeral.

> "He'll help grow the flowers, and he'll help grow that tree and some grass. You know, he said, that's a pretty nice job for a cat."

This book is a must for children and adults who need to understand more about the miracles of life and death and real immortality. True family strength is depicted in this book and few "explanations" of death and its place in life come close to the reassuring, common-sense approach put forth by Judith Viorst.

Possibilities for Teacher-Student Discussion

1. Have you ever had a pet of yours die? How did you feel? Did you talk with a parent or a friend when it happened?

2. When we say that something is "dead" what does that mean to you?

3. What are some different things that you have heard people say about what happens to something when it dies?

4. What do you believe happens to things when they die? Why?

5. What do your parents do when something happens to make you sad?

6. How is your family like that of the little boy in the story? How is it different?

7. Which of the characters in the book do you think was the best or most interesting? What did you like most about that character?

8. Have you lost a close relative or friend in the last few years? Try to describe what it meant to you when it happened.

9. Is it important to you to have a close family or close friends at times when you are very sad? Why?

10. Do you feel that dying is something bad, or horrible, or frightening? Has this book made you feel differently about living or dying than you once felt?

Ideas for Follow-Up Activities

1. Have a funeral for a classroom pet that dies. Allow the children to plan it. Have some of them think of some "good things" to say about the pet.

2. Visit a cemetery. Examine what is written on grave markers. How old were some of the people when they died?

3. Is there a pet cemetery in your area? Investigate. Visit it, if possible.

4. Some writing activities or themes:

    a) Make up gravestone epitaphs.

    b) Read some obituaries. Write a short obituary for a real or imaginary person.

    c) Write an obituary for a pet of yours or one that belongs to a friend.

    d) "When I die, I would like to come back to earth as...."

    e) "When I am very sad, the thing I most want is...."

    f) "My parents are the best in the world because...."

5. Make up a eulogy for yourself, a family member, a friend, or a pet. Recite it or write it down.

Rosie and Michael (New York: Atheneum, 1974). Illustrated by Lorna Tomei. (Gr. 1-4).

Here is a very honest exploration of the theme of friendship—a friendship between freckled-faced, pigtailed Rosie and casual, clutsy Michael. These two children (who could be anywhere between the ages of seven and ten) tell what it is like to have a real friend through good and bad times. Their feelings for one another are undaunted by unattractive appearance, mild rivalry, humorous but harmless pranks, or tense and dire emergencies.

Children love this book for its humor and for its visual appeal. Lorna Tomei's pen and ink drawings are excellent. The detailed illustrations give the reader a sense of the facial expressions, clothing, and exciting action which are important to the development of the two characters. The book also serves as a sort of primer on friendship—a set of conditions under which a true friendship will endure and overcome all problems and crises:

> "Just because I sprayed Kool Whip in her sneakers, doesn't mean Rosie's not my friend."

> "Just because I put a worm in his tuna salad sandwich, doesn't mean Michael's not my friend."

> "I'd give her my last piece of chalk."

> "I'd give him my last Chiclet."

> "That's what friends are for."

Possibilities for Teacher-Student Discussion

1. Do you have a friend whom you would do just about anyting for? Does that friend feel the same about you?

2. What are some things that friends do together or for one another?

3. What is the nicest thing you've ever done for a friend?

4. How do you feel about boys having girls as special friends or girls having boys as special friends?

5. Do you sometimes play tricks on a friend that you know will make the friend angry? How does this affect your friendship?

6. Tell us about a special friend of yours and tell all the good things you can think of about that person.

7. Do you sometimes call someone a name just for fun but not to be mean? How does the person feel? How do you feel when a friend calls you a name or makes fun of you.

8. Why are friends important to you? What would life be like for a person who had no friends? Have you ever been in a situation where you felt you had no friends?

9. What part of the book do you think showed the real secret to Rosie and Michael's friendship?

10. Picture yourself as either Rosie or Michael. What is there about you that would make people want to be your friend?

Ideas for Follow-Up Activities

1. Possible themes for writing projects:

a) "My best friend in the whole world is _____ because...."

b) "The meanest trick I ever played on a friend was...."

c) Make a list of funny names you could call a friend just for fun without making him/her angry. (In the book Rosie calls Michael "Banana Head" and Michael calls Rosie "Gorilla Face.")

d) "If I were in danger, I would want to be rescued by _____ because...."

2. Make a list of all the good things you can think of about yourself. Then list some things about yourself that you think are not so good. Ask a friend to do the same, and compare your lists.

3. Make up a story or a series of short stories about exciting or funny things you have done with a friend. Make illustrations to go with your stories. You might even wish to put them together in a booklet.

4. Put on a "Rosie and Michael" play or skit. Use ideas from the book, but make up some of your own, too. Let various members of the class play the parts of Rosie and Michael. Creative costumes could add a lot to your skit.

Alexander and the Terrible, Horrible, No Good, Very Bad Day (New York: Atheneum, 1972). Illustrated by Ray Cruz. (Gr. K-3).
Is there a person alive who hasn't had "one of those days?" Alexander has an almost unbelievably bad day and survives to tell us about it in this delightfully touching and entertaining book. Everything Alexander does seems

to have dire consequences. He wakes up with gum in his hair, trips on his skateboard, drops his sweater in a sinkful of water, finds only cereal in his cereal box, and gets car-sick on the way to school. And that's only the beginning.

The rest of Alexander's day is filled with putdowns, mistakes, accidents and minor catastrophes. He is rejected by his friends, his teacher, his brothers, his parents—even the pet cat. There is only one way out.

"I think I'll move to Australia," says Alexander. This book embodies the essence of what it must be like to a child to live in a world of chaos, confusion, and nonsense—a world over which he has little control. Young children love this book for its humor and its insight into the trials and tribulations of growing up. They identify very strongly with Alexander and have much empathy for him as he fearlessly plows through an avalanche of discord in his life. However, no adult could read this book without having those same feelings of identification and empathy. We've all been there.

Alexander pulls through unbowed. Lying in bed at the end of this terrible, horrible, no good, very bad day he philosophizes: "Mom says some days are like that. Even in Australia."

Possibilities for Teacher-Student Discussion

1. Have you ever had a day like Alexander's day? Tell us about it. How did you feel when it was over?

2. Have you ever had a friend or a brother or sister who was having a very bad day? Was there anything you could do or say that would help the person?

3. Are there times in school when everything seems to go wrong for you? Do you wish you could stay home from school after days like that?

4. Is there some really "neat" place you would like to escape to when you are having a bad day? What is it like? Does it help even if you just go there in your imagination?

5. If you had the power to make the world or your school just perfect for you, what things would you do?

6. What do you think was the worst thing that happened to Alexander during his very bad day? What is the worst thing that ever happened to you?

Ideas for Follow-Up Activities

1.   Make (recite or write) a list of words you would use to describe bad days you have had. Alexander used *terrible*, *horrible*, *no good*, and *very bad*.

2.   List or write about:

   a)   foods you don't like

   b)   things you don't like about school

   c)   some people that "bug" you

   d)   things you would like to do but people won't let you

   e)   places you would like to go to get away from it all

3.   Find out if a friend or classmate is having a very bad day. Try to do what you can to help that person through it.

4.   Make some pictures or put together a montage (explain) of magazine pictures which illustrate some bad things that have happened to you.

5.   Write a book about "The Worst Day of My Life." Illustrate your booklet with art work or magazine cutouts.

My Mama Says There Aren't Any Zombies, Ghosts, Vampires, Creatures, Demons, Monsters, Fiends, Goblins, or Things (New York: Atheneum, 1973). Illustrated by Kay Chorao. (Gr. K-4).
   This should be #1 on the required reading list for any parent or adult who deals with children in any facet of life. (Doesn't that include just about everyone?) It is a book in which a child's question is posed: "Just how honest and trustworthy are adults, anyway? Can I really believe everything they tell me?"
   Through a child's eyes we see a world of danger, inconsistency, fear, and confusion. The child knows his Mama loves him and means well, and he finds it difficult to push aside the realization that she is not always right.

> "And once she said I hadn't flushed and it was Alexander's. So ... sometimes even Mamas make mistakes."

> "My Mama says that a Zombie with his eyes rolled back in his head ... isn't clonking up and up the stairs. But how can I believe her when she told me Holly's middle name was Susan. And Holly's middle name is really Jane."

Kay Chorao's pen and ink drawings are simple, delicate, and touching with just the right amount of whimsical feeling. The warm and tender feelings that exist between the boy and his Mama are evident in the fine detail and facial expressions. She shows the boy's total spectrum of emotions and feelings — fear, mistrust, disappointment, resignation, contentment, joy, and "I told you so."

Everyone who reads this book, child or adult, will be stunned by the coincidence that—"Hey, that's just what happens to me!" For, of course, Judith Viorst has based the incidents of the book on actual experiences and dialogue with her son, Nicholas. The ultimate honesty of the text is revealed in Nicholas' words: "Sometimes even Mamas make mistakes. But sometimes they don't."

Possibilities for Teacher-Student Discussions

1. Do you believe in ghosts, zombies, werewolves, etc.? Where do you think these things come from?

2. Does your Mom (or Dad) sometimes make mistakes? Tell us about one of them. How do your parents react when they make a mistake that you are aware of?

3. Has your Mom or Dad ever told you something that you knew wasn't right? How did they find out that they were wrong? How did they react?

4. What imaginary creature are you most afraid of at night or in your own room at home? Tell us about it.

5. How do you think the little boy feels about his Mama even though she isn't always right and does make mistakes? How do you feel about your Mom?

Ideas for Follow-Up Activities

1. There were eight kinds of "scary" things listed in the title of the book. Continue the list and add as many more as you can think of. Examples: werewolf, leprechaun, witch, devil.

2. Write a short story or poem about catching your Mom or Dad making a mistake. Illustrate the story with your own drawings or cutouts.

3. Use monster drawings or cutouts to illustrate your own book of *My Favorite Monsters.*

4. Find pictures of various kinds of monsters and creatures in magazines. Cut them out and make a "monster montage" with them.

5. Construct large three-dimensional models of monsters, creatures, and "things." You could use paper rolls, boxes, paper, and paint. Make a display of the monsters created by your class.

6. Make a monster costume for yourself using old clothes, masks, makeup, or wigs. You may wish to put on a play or skit in your costumes.

7.   Make up a "ghost story" and tell it to your class in the dark. It might be even more interesting to record it on tape and play it back with weird sound effects or music. Maybe you could have a contest in your class to see who can produce the most frightening story.

Alexander, Who Used to Be Rich Last Sunday (New York: Atheneum, 1978). Illustrated by Ray Cruz. (ps-4).

Alexander is the same Alexander who had the very bad day. This time he squanders a dollar given to him by his grandparents one Sunday morning. In a matter of hours after he is given the dollar, Alexander is the unproud owner of a one-eyed bear, a melted candle, part of a deck of cards and some bus tokens. His two brothers make fun of him and gloat about their own "riches" — $2.38 for Nicholas and $2.40 for Anthony.

The three boys like money. "A lot. Especially me," says Alexander. Despite the suggestions of his parents to save his dollar, Alexander sets out to use his dollar in his own way. He loses bets, buys bubble gum, rents a snake, gets fined for swearing, loses money down the toilet, buys "valuable" items at a garage sale, and loses money doing magic tricks. The dollar soon dwindles to nothing.

The book is full of good lessons on thrift, wise consumerism, and investment. Children enjoy the book as they watch the hapless Alexander's dollar slowly drift away. They have all done the same thing at one time or another and delight in watching Alexander fall into his own trap.

The illustrations by Ray Cruz are excellent pen and ink drawings which add much to the action and dialogue of the story.

Possibilities for Teacher-Student Discussion

1.   Have you ever squandered money that someone gave you to save? What things did you buy? How did you lose some of it?

2.   What do you think Alexander should have done with his money?

3.   If someone gave you $10.00 right now, what are some things you would do with it?

4.   What are some things that small children like you can do to earn their own money? What were some things that Alexander did to earn money after his $1.00 ran out?

5.   What do you think was the most foolish thing Alexander did with some of his money? What is the most foolish thing you have ever done with money?

6.   What are some things that you are saving your money for now?

7.   Have you ever gone to a garage sale or a rummage sale with your own money? What things did you buy?

Ideas for Follow-Up Activities

1. Find pictures of things that you would like to buy if you had enough money saved up. Cut them out and make a montage.

2. You might want to hold a rummage sale in your classroom. Each class member could bring a few small items from home and decide on prices for them. Invite students from other rooms to your sale. Decide on what you will do with the money earned from your sale.

3. Visit a bank or savings and loan, and find out how to set up a savings account. Ask the people what they do with money that is deposited. Find out how to make deposits and withdrawals correctly. Math lessons could be structured around deposits, withdrawals, interest rates, compounding interest, capital investments, fractions, or penalties for early withdrawal.

4. Set up a bank or savings and loan in your classroom where children can deposit and withdraw money.

5. Make up a list of do's and don'ts on ways for children to use their money.

Other Books by Judith Viorst

I'll Fix Anthony (New York: Harper and Row, 1969). Illustrated by Arnold Lobel.

Try It Again Sam (New York: Lothrop, 1970). Illustrated by Paul Galdone.

The nine lessons in Unit Two might be entitled, "What's Really Going On?" and serve as an introductory program to theme exploration. Unit Three takes the child from the picture book to the junior novel in delving deeper into theme exploration with the books of Bill and Vera Cleaver. It will hopefully serve as a model for exploring themes in the works of other fine authors.

These units can be explored independently or in groups, allowing students to set their own pace. As doors to thought are opened and key questions and issues come into focus, incisive examination of issues may occur and anticipated schedules may need alteration.

Unit Two
An Examination of Theme
in the Picture Book and in Life
By Charlotte Lohrmann

Procedure:

1.   Share the quotations preceding the book summaries.

2.   Discuss the quotations. What do children think each writer is saying about life?

3.   Share the book. Either teacher or students may read aloud, or students may read independently in the literature center.

4.   Initial discussion groups should meet to explore the author's theme using the questions given as an initial guide.

5.   Suggestions should be made for observations of real life.

6.   A follow-up discussion group should explore group members' observations relating them to the theme and the initial quotations.

Lesson I
HONESTY AND JUSTICE

Quotations:

"Dare to be true; nothing needs a lie;
A fault which needs it most gains nothing thereby."
—George Herbert

"He who feeds men, serveth few;
He serves all, who dares to be true."
—Ralph Waldo Emerson

"Truth is as impossible to be soiled by any
outward touch as the sunbeam."
—John Milton

Lead-in Story:

Why Mosquitoes Buzz in People's Ears, by Verna Aardema (New York: Dial Press, 1975). Illustrated by Leo and Diane Dillon. (ps-3).

This is an African legend that tells about a mosquito who tells a tall-tale to the iguana. The iguana plugs up his ears with two sticks so he does not have to listen to such nonsense.

This leads to a chain reaction wherein the whole animal kingdom in the jungle is excited and disturbed. It also causes the death of an owlet and the refusal of Mother Owl to call the sun to rise. Eventually the problem is solved by finding that the mosquito is the primary cause of everyone's unhappiness. The mosquito learns her lesson, but her reaction still causes anger and botheration in the world today.

Concepts

1. Our own self-respect is worth more than the idea we are tempted to impress other people with.

2. Honesty gives us a feeling of security and satisfaction.

Life Situations

1. Correcting our own work fairly

2. Admitting our faults

3. Bringing honest excuses to school for absence

4. Telling who is to blame if someone else will be punished for the misdeed

Discussion Questions

1. How much help should parents give in homework?

2. What should you do if you see someone else cheating?

3. What should you do if you harm someone else's property?

4. Is it a good idea to have a set time to do assigned chores or lessons?

5. Is it a good idea to try to impress someone with a story about yourself that is exaggerated just to make friends?

Observations

1. People returning borrowed articles in good condition

2. Children telling parents the full truth about difficulties encountered at school

3. Parents working for the good of the family

4. Articles in the newspaper that stress the idea that "Honesty is the best policy"

Lesson II

COURAGE AND GOOD SPORTSMANSHIP

Quotations:

"The bravest are the tenderest,
The loving are the daring."
—Edward Taylor

"I dare do all that may become a man;
Who dares do more is none."
—William Shakespeare

"An ounce of pluck
Is worth a pound of luck."
—Annonymous

Lead-in Story:

King Orville and the Bullfrogs, by Kathleen Abell (Boston: Little, Brown, 1974). Illustrated by Errol Le Cain. (Gr. K-3).

King Orville was a very ambitious and selfish man. He also believed that he was the best in every endeavor he undertook. His wife, Queen Rosemary, was shy and preferred the company of her flowers. Their three daughters decided to marry the three sons of Queen Pamela, a stubborn and gluttonous woman, and King Francis, a poet and lover of nature.

King Orville and Queen Pamela have a clash of personalities when she judges Orville last in a game at the wedding festival. Orville turns the boys into frogs and imprisons Queen Pamela. Eventually the boys are freed from their frog-state when the king finds that human companionship is extremely important to him. The boys live happily with Flora, Dora, and Cora in their own castles.

Queen Pamela and King Orville learn a lesson in moral courage and good sportsmanship.

Kathleen Abell is a young Canadian author. She makes her home in Ontario with her husband, an orthopedic surgeon, and her four children. When not being a housewife and mother, she enjoys developing a three-hundred acre tract of land that she has turned into a magnificent wildlife preserve.

Errol Le Cain is an English artist whose work has only recently begun to appear in this country.

Concepts

1. Moral courage, rather than physical courage, is the type demanded today.

2. If we do not show that we are afraid, our fears will lessen.

Life Situations

1. Playing a game according to the rules

2. Keeping a promise

3. Being a cheerful loser

4. Working quietly when the teacher must leave the room

5. Preventing a group of children from teasing another child or hurting an animal

Discussion Questions

1. If you overhear a conversation that gives you information you know you should not have, what should you do?

2. If the umpire gives an unjust decision against you, what would be the best course of action for you to take?

3. Should we insist on doing what is right even though the crowd wants to do the opposite?

4. How can we be sure our ideas are right if everyone else seems to think differently?

5. Should we try to force other people to have the same ideas of moral courage that we have?

Observations

1. Police arresting a dangerous criminal

2. Firemen entering a burning building to rescue someone

3. Lifeguards risking their own lives to save someone

4. Driver dimming his lights for an approaching automobile

5. Losing team congratulating the winning team

6. Parents saying "No" to an action they know will only harm the child morally or physically

7. Someone who refuses to smoke pot or drink even though the crowd laughs at him for this action

8. Children trying to help when parents are having difficulties in their lives (divorce, separation, alcohol, illness)

Lesson III

GRATITUDE AND THE APPRECIATION OF SERVICE

Quotations:

> "Let the man who would be grateful think of repaying a kindness, even while receiving it."
> — Seneca

> "A thankful heart is not only the greatest virtue, but the parent of all other virtues."
> — Cicero

Lead-in Story:

The Goosehill Gang and a Stitch-in-Time Solution, by Mary Blount Christian (St. Louis, MO: Concordia, 1978). Illustrated by Betty Wind. (Gr. 1-4).

The Goosehill Gang find themselves involved in a community project when they notice how their town is becoming littered and run-down. They involve Marcus's mother because she has shown her appreciation to them by making her home available for meetings during the cold weather. She also embroiders a shirt for each of them with the name of their club. The boys are rewarded by the townspeople and Marcus's mother finds a job that she can perform from a wheelchair.

This is not a picture book in the true sense of the word and is a little more advanced than the other books in this unit. It does, however, show how most people are grateful when a service is rendered, or a kindness received.

Concepts

1. One method of showing appreciation is by a smile and a word of thanks.

2. Doing things for others is a good way of showing appreciation of what others have done for us.

Life Situations

1. Caring for our environment

2. Caring for things that give us pleasure (plants, books, homes)

3. Expressing thanks to our parents, relatives, and friends for their thoughtfulness

4. Refraining from hurting others who have been kind to us

5. Thanking the teacher aides, custodians, cadets, and others in the school for helping us with our problems

6. Writing letters to the Mother's Club or the PTC showing our appreciation for the field trips they sponsor

Discussion Questions

1. How can a shy child show appreciation?

2. What should we do if people make fun of us for expressing gratitude?

3. How can we show appreciation to our community for the things they have done for us? (swimming pools, parks, playgrounds, schools, libraries, etc.)

4. What should we do if we see someone defacing a public building (writing or scratching on the bathroom walls, putting gum on lunch trays, tearing library or school books, etc.)?

Observations

1. People caring for aged parents

2. People caring for and protecting trees and flowers

3. A family caring for a pet that is no longer useful

4. People attending services or meetings held in gratitude for a group of people or an individual who has helped

5. Monuments erected to public servants or heroes who have died

6. People thanking waitresses or clerks

7. Someone thanking a stranger for opening or holding a door

8. Pupils who thank the teachers, room mothers, and adults in the building for a special kindness

Lesson IV
SELF-CONTROL, INITIATIVE, AND VISION

Quotations:	"Impossible—let me never hear that foolish word again." —Mirabeau
	"They can conquer who believe they can." —Ralph Waldo Emerson
Lead-in Story:	*The Truthful Harp*, by Lloyd Alexander (New York: Holt, Rinehart & Winston, 1971). Illustrated by Evaline Ness. (ps-3).

Fflewddur Flam, king of Prydain, yearns to roam through his kingdom as a bard. He does not have the natural talent for music, nor the self-control to learn to play the harp, but the Chief Bard takes pity on him and gives him a magic harp.

During his wanderings, he sacrifices himself to help people, but is also treated harshly by the lord of another domain. Returning to his own castle and through recounting his adventures to the Chief Bard, Fflewddur Flam realizes that his "deeds were more gallant" than his dreams. The Chief Bard tells him that a good truth is purest gold that needs no gilding. "You have a modest heart of the truly brave, but your tongue gallops faster than your head can rein it."

The king learns through his adventures that fantasy and vision could be different. He also sees himself as one who must develop a more selective tongue if he is to grow into the kind of mature man that is needed to rule a kingdom.

Lloyd Alexander was born and reared in Philadelphia where he still lives. A children's version of the King Arthur stories started his interest in tales of heroes and led him to the classic collection of Welsh legends. Finally the mythical kingdom of Prydain flowered from his research and became the subject of books for older readers, including a Newbery runner-up, *The Black Cauldron* and two picture books, *Coll and His White Pig*, and *The Truthful Harp*. He has revealed that some years ago he bought an ancient Welsh harp and tried unsuccessfully to learn to play it. In time the strings broke, but Alexander refuses to suggest why this might have happened.

Winner of the 1967 Caldecott Medal for *Sam, Bangs and Moonshine*, Evaline Ness has also written and illustrated several of her own books. She is a successful commercial artist and now lives in New York after having spent her childhood in Pontiac, Michigan.

Concepts

1. Initiative can be developed by beginning along a few lines.

2. One who wishes to be a leader part of the time, must also be willing to be a follower part of the time.

Life Situations

1. Keeping back angry words

2. Refusing to repeat things that may harm another's reputation

3. Keeping your head in an emergency

4. Thinking up new ways to solve playground problems

5. Thinking up ways to make the classroom more attractive

Discussion Questions

1. Can everyone be a leader?

2. Should you follow your own ideas even if you think someone else's are better?

3. How can you develop initiative and yet follow the rules laid down by parents and teachers?

4. Can you keep your friends and yet develop initiative?

5. If you don't fight back on the playground, will others upset you if they call you "chicken"?

6. Has being frightened ever made you forget how to do something?

7. Someone tells you in confidence what would help a friend. Should you tell your friend?

Observations

1. Clerks or waitresses remaining calm in spite of an angry customer

2. A driver reacting quickly to avoid an accident

3. Someone speaking kindly to someone who has treated him unkindly

4. Parents planning the budget to include an expensive item

5. Parents planning to build or remodel a home

6. Notice how groups plan to improve the community with better facilities for the public

---

Lesson V
COOPERATION AND FRIENDLINESS

Quotations:

"Let us all hang together, or we shall all surely hang separately."
—Abraham Lincoln

"Do unto others as you would have others do unto you."

"Adversity is the touchstone of friendship."
—Anonymous

"A friend in need
Is a friend indeed."

Lead-in Story:

The Procession, by Margaret Mahy (New York: F. Watts, 1969). Illustrated by Charles Mozley.

This is a type of "Pied Piper" story. It shows how the characters help one another toward a single goal. The goal is to find out that, "life is strong as the music of trumpets, and warm as the flame of a dragon," that poetry sings and that life cannot be experienced totally from books.

A wandering fiddler knocks at the door to call a little girl to see the world; she goes with him. They are joined by a bird-winged man and a man with a fiery dragon. The procession is happy because they have happy feelings inside. Their happiness does not depend on the outward signs of a real procession such as the bugles and trumpets and drums.

They knock at the door of a prince who is protected. Finally, not only the prince but also his guards and tutor join the procession. They are happy in their common goal and in their companionship. The outer facade is shed and happiness is felt through experiencing the truth and beauty of the world.

Margaret Mahy is a librarian in New Zealand, a poet and a storyteller, and the mother of two little girls, Penelope and Bridget. Since 1962, she has been stirring the imaginations and tickling the funnybones of young readers in New Zealand with stories in their school journal. Now her books are being published outside her own country.

Charles Mozley is a British artist whose jaunty drawings are familiar to readers of many stories.

Concepts

1. The work of the whole group suffers unless each individual does his or her best.

2. Friendship allows each person to be himself.

3. A real friend will stand beside you even when the going gets rough.

4. Cooperation makes possible many undertakings which could not be accomplished alone.

Life Situations

1. Sending notes to classmates who are ill. Phoning to offer help or just a friendly chat

2. Protecting a younger child

3. Sharing books, toys, ideas

4. Helping a new student get acquainted

5. Being cheerful at home and at school

6. Organizing a new game on the playground

7. Working with a group on a bulletin board or class project trying to do a fair share of the work

8. Taking whatever part that might be assigned in a play or group activity

Discussion Questions

1. Your neighbor refuses to cooperate with you. What should you do?

2. Should you cooperate with kids who are doing wrong?

3. Should you sell tickets or candy in order to cooperate when you really don't like to ask people to buy things?

4. Should you help a smaller child when everyone will laugh at you?

5.   You find a stray animal and try to find it a home. What would you do if you were accused of stealing the animal?

6.   What should you do if someone constantly rebuffs you when you try to be friendly?

7.   Should you continue to go around with someone whose habits you do not like?

Observations

1.   Picnics or get-togethers of members of an organization or church

2.   Neighbors helping one another

3.   People feeding birds during the winter

4.   Members of a team helping one another

5.   The adults around the school cooperating with each other

6.   People welcoming a new neighbor in your subdivision

Lesson VI
AMBITION AND THRIFT

Quotations: "Remember that time is money."

                     "A penny saved is a penny earned."
                         — Benjamin Franklin

                     "Seek the higher things.
                     Through difficulties to the stars."

Lead-in Story: *The Emperor and the Kite*, by Jane Yolen (Cleveland, OH: Collins, William & World, 1968). Illustrated by Ed Young. (Gr. K-3).

This not only tells of a small child's love and loyalty to her father, but how her one ambition is to keep her father, the emperor, alive after he has been captured by opposing rulers. Djeow Weow, the smallest daughter of the family, is quite lonely as the story begins so she flies her kite each day. After her father's capture, she does not flee to a neighboring kingdom spending her time in sobbing and sighing, as the others in the family do. Instead, she builds a hut of twigs and branches, and manages to feed her father by tying food to the kite and sailing it up to his prison window.

After understanding the implications of a monk that she should try to free her father, she works at twining grass and vines and her own hair into a rope that will be stout enough to hold her father's weight.

By sailing the kite to the window with the rope attached, she manages to free her father. He regains his empire and accords his smallest child the honor of ruling beside him.

Jane Yolen is a free-lance writer and reviewer. She has written a number of books for young people and was, for several years, an editor of children's books. Her special interest in kites is due to the influence of her father, Will Yolen, the world's leading kite-flying expert. She lives with her husband and daughter in Conway, Massachusetts.

Ed Young is an artist and instructor of visual communication at Pratt Institute. He has illustrated several books for young people. Young has used a paper-cut technique in this book. It is an authentic Chinese art form. Each illustration was painstakingly cut from a single piece of paper and is suited to the retelling of a classic Chinese tale. Young was born in Shanghai, China. He and his wife now reside in New York City.

Concepts

1. Ambition may be good or bad depending on the results for ourselves and others.

2. Selecting an ambition early in life helps us to work harder.

3. Sometimes we cannot have the material things we would like because of the expense of the item.

4. The worthwhile things in life are free. They have no price tag.

Life Situations

1. Working steadily at a task, so we do not waste time

2. Going to bed early enough so that we save our energy

3. Keeping clothes clean and mended

4. Weighing the cost of an article against our need

5. Saving something from each allowance or bit of earned money

6. Selecting one school subject and working on it until you raise your grades

7. Choosing a reasonable goal for a week and trying to accomplish the task

Discussion Questions

1. We are told to have our teeth checked every six months. If they are in good condition, isn't this a waste of money?

2. You budget your time for a day, but others keep bothering you. What should you do?

3. You really want something, but your budget can't pay for it. Should you use your savings?

4. Must a person be famous to realize his ambition?

5. Is ambition always good?

6. Can one be ambitious and yet be friendly and unselfish?

7. What should you do if you cannot realize your ambition? (Did you set unrealistic goals? Did you really allow enough time for the project? Did you work steadily?)

Observations

1. Family budgeting and saving

2. Discount coupons in the newspapers

3. A student working despite the noise around him

4. Using leftovers in dishes that the family likes

5. Buying food bargains and freezing them

6. Remodeling a home or building

7. Athletes practicing to improve their skills

8. Listen to older people talk about what they wanted in childhood. Did they realize their ambitions? How do they feel about this?

Lesson VII
KINDNESS AND SYMPATHY

Quotations:

"No one is useless in the world who lightens the burden of it for anyone else."
— Charles Dickens

"The world is happy,
The world is wide;
Kind hearts are beating
  On every side."
— James Russell Lowell

Lead-in Story:

My Grandpa Died Today, by Joan Fassler (New York: Human Sciences Press, 1971). Illustrated by Stuart Kranz. (ps-3).

David and his grandfather loved each other and were devoted to each other. When his grandfather dies, David must struggle to understand and cope with death. The story tells how neighbors and friends help. David's friend, Bobby, comes to involve David in ordinary life again. As David is playing baseball he realizes that life goes on and that his grandfather is happy when David is doing the things that are good for him. David accepts death as part of life.

Joan Fassler has been an editorial assistant for *Seventeen-at-School*, a lecturer, and the moderator of "Conversations with the Very Young," a New York City radio program, and has done extensive research in child development. Her books for young children grow from her work with disabled children.

Concepts

1. Helping others brings happiness to one's self.

2. People are kinder to you when you are kind to them.

3. It is easier to be kind when you think how you would feel if you were in the other person's place.

Life Situations

1. An older child comforting a smaller one who is hurt or frightened

2. Doing an unpleasant chore without complaining

3. Giving up a chair or a newspaper to our parents

4. Giving the class a treat on our birthday

Discussion Questions

1. How can you remember to be unselfish?

2. Can you be unselfish when those around you are selfish?

3. Should you continue to be kind to people who don't seem to appreciate it?

4. Should you give some money to a church or charity even though you would rather buy something for yourself?

5. Your brother says that housework is for girls and he doesn't do any of it. What should you do?

6. You stop at a house to tell the people that their car has a flat tire, but the owner fusses at you for disturbing him or her. What should you do?

Observations

1. Adults sharing a newspaper

2. A classmate getting a chair for the teacher at a movie or an assembly

3. Parents neglecting their own desires or wishes in order to do something that the rest of the family wants to do

---

Lesson VIII

TRUSTWORTHINESS, WILLINGNESS TO SERVE, LOYALTY

Quotations: "So long as we love, we serve."
                         —Robert L. Stevenson

                        The Pledge of Allegiance

Lead-in Story: *The Hole in the Dike*, retold by Norma Green (New York: Thomas Y. Crowell, 1975). Illustrated by Eric Carle. (Gr. K-3).

On his way home from a friend's house, Peter, a little Dutch boy, hears a noise that frightens him. It is the sound of water trickling through a small hole in the dike. Peter knows this could cause a break and the flooding of homes and the land. He puts his finger in the hole to stop the leak and guards it through the night. When he talks with Peter in the morning, the milkman hurries to town and sends workers out to fix the leak. Peter does not consider himself a hero, but only a person who has done his job.

Norma Green has retold this story in an interesting and palatable manner. She is an editor and an artist. She says about this story, "I felt there was a need today for young people to read about courage and pride in one's country. This story seemed to be a way of passing on these messages in a memorable fantasy."

Eric Carle was born in the United States and grew up in Europe. He has produced bold and colorful images. He combines collage and painting which is based on careful research.

Concepts

1. Loyalty in acts is even more important than loyalty in words.

2. Patriotism means that we obey our country's laws and try to improve its life in every way we can.

3. The satisfaction of rendering service brings its own reward.

4. Self-respect and the respect of others are better than power or riches.

Life Situations

1. Accepting an assigned task at home or at school and doing it without supervision

2. Accepting an office in your club or school

3. Behaving on field trips and busses so that the people of the community know that you understand the values of your school

4. Helping in your church

5. Supporting the Student Council members you have chosen

Discussion Questions

1. You agree to take an office in a club, but find out that you cannot handle it. What should you do?

2. Is it right for others to clean up the mess you make during an art lesson?

3. When should you be materially rewarded for your work?

4. Does being loyal to your church mean that you should be unfriendly to others who do not belong to your church?

5. Does being loyal to a friend mean that you do not see that he or she has faults?

6. Should you obey the laws that others are constantly breaking?

7. How can you show patriotism in peacetime?

Observations

1. People serving on community projects without pay

2. Scout leaders and coaches for Little Leagues

3. Members of a family who are loyal to each other

4. Members of churches and clubs working for the good of all

5. Drivers who observe the speed limit, stop and yield signs, etc., even though a police officer is not around

Lesson IX
INQUISITIVENESS, SELF-RELIANCE, INDEPENDENCE

Quotations:

"Everyone is the son of his own works."
— Cervantes

"I would rather be right than be President."
— Henry Clay

"If a task is once begun,
Never leave it till it's done;
Be the labor great or small,
Do it well or not at all."
— Phoebe Cary

"I propose to fight on this line if it takes
all summer."
— U. S. Grant

Lead-in Story:

The Sometimes Island, by Anne Norris Baldwin (New York: Norton, 1969). Illustrated by Charles Robinson.

Curious about why Pine Island was sometimes called an island and sometimes a peninsula, Brian sets out to find out for himself. Being stranded on the island causes Brian to use his ingenuity and resourcefulness until he is rescued. However, he finds out for himself the difference between an island and a peninsula.

Anne Norris Baldwin was born in Philadelphia, Pennsylvania. She received her B.A. from Smith College and her Ph.D. in biochemistry from Harvard. She had done independent research at Stanford University in the field of biochemistry and written several scientific articles. *The Sometimes Island* is her first book for children. She lives with her husband and two sons in Portola Valley, California.

Charles Robinson was born and grew up in Morristown, New Jersey. Although he earned a living as a lawyer for ten years, he decided to earn a living solely as an artist. He now resides in New Vernon, New Jersey, with his wife and three children.

Concepts

1. It is necessary to learn to trust yourself and your ability.

2. Finding the answers to questions by ourselves leads to self-reliance.

3. The more we depend on ourselves, the more self-assured we become.

Life Situations

1. Doing your schoolwork and homework as much as possible without outside help

2. Finishing a chore or assignment instead of going out to play

3. Getting a job delivering papers, cutting grass, etc. to help earn your own spending money

4. Thinking out your own art ideas rather than copying from a neighbor

5. Not asking questions when you know where to find the answer

6. Taking care of your own room, clothes, papers, etc.

Discussion Questions

1. Your mother or father wants to help with homework before you have had a chance to think it out. What should you do?

2. You want to be a better reader, but you can't find any good books. What should you do?

3. You can't find a place at home that's quiet enough for study. What should you do?

4. You can get a job, but you can't play baseball or football if you do. Your family needs the money. What should you do?

5. If you follow the advice of adults are you failing to be independent?

Observations

1. Adults talking over a problem to find a solution

2. Pupils working by themselves and refusing to look at another's paper

3. Certain families have family prayer, others do not

4. A college student working to help pay his or her way through school

5. Your parents keeping the house in order and running it fairly smoothly after a day's work

Unit Three
Vera and Bill Cleaver and Their Works
By Laura Gorham

Vera Cleaver was born in Virgil, South Dakota, on January 6, 1919, the fifth child of eleven, two of whom were adopted. Her somewhat sketchy education in the public schools began in Kennebec, South Dakota, but the family moved often. Vera was the only child in the family interested in books and she says that when she discovered the library, she and her family "simply parted ways."[1] Vera grew up in Perry, Florida, but spent some time with her brother in Fort Lauderdale and at the age of fifteen, was working in Miami.

Both Cleavers say that they always knew they were going to be writers and do not want to be anything other than what they are. Vera Cleaver's first story was written at age seven for a writing contest in a Florida newspaper. "they sent me a letter and a piggy bank that looked like a beer keg, and that really set me on fire," she says, "but my parents weren't impressed. Instead they made me take piano lessons. They were convinced I was a child prodigy, but all I wanted to do was write."[2]

Bill Cleaver was born in Seattle, Washington, on March 24, 1920, and is the youngest of two children. His parents were divorced when he was five and he was sent to a private school in British Columbia. When asked about their formal education, Vera and Bill have agreed that they are graduates of the public libraries of the United States of America.[3]

The Cleavers met and married during World War II and have lived many places in the U.S. and Europe. In 1954, the Air Force offered Bill, then an Air Force sergeant, a job in Japan; Vera followed him to Japan and then to France. After this last overseas job, they decided to return to the United States and lived for three years in the vicinity of Boone, North Carolina, in a cabin in Goshen Valley. This experience was the inspiration for *Where the Lilies Bloom* and *Trial Valley*.

The Cleavers now live at 600 East Lake Elbert Drive, Winterhaven, Florida, where they have a two-story house on a hill overlooking a deep spring-fed lake which Bill believes began as a sink hole. The Cleavers work together in their home. Bill is the idea man and the finisher. He also does much of the research for their novels. He and Vera sit down together to discuss the characters and plot and when it is clear in her mind, Vera goes to the typewriter and works for four or five hours a day and tries to produce at least two finished pages of copy each day.

When asked about their life in Florida, Vera replied, "We have pets. We have always had pets and don't regard them as playthings. They are little beings with little lives of their own who need our protection.... We do not have children but do have quite an assortment of nieces and nephews to whom we are less of a mystery than we are to the adults in our families....

"I am unable to tell you which of our fictional characters is our favorite. Creating them is quite a task and it's an enjoyable one, but once the work at hand is finished, we don't go back to examine."

Where the Lilies Bloom (Philadelphia: J. B. Lippincott, 1966). Illustrated by Jim Spanfeller. (Gr. 4-9).

Mary Call Luther, a fourteen-year-old Appalachian girl, is called upon by her dying father to keep the family together — to keep her older sister, Devola, from marrying and to see that her younger brother and sister get an education. When he dies, Mary Call persuades the rest of the family to keep his death a secret so that they can continue their life as it is. During an incredible year, they struggle to stay alive and keep the secret. They go "wildcrafting" — gathering medicinal herbs and roots to be sold in town. Kiser Pease, anxious to marry Devola, will not be discouraged. He owns the land on which the Luthers live, but while he is ill, Mary Call extracts his promise that he will give them the land.

After a long cold winter in which Mary Call forces them to school in the bitter cold and feeds them on pennies a day, the roof of their house caves in and Mary Call, exhausted, tries to find them a cave. Returning home, she is met by Devola and Kiser who announce that they will marry and that it is time that someone takes the burden from her. Relieved, Mary Call agrees that perhaps her father put more on her shoulders than she was prepared to carry. She had done her best but could do no more.

Springboards

Put yourself into the positions of the Luthers — what would you have done if you were Mary Call, Devola, etc.? Mary Call underestimated Devola's intelligence. Have you ever underestimated anyone? How did you find out you were wrong? Do you ever feel that people expect more of you than you are capable of? Or less? Why do you think they formed that opinion of you? What steps can you take to change it?

Think of environments other than the mountains. What could you do to make a living off the land?

Activities

Have the students take the parts of the Luthers and the neighbors. The Luthers do not want to let anyone in the house and the neighbors are suspicious and want to come in. Afterwards, discuss the tactics used. Did the adults try to take advantage of the fact that the Luthers were children? Did the Luthers have to lie? What made the neighbors suspicious? Was it any of their business?

Arrange to take a field trip to the nearest wildlife area. Beforehand, assign each student a plant or tree to identify and know its healing properties and other uses. With a guide from the wildlife area, go "wildcrafting" having each student tell the rest of the class about his or her individual plant.

Ask students to compile a recipe and home-remedy book using native wild foods and herbs. This is a good opportunity to introduce the *Foxfire* books.

Trial Valley (Philadelphia: J. B. Lippincott, 1977).

Trial Valley is a continuation of *Where the Lilies Bloom*. Devola has married Kiser Pease and Mary Call Luther, at age sixteen, is raising her younger brother and sister. To add to her burdens, a young boy, Jack Parsons, is found abandoned in a cage in the woods. Kiser and Devola volunteer to care for him, but he has chosen Mary Call, who now has another mouth to feed. Her life is further complicated by Thad and Gaither's romantic interest in her. Thad comes from a wealthy Virginia family; he is a social worker. Gaither is a local boy. Both are vying for her affection.

Fearing that Mary Call does not want him, and not wanting to live with Kiser and Devola, Jack runs away in the midst of a raging storm. The climax of the story comes during the hunt scene. Mary Call, after finding Jack, falls into the flooding creek and Jack jumps in to save her and is swept away. Thad jumps in to rescue Mary, but Gaither, instead, saves Jack. This brings Mary to the realization that she and Thad do not share the same dreams and that she would not be happy with him despite her romantic dreams of the good life in Virginia. The story ends with all the children secure and Gaither waiting.

Springboards

Imagine that you were shut in a cage and left to starve. How would you feel? If your family had put you there, would you want to find them? Why did Jack Parsons want to stay with Mary Call instead of Kiser and Devola? Where would you have stayed?

If you were Mary Call which of the two men would you have chosen? Why?

Activities

Ask students to write a sequel to the story. What happens to the family over the next few years?

Write the rescue scene from Thad or Gaither's point of view.

Explore three or four possible endings to this story. Have students choose one they like best and have them defend their choice.

Have students pretend they are Mary Call and describe what Virginia means to her and her dreams of the future.

The Mimosa Tree (Philadelphia: J. B. Lippincott, 1970). (Gr. 5-7).

The Proffitt family of Goose Elk, North Carolina, moved to Chicago encouraged by their father's new wife, Zollie, to find a better life. Once in the big city, however, Zollie deserts the family, leaving blind Mr. Proffitt alone with his three children and no prospects. Bewildered by Zollie's defection and having no ability to deal with the dishonest hustles of big cities, Mr. Proffitt allows the burden of keeping the family together to fall on the shoulders of fourteen-year-old Marvella. The two younger brothers, Hugh and Dwain, provide the answer to the family's lack of income—taught by two local boys,

Frank and Mario, they learn to snatch purses. Marvella, knowing that this is wrong, at first tries to prevent it, but when the promised "government money" never materializes, she joins them. Mario dies of untreated epilepsy; Marvella cannot find a job; and the final shock that awakens Marvella to the "wrongness" of their life comes when Frank "accidentally" pushes his mother in front of a bus. Realizing at last that they are doomed if they stay, Marvella, under-age and with no driver's license and a broken-down car, drives them all back to Goose Elk. There they are warmly welcomed by their former neighbors and Marvella, free of the responsibility, weeps for their lost innocence.

Springboards

If you were suddenly transported to a strange city, where you knew no one and had no money, how would you survive?

Would you rather be like Frank and Mario or like Hugh and Dwain? Why?

The Proffitt's neighbors in Goose Elk are much friendlier than the people in Chicago. What do you suppose caused this difference? Can anything be done to make neighbors more friendly?

Marvella is concerned with being "good." What are the rewards of being "good"? Why does Marvella feel it is so important? Does Frank think it is important? What is more important to him? Why do you think people feel different about it? What is your opinion?

Activities

Have students act out the scene where Hugh and Dwain meet Mario and Frank. Discuss why each character acts as he does.

Describe the Chicago world as Mr. Proffitt sees it and as it really is. Students can either draw or write a description. Afterward discuss which world is preferred and why.

Have students choose which place they would rather live, Goose Elk or Chicago. Ask them to list disadvantages and advantages of each and explain why they prefer one to the other.

The Mock Revolt (Philadelphia: J. B. Lippincott, 1971). (Gr. 6-up).

A thirteen-year-old boy with the unlikely name of Ussy Mock is the hero of this story. Ussy is the son of a bank president in the small, hot, southern town of Medina, and he wishes he were anywhere but there. This is the story of Ussy's rebelling and his questioning of the values held by his parents and society.

At the beginning of the story, his two exotic friends, Turner and Directly Ensley sell their house and leave on a motorcycle for San Francisco, leaving Ussy alone in a town full of "deadlies." Lacking anything better to do, Ussy enlists in a farm camp and goes every morning with a truck full of other middle-class boys to pick crops for a nominal wage. He hopes to save enough money to run away to San Francisco.

At the farm camp, Ussy meets Luke Wilder, the son of a migrant worker who lives and works at the camp. Through Luke, Ussy becomes aware of the world of the poor—trampled pride, illness, filth, and starvation—his first glimpse of a life without personal dignity. For the remainder of the summer, Ussy struggles between resentment of a society that permits such degradation, and resentment of people like Luke and his parents, who do not seem to be willing to do anything to better themselves. At the same time, he is torn between pity for Luke and anger that Luke is able to play on his sympathy to extort money from him. He also feels guilty about his own inability to extricate himself from the situation. The story ends with Ussy still unsure about whether he is a humanitarian or a sucker.

Springboards

What was so attractive to Ussy about Turner and Directly Ensley? Do you know anyone like that? Why are you attracted to them?

Why do you think Ussy cut his hair like an Indian? Have you ever done anything similar? Why?

If someone stole your hard-earned money, how would you react? What if the person were poor and hungry like Luke? How would you feel about yourself? How would you feel about the other person?

Why did Ussy want to avoid Luke? What connection do you see between Ussy's wanting to run away to San Francisco and his feelings about Luke?

Activities

Have one student be the wage-earner and the other be someone looking for a handout. Have students make up dialogue. Then, have the class discuss the interchange and how each character probably felt about the interaction.

Each of us has a place he or she would like to run away to. Have students describe in several paragraphs what their place is like. Also include why that place is different or better than where the student lives now and what thoughts or situations cause them to want to run away.

Me Too (Philadelphia: J. B. Lippincott, 1973). (Gr. 7-9).

Lydia is another of the Cleaver's intrepid heroines—determined, independent, intelligent, and courageous. She is twelve-years-old and has a twin sister, Lorna, who is mentally impaired. During the summer of their twelfth year, their father deserts them and their working mother leaves Lydia at home to take care of Lorna. Convinced that their father left because Lorna is "different," Lydia is determined to teach Lorna so that when their father comes home, he will not be able to tell the difference between the two girls. She becomes even more determined to succeed when neighbors begin to talk about "inherited characteristics" and will no longer allow Lorna to play with her best friend, Billy Frank. The neighbors are afraid that they might grow up, fall in love, get married and have "retarded" children like Lorna. In the face of such bigotry, Lydia begins her classes.

Lorna, however, does not respond. Lydia refuses to accept that she cannot teach her sister and alternates between loving, pitying, and hating her twin. She also refuses to accept that her father is not coming back at the end of the summer and constantly invents situations and dialogues between the two girls and their father. Finally, a natural disaster awakens her to the fact that Lorna will never react normally—that she is powerless to help her sister. While out in the woods, a sink hole collapses beneath Lydia and leaves her hanging on a tree over a chasm. Her sister is the only witness, and finally Lydia realizes that not only will Lorna not think to go for help, but that Lorna would not even notice if she fell to her death.

Belatedly, her mother realizes that the responsibility is too much, and sends Lorna back to her "special" school and then talks to Lydia about her father, emphasizing that he wanted to go and most likely would never return. Freed from her responsibility and obsessions, Lydia is able to return to being a twelve-year-old.

Springboards

Have you ever wanted to be a twin? What would you like about it? What would you not like?

Imagine that you have a younger brother or sister who wants to play school. What subjects would you start with? How long would you make your classes? What would you do differently from the teachers you have had? What would you do the same?

Activities

Many children live in one-parent homes. If you can find a group of children who are willing, have them form a panel and moderate a discussion on that experience.

Invite a biology teacher to class to give a basic genetics lecture. Ask each student to choose one of his or her physical characteristics and do a genetic chart of that characteristic. Also discuss forms of retardation and the types that are inherited, their frequency, and their genetic patterns.

Have students make up an imaginary class schedule for Lorna. Invite a teacher that works with retarded children to explain the differences in education for these students. Suggest to students volunteer activities they can engage in to work with these children or their families.

Ellen Grae (Philadelphia: J. B. Lippincott, 1967). (Gr. 4-6).

The irrepressible Ellen Grae gets in trouble because of her tendency to tell tall tales. She and her constant companion, Grover, spend their school vacation on the river and in the woods of a small southern town fishing and digging for buried treasure. Another friend of Ellen's is Ira, an older man whom the people of Thicket think is crazy. His parents reportedly ran away and left him when he was a boy, and he now lives alone, wears no shoes, and will not talk to anyone but Ellen Grae.

One day, Ira confesses to Ellen Grae that his parents died in the swamp from a rattlesnake bite and that he buried them. Ellen Grae at first dismisses this tale as a strange man's ramblings, but after a treasure hunting expedition where they come across the sunken place that Ira says holds his parents' remains, Ellen Grae becomes confused as to how to handle the situation. Should she report the finding and expose Ira to the publicity and possible jail sentence, or should she keep it to herself? As she wrestles with the problem, she becomes depressed and distracted. Finally, she tells her parents who take her to the sheriff. At the last minute, much to her parents discomfiture, she reveals that she was just telling one of her tales.

Springboards

Imagine Ellen and Grover's typical day on the river. Is that how you would like to spend your summer vacation? What would you like to do that is different?

Why do you suppose that Ira will only talk to Ellen Grae? Why do you think the townspeople think he's crazy? Is he? What exactly do people mean when they say that? Why do they say it? Do you know anyone like Ira? How do you feel about that person?

Put yourself in Ellen Grae's position. Would you tell anyone about your discovery? Would you tell your parents? Your best friend? Law enforcement officials? Why or why not?

If you had been in Ira's position when the snake killed his parents, what would you have done? What could he have done differently?

Activities

All of us have had problems and have not known whether we should confide in someone. Have students write about problems they have had and how they solved them. Discuss these problems within groups and explore alternative solutions. Does talking about a problem help? Are there sometimes several solutions? Have students write down the alternative solutions after the discussion and select the solutions they prefer. How does one's thinking change? Why?

Ellen Grae tells tall-tales. Ask students to make up their own tall-tales and tell them to the class. Put tales into a booklet. This is a good time to introduce folk tales, jack tales, and oral history.

Lady Ellen Grae (Philadelphia: J. B. Lippincott, 1968). (Gr. 4-6).

Jeff and Grace Derryberry, parents of young Ellen Grae, decide that it is time for Ellen Grae to learn manners and values and to stop being a tomboy; so they arrange for her to visit her aunt and cousin Laura in Seattle for the school year. Ellen Grae and her friend, Grover, spend half of the summer trying to convince her parents that she is perfectly capable of turning into a lady without leaving home. She cooks dinner, wears dresses and Grover even gives her a home permanent, but to no avail. In Seattle, feeling lost in the cold, sterile environment, Ellen Grae continues to act lady-like and well-adjusted in hopes of being allowed to return home. While sailing with the neighbor children, Smith Smith the Seventh and Victoria, she purposely allows the boom to hit her. Later, in the hospital, she talks long distance with her father, but to her dismay, he has seen through the ploy and is extremely angry. Realizing the futility of further "accidents," Ellen Grae begins to adapt to her new life. Then, before school starts, her parents write and send Ellen a plane ticket home. At home again in Thicket, Ellen Grae tries to understand why she was allowed to return, but all her father will say is that even if he, Grace, and Ellen Grae do not all live together, they are still a family and "life is precarious."

Springboards

Which of Ellen Grae's tall-tales is your favorite? Why do you think she tells them? In what situations do you tend to embroider the truth? Why?

Look up "Geoduck" in the encyclopedia — what are other native life forms in the Seattle area? How are they different from the wildlife that Ellen Grae is used to in Thicket? Why do you think Ellen feels that Seattle is a sterile environment?

Imagine that your parents sent you away for a year. What would be the hardest thing for you to get accustomed to? What would you miss the most? How would you go about making new friends?

When Ellen Grae hurt her head, her parents did not let her come home immediately. Do you think that was a wise decision? Why or why not? Have you ever done anything similar? Why did you do it?

Activities

Have students choose a city to move to. Ask them to write an imaginary journal about their first week there. Give them a month to complete the assignment and suggest that they write to the Chamber of Commerce, listen to weather reports, and note news items pertaining to their city.

Have students write a letter home trying to convince their parents to let them return. Then discuss the letters in class and evaluate which approaches might be the most effective and why?

Grover (Philadelphia: J. B. Lippincott, 1970).

Grover Ezell's mother is dying and no one wants to tell Grover. His relatives are all too kind, and everyone conspires to keep the facts from him, but with a child's sensitivity, he suspects. His father is stricken and cannot communicate his feelings or help Grover to sort out his, and Grover is confused, angry, and bereft. His mother, upon returning home from the hospital, tries to help him understand and explains things to him, but like all the adults, is too caught up in her own personal agony to have much time for Grover. The pain and knowledge of slow, certain death become too much for his mother to bear, and she commits suicide. Grover's father is like a madman—unable to deal with his own grief and anger, he cannot deal with his son's. To Grover, his reaction seems selfish—his father berates his wife for leaving him alone, saying it was her Christian duty to endure. Throughout, Grover seems numb, but one afternoon the tension surfaces and his anger and bewilderment manifest themselves in the slaughter of a turkey that belongs to the town's black sheep, a lady who says spitefully, "You're the kid whose mother blew her brains out."

This symbolic act releases some of the anger and he goes to talk with his preacher about enduring life. The minister cannot answer, however, and Grover reaches his own conclusions: he does not know the answers, but neither does anyone else, it seems. He is simply going to keep on living and learning. By coming to terms with his confusion and his mother's death, he frees himself from depression and is free to get on with his own life.

Springboards

Does Grover know for certain that his mother is dying? Why do you think so? Why don't you think so? How do adults act when they are trying to keep a secret from you? How do you behave when you are trying to keep something from someone?

Imagine how you would feel if you thought one of your parents was dying? How do you think they would feel about it? What would they worry about? If you did not know, would you want to be told?

Do you agree with Grover's father when he said life was to be endured? Are there exceptions? Do you think that suicide is ever acceptable?

Activities

Ask a student to select a church near him or her. Make an appointment to see the minister or Sunday school teacher. Ask about the church doctrine on suicide and see if they will tell you their personal feelings about the subject. Investigate other religious doctrines.

Many people in history have committed suicide. Have students look up a few and then try to determine causes and prevailing opinions about suicide.

Have students alternate in parent and child roles. Have the parent explain death to the child. In preparation, have class read selections from Elizabeth Kubler-Ross' *On Death and Dying* (New York: Macmillan, 1969). After role playing is finished, open the topic for class discussion. (Many hospitals now have trained staff to work with dying patients and their families. Invite one of them either to join in or to conduct the class discussion. Invite specialists to encourage students to express their fears and doubts about death both for themselves and their family. In some instances, it might be a good idea to have a clergyman present to participate in the discussion.

Other Books by Vera and Bill Cleaver

Delpha Green and Company (Philadelphia: J. B. Lippincott, 1972). (Gr. 7-up).

Dust of the Earth (Philadelphia: J. B. Lippincott, 1975). (Gr. 7-up).

I Would Rather Be a Turnip (Philadelphia: J. B. Lippincott, 1971). (Gr. 4-6).

Queen of Hearts (Philadelphia: J. B. Lippincott, 1978).

The Whys and Wherefores of Littabelle Lee (Philadelphia: J. B. Lippincott, 1973). (Gr. 7-up).

Footnotes

[1]*Meet the Lippincott Author* (Philadelphia: J. B. Lippincott Co., n.d.).

[2]*Meet the Lippincott Author.*

[3]Doris de Montreville and Elizabeth D. Drawford, eds. *Fourth Book of Junior Authors and Illustrators* (New York: H. W. Wilson Co., 1978), pp. 88-90.

9 GIFTED AUTHORS—GIFTED READERS

In initiating a program of literature study with its emphasis on developing literature skills, we must never lose sight of our ultimate goal: creating readers who have found joy and satisfaction in a wide variety of reading experiences which not only stretch young minds, but touch young hearts. The teacher or librarian who chooses wisely the books to be shared—books filled with beauty in idea and language—will find enrichment as the books themselves enrich and stretch the pupils' conscious or unconscious awareness of true art.

Avid adult and young readers alike choose books not by title but by author. Ask any reader to name a favorite author and a long list will be forthcoming. While thematic units treating works by several writers can be challenging, a reading unit centered upon the characteristics of an individual gifted author must be a part of the literature program as well.

Fortunately, children who have been identified and placed in gifted programs have achieved literacy rather than "letteracy." These children have discovered the intrinsic rewards of the reading experience and do not need gimmicks to lead them to books. They do, however, need knowledgeable guidance to take them beyond their present stage of reading and to help them savor the literary morsels of gifted authors.

The literature units presented in this chapter are only the beginning of the literary feast. Hopefully they will serve as models for developing areas of literature study at appropriate grade levels either through study of the books of a single author or through exploring a theme as it is developed by a number of authors.

The three units presented here include:

Unit One: Exploring Basic Needs—Pre-School to Grade 1. A unit to assist very young children in an examination of values and basic needs.

Unit Two: The Many Worlds of Lloyd Alexander. Introducing fantasy worlds and superb literary style to second- and third-grade students.

Unit Three: Zilpha Keatley Snyder—Versatility Plus! Getting acquainted with an author whose versatility moves from realism to fantasy for grades four through seven.

Each unit summarizes selected titles and suggests activities that will extend reading enjoyment and, at the same time, develop a broader range of literature skills and understanding. Units Two and Three are centered around the works of one author and ideally should be introduced by allowing the children to meet the author in every way possible:

1. Bring the author to the school! (Impossible? Not when gifted minds get to work on achieving a goal!)

2. Use a telephone hook-up which allows children in the classroom to speak directly to an author in his or her home, office, or studio.

3. Write to the author and his or her publisher—encourage students to ask questions and offer comments that really show thought.

4. Use many sources of information about authors. Lee Bennett Hopkins' *Books Are by People* (New York: Citation Press, 1969) and *More Books by More People* (New York: Citation Press, 1974) contain delightful author interviews. The Gale Research series, *Something about the Author* (Detroit: Gale, 1971-) is an invaluable source of information. *A Treasure of Letters from Favorite Authors*, books one and two, contain actual letters, many in the authors' own handwriting with permission to reproduce the letters for students. These booklets of letters are available from Book Lures, Inc., P.O. Box 9450, O'Fallon, MO 63366.

5. Use the media! The "Meet the Newbery Author" sound filmstrip series from Miller-Brody Productions (342 Madison Ave., New York, NY 10017), is an excellent series to help bring authors alive as real people.

Unit One
A Basic List for Basic Needs—
Pre-School to Grade One

By Marigene Suellentrop

Out of all the thousands of picture books published over the years, it would be difficult to draw up a list of the one hundred very best. Certainly many Caldecott books would be included and the compiler could be allowed to include many personal favorites. Librarians would agree, nonetheless, that there are some titles that it would be a shame for a student to miss.

Let us consider as guidelines for the list some needs common to most. There is the need to achieve, to have security, to gain acceptance, and to experience beauty and diversion. One might contend that this is a catalog of "rights" of children: the right to be loved and feel secure, the right to exercise the imagination, the right to know beauty, to achieve competency and a good self-image, the right to express feelings and, lastly, the right to laugh. Picture books contain the material to fill these needs and satisfy these rights.

This unit will identify specific books containing these themes. Sometimes a book chosen to specify a particular need overlaps into another area, but here are books every student has the right to become acquainted with, to enjoy and "own"—enough for nearly an entire school year.

Nobody Asked Me If I Wanted a Baby Sister, by Martha Alexander (New York: Dial, 1971). (ps-2).

Oliver can no longer stand the fuss over his baby sister, Bonnie, so he packs her up in his wagon to find someone to give her to. When it seems Toby's Mom will take her, Bonnie demonstrates preference for Oliver. The book ends as Oliver imagines sharing life with Bonnie as she grows older.

Discussion

1.   Ask what the children enjoy about having a younger brother or sister and if there has been some task they were able to help the younger one accomplish (or how an older brother or sister has helped). Older students might write about an incident shared with a younger family member.

2.   List all the people you can think of who have helped you in any way today. Why is helping each other important?

Activities

1.   Use your own younger brother or sister as a model or use Bonnie as a model and write a short *Handbook for Babysitters*. List all of the things it would be necessary for someone to know to babysit at your house.

Look Out the Window, by Joan Walsh Anglund (New York: Harcourt, Brace & Jovanovich, 1959). (Gr. K-2).

Here is a small book with the special Anglund illustrations. This book makes every student realize his or her own personal worth "because you are the only one in this whole wide world that is you."

Activities

1.   On an unsigned slip of paper, list one thing you can do well—decorate a cake, whistle, set the table, make someone smile, work a hard

math problem, make your bed — some simple task you feel confident about. The teacher will write the list on the board to show everyone has a special ability that makes her or him a special person.

2. Collect "Easy to Read" biographies on a variety of people. Encourage children to select and read as many as they wish. Have a "Famous Person" sharing time. Children choose one famous person and tell about that person's qualities and accomplishments. Other students try to guess the person described.

Red Mittens, by Laura Bannon (Boston: Houghton Mifflin, 1946). (Gr. K-3).

This is a simple story with a gentle kind of humor. Little Joe's mother makes red mittens for him and he loves them so much he wears them all the time. One day he loses them and the cow, cat, and other animals help find them. They look high, low, and in the middle, so we have a book useful in reinforcing those concepts.

Activities

1. Young children love to help the storyteller and the characters look "high," "low," and "in the middle." With black magic marker, outline right and left mittens on red construction paper. These can decorate the bulletin board. If you prefer, staple lengths of yarn to the mittens and children can wear them as Little Joe did.

2. Share also Elsa Beskow's *Pelle's New Suit* (New York: Scholastic Book Services, 1974), which describes the wool-making process. Invite someone who knits to demonstrate the process and explain how much yarn is needed for one pair of mittens. Ask the children to check store or catalog ads to price mittens and yarn. Would it cost less to buy mittens or to make them?

The Five Chinese Brothers, by Claire Hutchet Bishop (New York: Coward, McCann, & Geoghegan, 1938). Illustrated by Kurt Wiese. (Gr. K-3).

There has been much recent criticism that this old standard has racial overtones and is guilty of stereotyping; children do not seem to be alarmed by this adult furor and continue to enjoy the book as much as ever. The five identical-looking Chinese brothers have special talents that are used to outwit the executioner and save all of them. The book has a folk tale quality plus a rhythmic repetition children enjoy. The theme of the weak putting down the powerful, stronger opponent is always a satisfying one.

Activities

1. Design a book jacket for this story which will give the reader clues to the story's content.

2. If you could have the special talent of one brother, which talent would you choose? Why? List all the ways you could use it.

The Runaway Bunny, by Margaret Wise Brown (New York: Harper and Row, 1942). Illustrated by Clement Hurd. (ps-2).

Clement Hurd, the illustrator, uses brilliant colors in a double-page arrangement at the end of each rhyme-like exchange between the mother rabbit and the little bunny. Their warm relationship is reflected in the conversation about the bunny who says he will run away. Mother always says she will come after him, so in the end he decides he will stay and be her little bunny after all.

Activities

Here is a delightful "pattern" book about things that belong together. Using it as a springboard for children's own creative writing can have satisfying results.

Place some "story starters" on the board: "If you were the ocean then I would be a _____ to _____ . If I were a giraffe, then you could be a _____ and _____ ." Children will soon develop their own beginnings.

Mike Mulligan and His Steam Shovel, by Virginia Lee Burton (Boston: Houghton Mifflin, 1977). (Gr. K-3).

Mike Mulligan and Mary Anne, his old-fashioned steam shovel, prove they can dig the cellar for the new town hall in Popperville. The distinctive drawings of Virginia Burton enhance this favorite, and the story has enough suspense to satisfy this media generation. It doesn't take long for children to recognize Burton's art in this and *The Little House*.

Activities

What fun to discover the world of machines and the many uses of each. Allow children to search newspapers, magazines, books, and any other sources they can find for pictures of machines. Children should mount the pictures and give the following information about each:

1. the name of the machine

2. what it is used for

3. who would use it

4. how many other uses they can think of for this machine

Arm in Arm, by Remy Charlip (New York: Parents Magazine Press, 1969). (Gr. 1-4).

This is a wildly funny book with pages busy with illustrations. Young students enjoy it, but the older students seem to enjoy its humor more. It is described as a "collection of connections, endless tales, reiterations and other echolalia." It begins with "two octopuses got married and walked down the aisle arm in arm in arm in arm...." Some pages have print that turns and spirals, so it is really better to read alone or in small groups.

Activities

Explain to the students that Remy Charlip teaches the art of mime. (If possible, have secondary drama students visit the class to demonstrate mime.) Since all of Remy Charlip's books are appropriate for dramatic play, locate as many as possible for students to enjoy. Hold a "Mini-Mime Festival" where students can try their talents in acting out one or more scenes from a Charlip book.

Andy and the Lion, by James Daugherty (New York: Viking, 1938). (ps-3).

"A modern picture story of Androcles and the lion," done in yellow, black, and white illustrations and dedicated, surprisingly, to the two New York Library lions. It is the story of Andy's kindness to a circus lion and the gratitude that results. Daugherty's illustrations are so concise it could be used as a wordless picture book. An imaginative, fun book.

Activities

Children might enjoy as a companion book *Gia and the One Hundred Dollars Worth of Bubble Gum*, by Frank Asch (New York: McGraw-Hill, 1974). It is also a sort of Androcles and the lion story. Then, using a round-robin technique, let the children invent their own oral tale of kindness to an animal and what happens as a result. Take turns adding events to the story. Older students could write their own individual stories.

Wait for William, by Marjorie Flack (Boston: Houghton Mifflin, 1935). (Gr. K-3).

Who has never been too weak, too little, too clumsy? Children identify with William who gets to ride the elephant in the circus parade. When the ride ends, his companions wait while William ties his shoe and walk slowly with him listening to his tale of his marvelous ride.

Activities

1. Decide what you will do today to help some younger student, or a classmate. Hold the door for someone to pass ahead, or let someone go first in line and feel yourself grow larger and stronger!

2. Be a *secret* pal to someone today. Choose a classmate, a teacher, or a family member. Decide what you can do for that person that will help him or her in some way. Do the task you choose *secretly*. Let the person guess who her or his secret helper is.

The Story about Ping, by Marjorie Flack (New York: Viking, 1933). Illustrated by Kurt Wiese. (Gr. K-2).

Ping is a little duck who lives on a houseboat on the Yangtze River with his family, including 42 cousins. They spend each day on shore, returning to the boat at night. One day Ping is left on shore and nearly meets his end. As the story closes, Ping is reunited with his family, but not without a spank for being last.

Activities

Make duck puppets from white socks. Cut yellow construction paper bills to glue (or staple) on. Follow the leader as the ducks return nightly to the houseboat, taking care not to allow the leader to spank too hard. Using the puppets, have each student dramatize a *new* adventure for Ping.

Bedtime for Frances, by Russell Hoban (New York: Harper and Row, 1960). Illustrations by Garth Williams. (Gr. K-3).

Like Frances the badger, most children postpone bedtime as long as they can and at some time or another experience fear of the dark. Frances is fearful of the dark shapes and strange sounds in her room, and Father Badger helps her overcome her fright.

Activities

1.   Play the record about being afraid from *The King and I*—"Whenever I feel afraid I hold my head erect, and whistle a happy tune so no one will suspect I'm afraid." Whistle a chorus. Whistling is becoming extinct and effort should be made to promote it!

2.   Visit the library and have each child choose an animal book (nonfiction). After browsing through and book and examining the pictures, ask each child to tell what dangers the animal might fear when bedding down for the night. Are they real or imagined?

I Need a Friend, by Sherry Kafka (New York: Putnam's, 1971). Illustrated by Eros Keith. (Gr. K-2).
> "All by myself I can play alone
> But I need a friend for sharing."

The girl in the book discusses various things she can do alone, but concludes that she needs a friend to complete and enlarge her activity. Careful observers note that the illustration background shows a friend moving next door, together with a cat, and anticipate a happy ending.

Activities

Working in teams of two or four, students can do a creative writing project by completing, "All by myself I can _____ . But I need a friend to _____ ." Their text, plus illustrations, could be bound into a class book.

The Snowy Day, by Ezra Jack Keats (New York: Viking, 1962). (ps-1).
This outstanding author-illustrator's mood book won the Caldecott medal in 1963. It is a simple story of a little boy's day as he plays alone in the snow and tells his mother about it while he prepares for bed. The next morning there is new snow, and he goes out to play in it again, this time with a friend.

Discussion

What makes snow? How can we find out? What problems can snow cause? What joys can snow bring?

Activities

Notice the artist's use of collage. Look at the variety of snowflakes drawn on the book's inside cover. With scissors, snip folded paper snowflakes of your own and mount them on blue construction paper. These are effective displayed thus or simply unmounted in classroom window panes. The book and this activity are good for winter's first snow.

A Hole Is to Dig, by Ruth Krauss (New York: Harper and Row, 1952). Illustrated by Maurice Sendak. (ps-1).

More humorous drawings by Sendak add to this book of definitions that is full of imaginative language play. Examples include "a nose is to blow" and "steps are to sit on."

Activities

Make your own list: Gum is for chewing, trees are to climb, roses are for smelling, etc. Keep going! How many can you list!

In the Flaky Frosty Morning, by Karla Kuskin (New York: Harper and Row, 1969). (ps-3).

A snowman tells how he comes into being, only to return to "snowman soup" in the sun the next day. The rhyming text is brief and the illustrations are colorful, making this an appropriate wintertime book.

Activities

1.   If possible, go outside and make a snowman. If the teacher is not the outdoor sort, students can outline a snowman on blue construction paper, filling in the body with glued-on cotton and adding a hat, scarf, etc., from scraps of material or bits of colored construction paper.

2.   Let the children suggest unusual names for the snowman. Vote on the name to be chosen. Explain the term "autobiography." Ask each child to pretend that he or she is the snowman and write an "autobiography of a snowman." Encourage the children to add many events to the snowman's life that are not mentioned in the book.

Frog Went A-Courtin', by John Langstaff (New York: Harcourt, Brace & World, 1955). Illustrated by Feodor Rojankovsky. (Gr. K-3).

This Appalachian mountain ballad, which has roots in Scotland, was an adaptation that won the Caldecott medal. It is the story of Miss Mouse's courtship by and wedding to Frog and culminates with the old tom cat breaking up the wedding breakfast.

Activities

Sing it, of course! This is how the mountain people told the story. After the class learns the words, various students can dramatize the story as the choral background is sung so that everyone can participate.

Make Way for Ducklings, by Robert McCloskey (New York: Viking, 1941). (Gr. K-3).

Another favorite Caldecott winner (1942) is this story of a family of ducks whose mother leads them through city traffic to their new home in Boston's Public Garden, with the help of a policeman.

Activities

Using the card catalog, see what the library has about Boston. Watch a filmstrip or read an article in *National Geographic*. See the article on Boston in *World Book Encyclopedia*, and read about Beacon Hill, Boston Common, and Public Garden. Look at the map contained in the article, and find the places mentioned in the book. Trace the route the ducks took in locating a new home. Younger students could color a picture the teacher has mimeographed, a drawing of Mr. and Mrs. Mallard and the eight ducks. There are various ways to enjoy this tale of reassurance and love.

A Kiss for Little Bear, by Else Holmelund Minarik (New York: Harper and Row, 1968). Illustrated by Maurice Sendak. (Gr. K-3).

Sendak's illustrations make a delightful accompaniment to this "I Can Read" book about Little Bear's picture delivered by Hen. Grandmother's thank you kiss eventually arrives via Hen, Frog, Cat, and other animals. Two skunks involved in the unusual delivery get married at the end of the book and Little Bear is best man at the wedding.

Activities

This story reflects a warm relationship between Little Bear and his grandmother. After discussing what they would like to give a grandparent, and why, students could draw and color on small squares a "gift" to be attached to a "Grandmother Tree," a branch stuck in a container of sand. On the reverse side of the gift, identify what is inside. These "gifts" might be a "gift of self," i.e., writing a letter or making a card to send grandparents who live far away; picking up toys, closing doors, etc., without being told when visiting a grandparent.

The Little Engine That Could, by Watty Piper (New York: Platt & Munk, 1930). (ps-3).

This favorite is nearly as old as Peter Rabbit. It is a cheerful story of the Little Blue Engine that pulls the trainload of toys and good food for good boys and girls up over the mountain, not because he is new or strong, but because he says "I think I can." This example of determined effort may bolster the confidence of a reluctant student and encourage him or her to say firmly "I thought I could."

Activities

Younger children love to help the train as the teacher reads, "I think I can," train-fashion. Students can write on a slip of paper something they could do if they tried a little harder, or something they hope to accomplish during the school year. Slips should be folded (not read) and collected. At the end of the year, slips can be given back to their owners who evaluate how well the task or deed was accomplished.

The Boy Who Could Make Things, by Edna Mitchell Preston (New York: Viking, 1970). Illustrated by Leonard Kessler.

This is a story about love and families and relationships and, perhaps, even Creation. The Boy makes a house with furnishings for the family of Little People he made, but the family never behaves properly. The boy must always spank them and put them back in the box. It seems they will never live happily ever after. Finally he draws a heart on each and miraculously they begin to live as a loving family. The moon assures the boy they will live happily ever after and when he asks, "How did they learn? When did they begin? Why did it start?" the moon answers, "You know. You know."

Activities

Obtain as many old magazines as possible (always useful in the classroom). Let children browse through the magazines to find, clip, and mount one or more illustrations showing the many forms of love. Each child should write captions for the illustrations selected. For example, a man or woman cooking might be captioned: Love is feeding a hungry family.

Nothing Ever Happens on My Block, by Ellen Raskin (New York: Atheneum, 1967). (Gr. K-4).

As Chester sits grumpily wishing something would happen, all kinds of wild, exciting events are taking place directly behind him, and he is never aware. This humorous book is good for practicing observation.

Activities

Using the opaque projector, show pages from *Find the Cat*, by Elaine Livermore (Boston: Houghton Mifflin, 1973). Find the cat somewhere on every page. Children often accomplish this before the teacher does. Folk tale characters are hidden in the pages of *Anno's Journey*, by Mitsumasa Anno (Cleveland, OH: Collins-World, 1978). Ask each child to be prepared to tell the class about something he or she saw for the first time going home from school by the usual route.

Where the Wild Things Are, by Maurice Sendak (New York: Harper and Row, 1963). (Gr. K-3).

A 1964 Caldecott book, this is the fantasy of a small boy who, after being punished for acting wildly himself, sails away to the land of the wild things. When he decides to return, he finds supper waiting—still warm. Creatures get larger as we turn page after page.

Activities

Discuss with the children acceptable and unacceptable ways of handling anger. Let children find, cut out, and mount pictures of people with a variety of facial expressions. Discuss each picture. Bring out possible causes and constructive solutions for negative feelings.

Horton Hears a Who!, by Dr. Seuss (New York: Random House, 1954). (Gr. K-3).

Written in typical Seuss verse and illustrated in his usual style, this book tells about Horton, the elephant, who goes to great lengths to save the tiny Whos because "after all, a person's a person, no matter how small." This book emphasizes the importance of the individual and, incidentally, the effectiveness of group effort.

Discussion

1. Have you ever allowed someone to do something for you that you could have done for yourself? Why? How did you feel when the job was done?

2. Who was entitled to "mother" the new "bird," Horton or Mazie? Why?

3. What is responsibility? Is it important for people to be responsible?

Caps for Sale, by Esphyr Slobodkina (New York: Scholastic Book Service, 1976).

"A tale of a peddler, some monkeys and their monkey business." While the cap peddler naps, monkeys steal all his caps. The page full of monkeys in the tree all wearing caps and laughing is a very funny scene. The peddler finds a clever way to regain his caps.

Activities

Let young children participate in the storytelling as the peddler scolds the monkeys in his effort to get back his caps. They'll catch on fast. Each child can bring a cap to school and the group will be able to dramatize the story. There are many monkeys, so all will be needed in the dramatization.

Alexander and the Terrible, Horrible, No Good, Very Bad Day, by Judith Viorst (New York: Atheneum, 1972). (Gr. K-3).

Not only children, but adults as well, can relate to the story of Alexander's frustrating day. From when he wakes up with gum in his hair to when he has to wear his hated railroad train pajamas to bed, it all goes so wrong that he considers a move to Australia, but his mother says some days are bad there too.

Activities

Students need to be assured of the freedom to express feelings, so let them tell what makes some of their days terrible. Then, as one-sentence alternatives, let them complete "It's a good day for me when _____." Read them or display them.

The Biggest Bear, by Lynd Ward (Boston: Houghton Mifflin, 1973). (Gr. K-3).

Johnny Orchard wants a bear skin displayed on the family barn like every other farmer has. When he comes into possession of a bear cub it creates all kinds of mess, and in attempting to lose this now huge creature, both boy and bear are captured in a circus trap. Johnny's problem is solved and the bear is assured a good home with the circus.

Activities

Place children in small groups. Present the problem, "Suppose there were no circus for the bear. How could Johnny solve the problem of keeping the bear alive and out of trouble?" Allow 10 minutes for group problem-solving. Let a spokesman for each group present and defend the group's solution.

Brian Wildsmith's Wild Animals, by Brian Wildsmith (New York: Watts, 1967). (Gr. K-3).

For a riot of color, any Wildsmith book could be used, but since children enjoy animals, this one was selected. The book begins with a discussion of the words used for groups of animals and proceeds to illustrate these words on double pages. This is a series of pictures, no story.

Activities

Wordless picture books are ideal for motivating composition. Children can study the pictures and write or dictate vivid descriptions of their favorite animals. Encourage the use of a variety of descriptive words.

Crow Boy, by Taro Yashima (New York: Viking, 1955). (Gr. K-3).

This is the story of a shy boy in a village school in Japan, a boy totally rejected by his classmates for five years, until a new teacher, Mr. Isobe, is instrumental in helping him display a special talent. From then on, the children accept Crow Boy as an important person.

Activities

This most important book should help gifted children to see that all people are gifted in some way. Begin a list of "gifts," encourage children to go beyond obvious talents in music, art, and mental ability to unusual gifts. Let the list grow and grow and grow! Emphasize that many "gifts" are useless unless they are developed. Short biographies should be introduced to allow children to see how famous people developed those gifts which led to outstanding achievement in their fields.

Unit Two
Lloyd Alexander—An Author Study Unit for Grades 2-4
By Peggy Klein

Lloyd Alexander is an excellent choice for a literature study unit for several reasons. His titles include picture books for younger children, stories for middle-grade students, and the Prydain series for upper-grade students. Children who meet the superb literary style of Lloyd Alexander early in life will not long be satisfied with books that are less well written.

In addition, the world of fantasy has particular appeal for gifted children; for it is an infinite world of ideas and images as contrasted with the finite real world in which so many limits are set. As Lloyd Alexander himself says:

> Unleavened by imagination the variety and richness of life turn into flat abstractions. When we have a meaningful experience with imaginative literature we should not consider it a legal freakout or an indulgence which we allow ourselves for the sake of something to do. Rather, it is one of the ways of gaining an active awareness of ourselves as individuals, an awareness of our society, and perhaps an encouragement to make it better.

Lloyd Alexander was born January 30, 1924, in Philadelphia. As a child he was an avid reader and his favorite place was a bookstore with two shelves in the back for children's books.

At the age of fifteen, Lloyd announced to his parents that he wanted to be a poet. His father immediately pointed out that that was not a very lucrative career but his mother encouraged him and his father decided he could be a poet, as long as he had another job to sustain him. The book *King Arthur and His Knights* led Alexander into the realm of hero tales and legends at an early age.

Alexander's first job was as a messenger boy for a bank. He then returned to school but found the local college too elementary and rturned to work.

With the advent of World War II he joined the army hoping for adventure; what he felt was a main ingredient in learning to write. In the army he was assigned to an intelligence unit and travelled with them to Wales. He immediately adopted Wales as the land of all his heroes, truly an enchanted kingdom. After the war he was stationed in Paris. There he met and married his French wife, Janine. They have one child, Madeleine.

Alexander attended the University of Paris (Sorbonne) following his discharge from the army. Feeling homesick, he returned to Philadelphia, tried writing for adults, and had his first three novels rejected. He then worked at a succession of jobs and wrote for seven unsuccessful years. Finally, he wrote about those hard times and his novel was accepted for publication. From this experience he learned to write about things he knew and loved. His love of cats and music is evident in many of his children's books.

When doing research for his book, *Time Cat*, he came across Welsh legends. The heroes of his past and the Wales he had known came back to him and resulted in the tales of the Prydain cycle.

Introducing the picture books of Lloyd Alexander to children who are eager to test their new-found reading ability, and sharing aloud many other books of this talented author will open the door to the rich literary experiences awaiting children in the Prydain series as soon as they are ready for them.

The Cat Who Wished to Be a Man (New York: Dutton, 1973). (Gr. 4-7).

When Lionel asks his master, Magistor Stephanus, to change him into a man he is warned of how awful men can be. Lionel is determined however and eventually succeeds in getting his wish granted. As soon as he gets to the town of Brightford he begins to discover that all his master had told him about people was true! However, his master had forgotten to tell him that there were some good people. Lionel finds that out for himself and must then decide whether to stay a person or return to his former self. The ending will definitely surprise you.

This book is an excellent choice for reading aloud to gifted classes in grades two and three.

Activities

The book is filled with expressions such as "look a little green around the gills." The children will sympathize with Lionel as he struggles to understand the people around him. Have students make a list of expressions found in the story and others that are commonly used in our everyday language and then define them.

Examples:

> tickled pink—pleased
> cock and bull story—a way out, made-up story

Another group might list the cat characteristics that Lionel has and show how each characteristic was helpful.

Examples:

> keen sight—helped him win money at gambling booth
> agility—helped him duck and avoid Swaggart

A third group could investigate the use of names in this book. What does it mean to swagger? Why is the Mayor named Pursewig? Does it describe him? What about Master Fuller? What do you think his business was? What can you find out about any of the other names?

Coll and His White Pig (New York: Holt, Rinehart and Winston, 1965). Illustrated by Evaline Ness. (Gr. K-3).

Children who have read or heard any of Lloyd Alexander's books about the land of Prydain will recognize Coll. He is a character from those books and in this picture book he again participates in an adventure based on an incident from *The Book of Three*.

Coll's pig, Hen Wen, has been taken by a mysterious band of horsemen. Coll, who is now a simple farmer worried about his crops, reluctantly goes in pursuit. Hen Wen has been taken by the Lord of the Land of Death himself. On this adventure Coll is helped by some extraordinary characters: Ash-Wing, an owl; Oak-Horn, a stag; and Star-Nose, High King of the Moles. Together, these strange partners rescue the far-from-ordinary pig and return Coll to his farm and crops.

Activities

1. Young children will enjoy this story of the animals who can be understood because Coll ate the Hazel Nuts of Wisdom. Have each child find

a picture(s) of the animal he or she would like to be able to talk to. Then, let them eat some Hazel Nuts of Wisdom and tell just what they would talk to their animal about. These stories could be tape recorded or written in books for the children to enjoy again and again.

2. In this book can be found some very basic symbols used by writers. The animals themselves are the owl — wisdom, the stag — swiftness and grace, and the mole — persistence. Discuss the idea of symbols with your class and then have them find the meaning in the pig, the Lord of the Land of Death, the plow made from a sword, the beanpoles made from old spears, etc. See how many symbols you can find!

The Four Donkeys (New York: Holt, Rinehart and Winston, 1972). Illustrated by Lester Abrams. (ps-2).

The Four Donkeys is the story of a tailor, a baker, and a shoemaker, each on his way to the town fair. They are each concerned with how well they will do and what rewards they will have for their labors. When misfortune strikes all three, they learn a valuable lesson in cooperation and come home much wiser for having made donkeys of themselves.

Activities

1. Young children may not know about careers such as the shoemaker and the tailor. An interesting introduction to a unit on careers could come from the reading of this book. The children could look up the tools used by a baker, tailor, shoemaker, printer, and other people who produce things by hand. A visit to a factory and a discussion of the difference between things made by hand and things made by machine — a craftsman and an assembly line worker — could give young children a better appreciation of handmade goods.

2. Another activity could involve some creative writing. Discuss with the children the characteristics shown by each man in the story. Is the tailor a proud man? Who is the most stubborn one in the story? What do they each learn from being a donkey? Introduce sayings like: stubborn as a mule, slippery as an eel, and friendly as a puppy. Talk about sayings like these for each animal and then turn the children loose to make up more sayings of their own.

The King's Fountain (New York: Dutton, 1971). Illustrated by Ezra Jack Keats. (ps-3).

The King has decided to build a huge and beautiful fountain in his garden. If he does, the town below will not get any water and the people will all be thirsty. A poor man in the city realizes this and goes to the wise man, the glib merchants, and the strongest man in the village to get them to go to the King and stop the building of the fountain. But none of them will go. Only one man realizes the danger and can do the task — the poor man himself. Can he face the King and be wise, glib, strong, and brave? This story shows man's ability to act and call upon his resources when the situation demands his action.

Activities

This story should make a good play. Parts for everyone would include those of the townspeople and palace guards. It could easily be staged and parts written for all the characters. Older classes might enjoy collecting articles from newspapers and magazines for a bulletin board entitled "They Could Do It" or "Mission Impossible?" Articles on people who reacted with more than human strength and did what had to be done in emergency situations or simply showed real courage in standing up for what they believe could be posted on this bulletin board.

The Marvelous Misadventures of Sebastian (New York: Dutton, 1970). (Gr. 4-up).

Lloyd Alexander has dedicated this book to "willing listeners." There are no illustrations in this book because the words conjure up very vivid pictures themselves. While intermediate children would most enjoy this book, it would also be a good choice to suggest for family reading at home. Gifted second-and third-grade students should thrive on hearing parents read the book aloud.

Sebastian is the unlikely hero of this tale of fantasy in the land of Hamelin-Loring. He is the fourth fiddler in the orchestra of one of the nobles of Hamelin-Loring until an unfortunate accident causes him to lose his position. He takes to the open road in search of a place to earn his fortune and instead meets tragedy in the loss of his fiddle. Having nothing with which to earn even a meal, Sebastian falls into strange company, ends up helping a princess, and discovers a very unusual fiddle. All of these ingredients lead to high adventure — the nightmare of trying to escape the cruel Regent of the country, and eventually, a decision on how to spend his life.

Activities

The Kingdom of Hamelin-Loring provides excellent material for a discussion of a kingdom versus a dictatorship. The Regent has taken over power in the country. How was he able to do this? What are the powers of a King? How are the powers of a Regent different? How do the people of the country feel about their Regent/government? Would you like to live in a dictatorship? Why or why not? Can a dictator be good?

All of the above questions and more could be brought out and a unit on government follow. The book might be a prelude to a unit on democracy and how we moved from a constitutional monarchy (England) to our own form of government.

The world of eighteenth century music is also authentically represnted in this book. The social hierarchy, the ranks of noblemen and peasants and their places in the society could be discussed and researched using this book as a reference and a starting point.

Time Cat: The Remarkable Journeys of Jason and Gareth (New York: Holt, Rinehart and Winston, 1963). Illustrated by Bill Sokol. (Gr. 2-4).

If you were banished to your room for being bad and found the adventure that Jason found, you'd beg to be punished! To Jason's surprise, his cat, Gareth, begins to talk to him. When he tells Jason of his power to visit other time periods and invites Jason along, the danger, adventure, and learning begin. Together Jason and Gareth find out what it was like for cats and people in ancient Egypt, Celtic Rome, Ireland, Imperial Japan, Renaissance Italy, Spanish Peru, the Isle of Man, seventeenth century Germany, and Colonial America.

Activities

This book is geared for the upper elementary grades; it is illustrated with line drawings. Primary grades would enjoy the story and the adventures of the boy and cat and could draw pictures of Gareth, and describe the cat, perhaps even using the initials of the word: C—courageous, A—affectionate, T—talented, etc.

For the intermediate grades this book would be a marvelous introduction to a history study of any of the time periods included. Students could research and report on the rulers, forms of government, etc. of any or all of the times. Others could research the dress, social customs, and daily life of each period.

With all of this information, a great comparison/contrast could be set up. It would be a good lesson in comparing/contrasting and would also show the vast amount of change that has taken place throughout history. Similarities and differences are sometimes hard for students to see. This book would be an excellent source for finding similarities and differences from the obvious—they wear different clothes—to the subtle—most primitive people were very superstitious.

The Truthful Harp (New York: Holt, Rinehart and Winston, 1967). Illustrated by Evaline Ness. (ps-3).

Have you ever heard of a king who didn't want to be king? Well, Fflewddur Flam, the delightful king of a kingdom he can stride across between mid-day and noon, doesn't want to be king. He wants to be a bard and play the harp. So he practices and practices and then goes to the Chief Bard to get permission to become a Bard. But once there he forgets all he knows and flunks the test. Poor Fflewddur! The Chief Bard takes pity on him and gives him a magic harp on which even he can make beautiful music. Fflewddur sets out on the road to be a Bard. His adventures with this wonderful harp and the lessons he learns about himself are all revealed when he returns to the hall of the Chief

Bard. There he learns the true worth of his misadventures and finds out something very important about himself.

Activities

1. Children will enjoy hearing this tale of Fflewddur and his harp whose strings break when he lies. One little lie leads to another and soon we aren't sure what is true anymore. A class discussion of lying and "stretching the truth" which is so common in the early grades would be most appropriate here. Encourage the children to tell stories from their own experience and ask them if a string on their harp would have broken. That phrase could then become a classroom reminder to tell only the truth to classmates and the teacher.

2. Discussion can center on the realization of one's worth. Fflewddur discovers that he does good things without embroidering them into fantastic tales. A class could make a collage of pictures and words describing themselves as they dream or wish to be.

Cut out a large paper doll shape of a girl or boy and use this as the background on which to paste the pictures and/or words. These could then be mounted around the room. Another paper doll could also be made to show them as they are and the two could be put together to show perhaps that they are not as different as they think.

The Wizard in the Tree (New York: Dutton, 1975). Illustrated by Laszlo Kubinyi. (Gr. 4-7).

When Mallory sees the grey wisp curling out of the trunk of her oak tree she doesn't know what adventures lay in store for her. Helping a wizard who has lost control of his magical powers isn't easy. Especially when he can't control what he turns into. Mallory finds herself protecting a pig from being slaughtered, riding a stag, and all the while trying to help her wizard regain his powers and get to Vale Innis where all the other enchanters have gone.

This tale of a young girl's adventures is set against a background of progress in the England of squires and tenant farmers. It deals with the changes involved in industrialization and "progress."

Activities

1. Young children will sympathize with Mallory when she asks her wizard for three wishes and finds that he won't grant them. Ask the children what they would wish for if they had three wishes. From there they could go on to a creative writing exercise. A story of their meeting of a wizard or witch and their three wishes or the results of their three wishes could be dictated or written individually.

2. For the intermediate grades this book would be an interesting introduction to the system of squire and tenant, the feudal arrangements of landowner and farmer. A typical village and farm-estate could be mapped out

or drawn or built from boxes and milk cartons. This could then be compared to the cities and farms of today.

Other children might be interested in the village inn and its place in the towns of early England. Many had very interesting and descriptive names. These could be researched and then the students could make up signs to illustrate the taverns' names. (Many had signs that told people who were illiterate what kind of business the establishment was.)

Unit Three
The Magic of Zilpha Keatley Snyder
By Mary Vishy

"Zilpha Keatley Snyder, is that your real or spiritual name?" Amanda from *The Headless Cupid* might ask. Zilpha is her real name and she writes imaginative children's books based on the difficulties kids experience in their daily lives. Her characters are not just sugar and spice, but children who feel jealousy, get angry and frustrated, and are not above telling lies. She usually adds fantasy to her stories by including an element from the realm of the supernatural.

Snyder was born May 11, 1927, in Lemore, California, the daughter of William Solon (a rancher and driller) and Dessa Jepson Keatley. In 1950 she married Larry Snyder, a college instructor in music. She attended Whittier College where she received her B.A., and continued her education at the University of California at Berkeley. She taught public school in California, New York, Washington, and Alaska for nine years. Then she became a master teacher and demonstrator for education classes at the University of California, Berkeley.

Zilpha Keatley Snyder decided she was a writer at the age of eight and "wrote continuously and unsuccessfully" until she graduated from college. At that time, marriage, teaching, traveling, and motherhood consumed her energies. She wrote almost nothing for about ten years. When things began to slow down, Snyder had been teaching the intermediate grades for several years and had school-aged children of her own. She paused and started to write again. This time it turned out to be for children.

She credits her teaching experience and her own children as sources of inspiration and incentive. "My own kids have also served constantly as both guinea pigs and critics and they have been very patient and conscientious in both roles."

Books and Activities

Eyes in the Fishbowl (New York: Atheneum, 1968). Illustrated by Alton Raible. (Gr. 5-9).

To Dion, Alcott-Simpson's represents an escape from a cold, ordinary world. Since the age of eight, he has been fascinated by the elegance of the store, but one day something strange begins to happen. It involves a mysterious girl named Sara who seems quite at home in Alcott-Simpson's after closing hours. Who is she and where did she come from? Who are "the others" she speaks about? The more Dion sees of the girl and learns of the unusual occurrences in the store, the more suspicious and confused he becomes. Finally, he learns the truth and power behind the mystery, but it is almost too late.

Inquiry

1. Why do you feel Dion is so frustrated with his father?

2. How do you think Dion felt when he entered Alcott-Simpson's?

3. Dion writes a song that he feels is quite good, but he chooses to put it in his drawer rather than share it. Why do you think he does this? What have you created that you are proud of? Why are you proud? Did you share it or keep it a secret? Why?

Opportunities

1. Write a story about a department store after closing hours. You might want to expand the story with illustrations and produce a picture book to share.

2. Draft a blueprint for an elegant department store such as Alcott-Simpson's. Use your blueprint to produce a bulletin board mural. Add details and special features.

3. Design a newspaper advertisement of special luxury gifts that might be featured during the Christmas season, "Gifts for the Friend who has Everything." Share your ad with a friend. Ask which gift he or she would choose. Find out why.

4. Have the students fill out applications for employment at Alcott-Simpson's. They may devise a fictitious character and information, or elaborate on themselves. Go to a local department store and ask for an application blank to use or modify.

The Headless Cupid (New York: Atheneum, 1971). Illustrated by Alton Raible. (Gr. 5-9).
When the Stanley children acquired a new mother they also gained an older sister named Amanda. What would she be like?
The Headless Cupid is the story of Amanda's rocky transition into the Stanley family. From the day she arrives in her ceremonial costume complete with a familiar spirit, Rolor the crow, David and the other Stanley children are

amazed by this practicing student of the occult. Amanda soon has fresh participants for her mystical activities. She conducts a series of tests, initiation ceremonies, and a seance with her new troop. Somehow these do not turn out as Amanda or anyone else has expected.

Everything seems quite harmless until Amanda discovers a headless cupid that proves the old Westerly Place had once been inhabited by a real poltergeist. Then a new problem arises—is Amanda playing tricks or had the poltergeist returned?—David thinks he knows the answer, but it takes the perception of little brother Blair to solve the mystery.

This was a Newbery Honor Book in 1972.

Inquiry

1. Why do you think Amanda acts so cool toward Molly?

2. What kind of initiation ceremony have you seen? Describe the ceremony as you remember it.

3. What spiritual name would you choose? Explain why.

4. What treasured possession would you offer as a "sacrifice"? What makes you value this item?

5. Sometimes activities attributed to ghosts or magic have very logical explanations. What situations can you think of where spirits have been replaced by logic?

Opportunities

1. Prepare and present a mind-reading routine to mystify your classmates. The following example from *Fun with Stunts*, by Effa Preston, is for teacher reference: Mind Reader—Tell the audience you and your assistant can give them the name of any person present that they may select. You leave the room and the audience selects a person. Your assistant is pledged not to mention the name to you but he will convey the knowledge in a mysterious fashion; you will read his mind. Choose your assistant, take him aside and tell him you will ask him three questions. The first two words in his answers must begin with the initials of the person selected. If the person chosen is named Mary Norton, the question could be, "How old is your niece?" The answer might be, "Merely nine but she acts twenty." All answers should have the first two words begin with M.N. Look over the group and see who has those initials.

2. Design your own ceremonial costume. Remember to include:

    a) a family heirloom
    b) something borrowed
    c) something very old

    d)   nothing white

Assemble your costume or share by drawing a picture and explaining.

3.   Turn an everyday activity into a ceremony. Instead of following the usual routine, schedule a special time for the ritual. Examples: Ceremony of the Completed Assignment, Ceremony of the Lunch Count.

4.   Write a recipe and directions for your own ceremonial brew? Would could the "brew" be used for?

Black and Blue Magic (New York: Atheneum, 1966). Illustrated by Gene Holtan. (Gr. 3-7).

It is the first day of vacation, and Harry is already melancholy over the prospects of a long boring summer. Yet this is to be the most magical summer of Humpty Harry's life. By some turn of fate, Harry is given the gift of soaring flight by the strange Mr. Mazzeeck. Awkward when earthbound, Harry has some interesting and slightly hazardous episodes learning to use his gift.

Not only do Harry's muscles benefit from his high flying, but his neighbors are also influenced by his angelic presence. Harry develops some basic coordination, and his boarding-house life is permanently improved.

Inquiry

1.   What is Harry's most obvious personal problem? Have you ever had this problem? How did you feel? What did you do to solve it?

2.   What would it be like to grow wings and fly? How would your wings look and feel? Where would you fly?

3.   Aside from wings, what is Harry's rare gift? Do you consider this to be a true gift? Explain.

Opportunities

1.   The Sorcerer's Suitcase:
    a)   Construct a replica of the sorcerer's suitcase and place your own magical items in it. Give a sales talk to your classmates regarding items in the case.

    b)   Design a board game called "The Sorcerer's Suitcase." Playing pieces should be named after characters in the book and represent their personalities.

    c)   Do research to find out what other storybook characters could have used items from Mr. Mazzeeck's case. Share your findings or create a quiz for your classmates.

2. Possibilities:
    It just might happen! Complete the following possibilities from *Black and Blue Magic.* Remember there can be more than one correct answer.

    1. When Harry sees the poster wink at him in the attic, it is a possibility that _____.

    2. When Harry drops the bottle of medicine on the stairs, it is a possibility that _____.

    3. When Harry returns the suitcase to Mr. Mazzeeck, it is a possibility that Mr. Mazzeeck _____.

    4. When the hot water heater breaks, it is a possibility that _____ _____.

    5. When Miss Thurgood leaves, it is a possibility that _____.

    6. When Mr. Mazzeeck gives Harry the silver bottle of volo oil, it is a possibility that the bottle _____.

    7. If Harry does not go slowly when learning to use his new wings, it is a possibility that _____.

    8. After Harry gets soaking wet in the monkey moat, it is a good possibility that _____.

    9. When Harry stops to help the small children in the rowboat, it is a possibility that _____.

    10. When Miss Clyde bats her eyelashes at Mr. Brighton, there is a possibility that _____.

    11. What is the difference between a possibility and a probability? _____ _____.

Go back through your list of possibilities and put a star in front of each answer that is also a probability.

The Egypt Game (New York: Atheneum, 1967). Illustrated by Alton Raible. (Gr. 3-7).
    April has come, very reluctantly, to live with her Grandmother Caroline at the Casa Rosada. She came because her beautiful and glamorous mother, Dorothea, sent her away. April's reluctance is soon forgotten when she is confronted with Melanie and her imagining games.
    After only one month, the most imaginative game of all comes into existence. In the back of the A-Z Curio Shop, in an abandoned storage yard, Melanie and April start the Egypt Game. Both girls have read a great deal

about Egypt, so they are chiefly responsible for designing the temple, sacred altars, and rituals. But before long there are six "ancient Egyptians" who meet everyday after school. It is fun until the oracle tells the truth once too often and a murderer appears in the neighborhood. April and the Professor, the man who owns the storage yard, have a terrifying experience as they become much too involved in both.

This was a Newbery Honor Book.

Inquiry

1.   Why are the children afraid of the Professor? Have you ever been afraid of a person? Who was it? Why were you afraid?

2.   What imagining games have you played?

3.   Describe April's actions when meeting new people at the Casa Rosada. Why does she act this way? What act have you used on others? When did you use it? Why did you feel it was necessary?

4.   Why is Melanie worried about April's first day at Wilson School?

5.   How do April and Melanie feel when Ken and Toby find out about the Egypt Game?

Opportunities

1.   Construct altars for Nefertiti and Set. Find appropriate items for each, or, plan two bulletin boards. Dedicate one to Nefertiti, the goddess of goodness, love, and beauty. The other should be decorated in honor of Set, the Evil One. (Halloween is a good time for this activity.)

2.   Create a hieroglyphic code of your own. Look up recipes for invisible ink. Send secret messages in your code using invisible ink.

3.   Design a hieroglyph or sign to serve as your trademark. Make several sheets of personalized stationery to use.

The Velvet Room (New York: Atheneum, 1965). Illustrated by Alton Raible. (Gr. 3-7).

Robin is always "wandering off," looking for a private refuge from the confusion she feels inside. It is not until Robin's father finds a permanent job at the McCurdy Ranch, after three years of migrant work, that Robin has a place to wander to. She is attracted to Bridget's neat little cottage with its kindly owner and unique assortment of pets; and finds Palmeras House, a deserted mansion, fascinating. The key to unlock this intriguing house comes from Bridget.

As Robin explores the old mansion, she finds her haven. In the Velvet Room, the still furnished library of the deserted house, Robin spends many happy, secure hours wrapped in her thoughts and treasure of books.

When Robin has to choose between the Velvet room and leaving the McCurdy Ranch with her family, the decision is very difficult. Bridget and a bunch of thieves enter the picture to influence her choice.

Inquiry

1. What is life like for a migrant worker? What would you like about this lifestyle? What would you dislike?

2. What attracts Robin to Bridget's cottage?

3. If you had your own Velvet Room, what would it be like? How would it look? Feel? Smell? Where would it be located?

4. What causes people to think deserted houses are haunted?

5. What experiences are Gwen and Robin able to share?

Opportunities

1. Draw a representation of your Velvet room. Furnish it with items that make you feel relaxed and secure.

2. Arrange for the students to visit a local farm as volunteer migrant workers. Students might weed a garden, pick beans, etc. Set up a punch card system to record individual work records.

3. Collect information about other "haunted" buildings. Share your building's legendary ghost. Example: Old Courthouse (St. Louis) — the ghost of Dred Scott.

The Witches of Worm (New York: Atheneum, 1972). Illustrated by Alton Raible. (Gr. 4-7).

Loneliness can be a very painful, destructive force. Once again Joy, Jessica's mother, goes out for the evening leaving Jessica to her own devices. Unable to conceal her disappointment, Jessica runs to the hillside cave where she and Brandon have spent many fun-filled days. But Brandon no longer comes to the cave, so she is left alone with her book on witchcraft and her thoughts. As isolated as Jessica feels, she is not alone on this occasion. Toward the back of the cave she hears a scratching noise and a tiny worm-like animal appears. It is a scrawny, newborn kitten. Jessica does not want the disgusting eyeless creature, yet something compels her to take it home to Mrs. Fortune.

Mrs. Fortune advises that the kitten is too young and needs its mother, but there is no mother cat to be found. So Jessica becomes the reluctant owner of the ugly kitten, Worm.

As the kitten grows, Jessica can see it is an unusual animal. It doesn't look or act like an ordinary cat. Then one day, when only the cat and its owner are present, Worm begins to talk. Worm's messages cause Jessica to tell many lies. Jessica covers for these by feigning amnesia.

Finally, when Mrs. Fortune catches her in a lie about Brandon's trumpet, Jessica is forced to act. She decides to exorcise the demon from Worm to stop the problems. During the events that follow the exorcism, Jessica finds out the truth about the witch's cat.

Inquiry

1. Why is it necessary for Jessica to spend so much time by herself? What does Jessica do with her free time? What do you do when left by yourself? How do you feel?

2. Do you think Worm really speaks to Jessica? Explain your answer.

3. What reasons might Jessica have for lying to Mrs. Darby? Mrs. Post? Her mother?

4. How does Jessica react to the school counselor? How would you react to a visit with the counselor? What do you think the counselor's job involves?

Opportunities

1. Visit the junior high school to interview one of the counselors. Be sure to call for an appointment in advance. Find out exactly what his job involves.

2. Have the students write five lines to finish these phrases:

   Loneliness is....

   I felt lonely when....

3. Have the students develop a booklet on pet care for the animal of their choice. Include information on feeding, grooming, stages of development, and habits.

4. To find out about a more traditional witch, read *The Witch of Blackbird Pond* (Boston: Houghton Mifflin, 1958), by Elizabeth Speare.

The Truth about Stone Hollow (New York: Atheneum, 1974). Illustrated by Alton Raible. (Gr. 4-6).

Amy has always had a curiosity about the world around her, so it is only natural for her to wonder about Stone Hollow. The children of Taylor Springs say it is haunted and no one dares go there. Even the school bully is afraid, and Amy is too scared to go alone. Then, Jason Fitzmaurice appears at school. He is an odd-looking boy with peculiar ideas and behavior. When Gordie Parks beats him up, he refuses to defend himself. Yet he has already been to the haunted Stone Hollow where Amy longs to go, and is willing to go again.

Jason and Amy form a secret friendship that leads to the Hollow. Here they find traces left by the Indians and moonshiners. There is also a very special place where Jason can see visions of the past right before his eyes. Jason tells Amy many stories, but none seem to be true. She has many doubts and questions about his so-called sightings at first, but then something happens to make her wonder.

Inquiry

1. What does Amy do to adjust to the Taylor Springs School? What have you done to fit into a certain group?

2. What frightens you? Why?

3. The adults around Amy leave many of her questions unanswered. Why do you think they do this? When do adults seem to avoid your questions? Why do they refuse to answer?

Opportunities

1. From the book, *The Truth about Stone Hollow*, we find that each of us perceives something as being true according to his or her own experience. "View" objects without the aid of eyesight. Write down your description. Compare your notes to another description of the same item. Discuss why the notes are different.

2. The Stone brings images of past events to Jason's eyes. Find an object at home that conjures up a vision of the past. Write a descriptive paragraph or poem about your visions. Then find someone who will share the "facts" about your object. Compare the two ideas.

3. Share the picture book, *The Blind Men and the Elephant* (New York: Scribner's, 1959), by Lillian Quigley. Discuss the truth each man shares.

General Opportunities

1. Have your class videotape a scene from one of these books to share with others. Your tape might be used as part of a book review. Suggested scenes:

From *The Headless Cupid*—the Stanley children at the dinner table during the hands-off metal initiation test

From *The Egypt Game*—the ceremony of the Oracle

From *The Velvet Room*—Robin preventing the thieves from burning the deserted mansion

From *Black and Blue Magic*—Harry's first reaction to his wings or Mr. Mazzeeck bestowing his gift

2.   Develop character blocks or silhouettes. Cut descriptive words from magazines to describe your character. Glue these to your block or silhouette until it is completely covered. Polymer over the finished product. Read the descriptive words from your block. See if others can pinpoint your character. (Do you think this activity will prompt the remark, "Who's the new character on the block?")

3.   Design an emotion chart like the one on page 165 for your book. Have the children chart 5 to 10 emotional experiences that occur in the story. They must decide how strong the feeling is and rate it on the scale. (Ten is most emotional.) Beneath the chart a short paragraph is written to correspond to the numbered emotion on the chart. This paragraph tells what the emotion is, when the character feels it, and why.

10 _____

9 _____

8 _____

7 _____

6 _____

5 _____

4 _____

3 _____

2 _____

1 _____

          1   2   3   4

The Witches of Worm

1. Jessica is disappointed when Joy goes out on a date and leaves her alone. She does not feel worse because this has happened so many times before.

2. Jessica is annoyed with nosey old Mrs. Post and wants to get even. When Mrs. Post stops by to check on Jessica, Jessica lies about seeing a man sneaking into the building.

3. . . . .

4. . . . .

10   AFTER THE PROCESS: THE PRODUCT

If literature can stimulate young minds, expand imaginations, and serve as a catalyst for imaginative thought and creativity, why then have not more literature programs been successful in nurturing selective and eager readers and creative writers among our students? The answer lies, perhaps, in the misuse of literature rather than in its use. Certainly students will be exposed to the minds of many great writers in any literature program. When the elements of literature are examined either through teacher explanation or through the discovery approach (as recommended in this text), students should gain greater understanding and thereby a deeper appreciation of the writer's art. But do they? Sadly, the answer is all to often no.

Before children can read, they must acquire skills in comprehension and decoding. But before a child truly becomes a reader in the fullest, most meaningful sense of the term, she or he must discover with the help of other enthusiastic readers the joy to be found in the reading experience; and from those who know the joy of creating the written word the child must learn the true sense of satisfaction that comes from expressing original thought. The study of literature and the use of patterning (for example) as a writing technique are only tools. Basic techniques in reading and writing may provide the child with necessary tools for expression but they cannot release those pent up forces within each child which we label creativity and imagination. Only a caring, knowledgeable, risk-taking teacher, who is not afraid to express the emotions engendered by a truly powerful piece of literature, can demonstrate that which literature is really all about. Creativity already exists in the gifted child. The role of the teacher is to create an environment to help the child find creative outlets in reading and writing.

Simply put, the teacher of the gifted must be a giver in every respect. Knowledge, technique, and experience are not enough. The teacher of the gifted must be able to tune in on another's wavelength, to give not only out of knowledge but out of the fullness of the heart, to be human above all and to delight in the discoveries of a young mind unhampered by outdated rules, moving in new directions, establishing new relationships.

On a snowy evening in March, 1979, author, Gertrude Bell, watched with great amazement and pride as a group of gifted seventh grade students performed their original staged adaptation of her novel, *First Crop* (Independence, MO: Independence Press, 1973), before a packed house at Lindenwood College. The performance was far more than a technical triumph of scenery, lights and action. It was a genuine expression of love from students whose hearts had been touched by the words of this writer and who, through the help and direction of a giving teacher, found the outlet for creative expression of this literary experience in drama. A case history of the production follows.

Dramatization:
A Case History

No greater challenge can be given to gifted students than that of adapting a junior novel for production as a play. The technical expertise required to bring a novel to life on the stage is considerable. This frustrating, difficult, and extremely rewarding task was undertaken by a group of very talented junior high students under the direction of teacher, Beverly Hopkins, who tells of the problems and the joys involved in such an undertaking:

"The ten seventh grade students who worked on the drama production were selected for our gifted/talented program (Probe) during January. This was after a rather lengthy evaluation process that took place during the first semester. The ten students were selected from among forty-three recommendations.

"After the students were chosen, I decided that I wanted them to be involved in some type of group project in order to build acquaintance and enhance their sense of identity as a group. It was after I had searched my files for materials on group dynamics and group simulation activities, that I received the call asking if some of my Probe students would make a fifteen-twenty minute presentation for Ms. Bell and the library supervisors at Lindenwood College.

"I was initially hesitant, but since the simulation activity I had selected really seemed to be lacking in long-range group cohesiveness strength, I decided such a presentation might be just what was needed for my new seventh graders. In retrospect, I realize I could not have made a wiser decision.

"As with any successful project, cooperation from other faculty members is tremendously important. Our librarian, Mrs. Frances Hall, collected Ms. Bell's books from various district libraries and saw that each of my students had one checked out to read. Almost all of the students read *First Crop*; one had read five of Ms. Bell's books. Then the real work began.

"We met for one-half hour as a group; I presented seven or eight alternatives for projects that could be used in a group presentation. Should I admit that secretly I hoped they might not choose drama since drama was not one of my strong areas? They voted and unanimously chose to do an original dramatization. The bell rang, and I immediately rushed to find Mrs. Karon Noll, our Creative Writing and Drama teacher. Fortunately, Karon was unruffled about the idea and most cooperative throughout the entire 'ordeal.'

"Our group met again so that I could explain exactly what had to be done. Subsequently, original scripts of *First Crop* began to appear in my office. Some were too short; some were not what I felt the students were capable of writing; three were excellent. In fact, of the three best, I could not choose one above the other two. That's how three scripts came to be combined. Parts of each were cut and taped on sheets of 8½" by 14" paper. Naturally one student had written on both sides of her paper, so that presented a copy problem. However, our A-V technician endured, and after he had carefully followed the arrows and 'underneath' notes, we had one dozen semi-readable copies. I did not want the scripts typed, feeling the students could learn a valuable lesson from seeing their actual work reproduced for others to use regardless of its appearance. There were moments when I became convinced that this was a mistake, and I'm still not sure whether or not any valuable lesson was learned.

"We met again after I had re-read and made notes on the students' drama preferences from a Renzulli Interest-A-Lyzer. This I felt would be helpful if any student should be reluctant to select a specific task for the production. Actors, actresses, props and scenery personnel then volunteered or were selected.

"Six rehearsals, including one Saturday morning, followed the memorizing of lines and gathering of props. One main character suffered a bout of pneumonia and there were numerous conflicts with rehearsals, but somehow we survived the traumas. One scene rehearsal was videotaped.

"As the cast rehearsed, [the] props people drew and painted scenery. Our student director completed the program details, listing the cast of characters, props, and scenery personnel, and a brief summary of each scene. The narrator designed the program's cover. One of my ninth grade Probe members volunteered to serve as an assistant during the rehearsals and served as our photographer for the final production. The students decided on sound effects, and once again our A-V technician was an invaluable source of help — all we lacked was the goat.

"Upon reaching Young Auditorium after dinner at McDonald's, we breathed a sigh of relief when we discovered that our scenery fit, even though the log cabin interior had to go over a permanently mounted chalkboard, and the blacksmith's interior had to drape around a corner. The tape held, and Avon helped produce a realistic Bennie. Bennie's rabbits were courtesy of two other cooperative faculty members.

"Since our final rehearsal had lasted thirty minutes, I was amazed when the final production was completed in its allotted fifteen minutes and perhaps even more amazed by the positive reaction from the audience. Was it really that good? When Ms. Farley suggested that we take our show on the road, I suggested she take it! Perhaps, Mrs. Polette, it can be taken in your book. That way we can forget such realities as pneumonia, Avon, the unpainted tree stumps, and a room full of potatoes, rocks, a hoe, wheelbarrow, bellows, and two cardboard goats.

"The intrinsic reward for their accomplishments was so obvious after the play was over that I could not help but feel a warm glow inside. I was pleased, too, to glance at each student and see the intense interest with which each greeted Ms. Bell's speech. It was touching to see the old and the young meet on a common ground of understanding that resulted from the writing efforts of one and the interpreting efforts of the other.

"As I've said many times before, working with the gifted is a very frustrating and rewarding experience. I'm grateful for both in this case, for above all, these ten students have been given a moment that will last a lifetime in their memories."

FIRST CROP
By Gertrude Bell

Adapted for the stage by the Enrichment Language Arts Class, Florissant Junior High School. Adaptation done with permission of Independence Press, publishers of *First Crop*, by Gertrude Bell.

Narrator: The time is 1861. The place is Jackson County, Missouri. Ambrose Patton is a young boy who wants to search out his grandpa in the Nebraska Territory. His grandpa is a soldier in the Civil War, but standing between Brose and his grandpa are a few major problems like Liza Morton (and her baby) whose house was burnt down by the fighting soldiers, just like

Brose's house. How will Liza find shelter, warmth, food, and take care of her baby all by herself? Then there's Bennie, a boy who can hardly do anything but set snares for rabbits.

Sometimes Bennie's best intended actions do not work out the way he plans. Finally, there's the Johnny Reb Ambrose finds in Liza Morton's burning house. But once the Johnny Reb is well and back on his feet again, he's a big help. Ambrose and the friends he gathers are trying to hide from the fighting troops.

All of this would not have happened if Order Number 11 had not been issued, but Order 11 forced all remaining inhabitants to leave their homes.

SCENE 1

Brose: You know I'm going to the Nebraska Territory, don't you Bennie; a long, long ways? Maybe it'll be frosty when I get there, and these are all the clothes we have, and no shoes. Maybe I won't have enough to eat, and ---

Bennie: I can snare lotsa rabbits an' there's apples to take. If the judge ain't comin' back, he won't keer.

Brose: I'll have to work along the way if I can find someone to hire me, so I can buy cornmeal and salt and pork.

Bennie: I'll work good. I'll work awful good.

Brose: We'll manage. We can't travel until the mule's better, but we've got to have meat. You reckon you could set a snare or two before sunset?

Bennie: Sho! Sho! (Bennie jumped up numbly, grinning, then he sobered) You won't go 'way 'thout me, Brose?

Brose: I promise. I'm going for more potatoes, and then I'll get ready to build a fire when it's too dark for the smoke to show. (Bennie trots off happily)

Brose: I don't think you'd better go into the woods very far, Bennie.

Bennie:	I ain' goin' a-tall; that's where foxes drug the judge's hens. Feathers evah place; I ain't gonna temp' no foxes. I knows a fence row over to'ards Hamp Morton's. (Bennie runs off)
Brose:	(Starts digging up yams) I'd give anything for some salt. (Gets leaves for fire)
Bennie:	(Bennie puffs in) Ghosses! in Hamp Morton's cabin! Heard 'em plain, mostly a baby cryin'. Brose, I ain' gonna set no snares where ghosses is at!
Brose:	You don't have to. Sit down and puff while I see if I can start a fire. We can manage on yams and apples tonight. (Bennie sits down) Hamp's house wasn't burned down?
Bennie:	Uh-uh, no smoke from the chimbley, so that's how I know it's ghosses, Miss Morton would have sidemeat fryin' an' pone bakin'. (Brose starts fire) What you cookin' us Brose?
Brose:	Potatoes and parched corn.
Bennie:	Wish I'd got usa rabbit.
Brose:	You will tomorrow. You reckon the corn's going to dry out enough so we can make cornmeal out of it?
Bennie:	Reckon the mill's burned up, too. (dolefully) Nothin's left, 'cept you and me and the ghosses.
Brose:	Tastes awful without salt! (Throws rest of potato down) I'm going to see about Hamp Morton's cabin. (Trudges off)

SCENE II

Baby:	(Crying)
Brose:	(Knocks on door) It's Brose Patton, Missus Morton.
Liza:	I've---I've got a gun aimed right at that door! (Shrill and shaky)

Brose:	Honest, it's Brose ma'am, come to see if you need anything.
Liza:	Come in. (Backs off) How'd you know I was here?
Brose:	Bennie heard the baby crying. He came over here to set snares. Didn't the soldiers come here?
Liza:	(Nods) Yesterday. They---they said that I had to leave. They didn't believe me when I told them Hamp was in the Union Army. Said it didn't matter anyway, I had to go (chokes back a cry) (baby wails) They said they'd give me 48 hours to get out of there or they'd b---burn the house.
Brose:	Can't you go to your folks?
Liza:	Mama died; papa went back to Ohio, that's where we come from.
Brose:	Where's Hamp?
Liza:	Up around St. Joe the last letter I had.
Brose:	What's the matter with the baby?
Liza:	She's hungry. (Angrily) I can't feed her and the cow, they stole the cow. They didn't need to do that. I told them Hamp was in their army. Enlisted first thing, he did, and I wanted him to, but---
Brose:	Didn't they offer to help you get away?
Liza:	No, just said I had to be gone tomorrow, that they'd come back to burn the house.
Brose:	Then you'd better be gone when they come back.
Liza:	Where?
Brose:	You'll have to hide. Take whatever you can take easy, like quilts and cover---lids and a cooking pot, and whatever food there is. I'll help you move into a hiding place and we'll take whatever you can save. You got cornmeal?

Liza: A smidgen, there was plenty of sidemeat, but they took that. I ain't been eatin' much.

Brose: Make the meal into corn cakes. I'll start you a fire. Gather up everything there is to eat. Bedding---stuff for the baby---

Liza: I've got money.

Brose: That's good. Hamp have a cart maybe?

Liza: There's a wheelbarrow out by the woodpile Hamp thought---(baby cries)

Brose: I'll get it. (Brose runs off)

Liza: (Brose runs in) Is there anything you want Brose? Better than having it burned up tomorrow!

Brose: Food and a way to keep warm, can't take much though! Let's hurry. (They pack the stuff in the wheelbarrow; Brose directs Liza to the hiding place in the woods and coils up a rope)

Liza: Where you goin'?

Brose: I'm going to steal a goat for the baby.

                          SCENE III

            (Brose enters)

Gustus: Whose there?! Stop or I'll shoot!

Brose: Gustus?

Gustus: Who's there?

Brose: I'm Brose Patton. I've come to steal a goat.

Gustus: (Steps out with gun) An honest thief, eh?

Brose: It's Liza Morton, she needs a goat to feed her baby.

Gustus: With Hamp in their own army! Her house--did they burn it?

Brose: They gave her until tomorrow. Why didn't they burn you out?

Gustus: Too good a place to waste I guess, how 'bout your place?

Brose: They burned the house and the barn, rode their horses through my corn, shot my mule, and killed my two calves. Soon Bennie and Liza will be taken care of and I can go to the Nebraska Territory to find Grandpa. Why did you come back?

Gustus: For the gun, had it hidden in the barn. This is bad. Men were murdered yesterday for nothing but hate!

Brose: (Shrilly) But we didn't do anything! We didn't fight anybody. The goat--I can't pay you back now--but----

Gustus: Take all you want. I was going to turn them loose for wild animals. (Gustus leaves)

Brose: Now where's the goat pen?
                  (Brose leaves)

SCENE IV

Brose: Gustus gave me the goat. He said he hoped the baby would be alright. You know how to milk a goat?

Liza: Of course. Here hold her. (Liza hands Brose the baby and begins to milk the goat) Let me have her Brose.

Brose: (Handing baby to Liza) How you gonna get her to drink?
                  (Liza dips a bit of rag in the milk and sticks it into the baby's mouth)
                  (Brose ties the goat to a tree)

Liza: (Walks over to the fire) Thank you, Brose, I think she would have died very soon. So little--only six weeks old.

Brose: What's her name?

Liza: Martha, for Hamp's mother. We decided that before she was born. Did you say you saw Gustus?

Brose: Yep. He said he didn't think very many people would be heading for Westport, but you never know.

Liza: When Hamp comes back and the war's over, if she ever has a little brother, I'll name him Ambrose.

Brose: Liza, I think I'll go over to your place and see what's happnin'.

SCENE V

(Brose is running back to camp in the woods)

Brose: (In a hushed voice) There's a wounded man in your house. Musta got trapped in when the army came.

Liza: Can you bring him here? We should try to help him.

                (Brose runs off and comes back a little later dragging the wounded man)

Brose: He's heavy! Maybe he's not hurt too bad.

Liza: Help me, and I'll try to treat him.

Brose: O.K. I'll try to make him understand he's got to help us if he can.

Johnny Reb: (Mumbles) Becky

Liza: Listen! You'll have to help us get you up. We can't do anything for you here, but----

Johnny Reb: (Softly) Try...

Narrator: The Johnny Reb was in a bad way. Careful as they'd tried to be, his wound was bleeding again. They'd have a bad enough time explaining a wounded Johnny Reb if any bushwackers caught them. They couldn't possibly explain a dead one. This added to Brose's troubles.

Bennie: Brose, that's a Secesh soldier! What did you bring him here for?

Brose: I don't know.

Liza: (Heating water) I've got a clean rag that will do for bandages. Brose, don't you know *anything* about doctoring?

Brose: I know if the bullet is still inside him, he's in trouble.

Liza: It isn't. There's a hole clear through his shoulder.

Bennie: I'm leavin'. Ain't gonna stay heah with no Confedrut soljer. Phelie tole me 'bout them. I'm going ta Wes-Port and look for somebody agreeable.

Liza: Will he get lost?

Brose: Not unless he wants ta. I'll doctor the soljer while you feed Martha.

Liza: Martha went to sleep soon as she was fed. Turn him just a mite so's I can clean that other hole. I saved him some milk, but one goat gives *so* little milk, wish we had two.

Brose: I reckon I could find another goat. I turned them loose like Gustus aimed to do.

Liza: I'll go help find one.

Brose: You stay off that foot; I can manage by myself.

Liza: I wish that Bennie would come back. If somebody caught him, he'd blab everything he knows, Brose!

Brose: Yep. But what would anybody be doing back at the judge's place?

Liza: I wish we could get this Johnny in the dry.

Brose:	(A little grumpy) Well, we can't.
Liza:	Brose, I'm sorry. (She looks up at Brose) You'd be gone by now if it wasn't for us, wouldn't you?
Brose:	I doubt it. Well, I guess I'll get started.
Liza:	Be careful. (Brose goes away) (Liza continues to doctor the Johnny)
Brose:	I found them. They weren't far off.
Liza:	Good. Now we'll have plenty of milk. The Johnny came to enough to drink some. I could cook potatoes to a mush with the rabbit, don't guess that would hurt him none. Who do you think he is?
Brose:	I don't know.
Liza:	Roll up in your blanket and hold Martha while I go get some milk for this Johnny to drink. (Brose takes the baby)
Brose:	Where's Bennie?
Liza:	I sent him out to set some snares. When he comes back, I intend to send him out for apples.
Brose:	(Laughs) That'll keep him busy.
Bennie:	Ain't I done good! (Two rabbits are in his hand)
Brose:	That's fine, Bennie.
Bennie:	How come they run us out? How come we gotta hide? Who done this to the judge an' me?
Brose:	I don't know.
Johnny:	That war. Every coyote, including me and Liza's husband, that couldn't think of any way but shooting to settle our

| Narrator: | differences. You go ahead and sleep, sonny. Won't anybody stumble onto us, honest. |
| | (Everyone goes to sleep) |

| Brose: | Mornin', Johnny. |

| Johnny: | Mornin'. You got any good ideas? Someday this war is goin' ta 'in. You got any plans? |

| Brose: | No. |
| | (Bennie and Liza wake up) |

| Bennie: | C'n you make fried peach pies like Phelie's? |

| Johnny: | Don't help to think about what you can't have, Bennie. |

| Liza: | My foot's just fine this morning. |

| Johnny: | Uh-huh. Till you walked half a mile on it totin' a load. |

| Liza: | You need lot's of good red meat, bread and fat. The blood you lost, it's a wonder to me you aren't dead! |

| Brose: | I reckon I'll be headin' for the Nebraska Territory today. |

| Bennie: | I'm a-goin' with Brose to the Nebraska Territory. |

| Liza: | (Sharply) You'll do nothing of the kind. I'm gonna be needin' you bad. |
| | (Liza, Bennie, and the Johnny Reb get up, too. The whole group walks over to where they eat while Liza fetches some food from the "kitchen") |

| Narrator: | Ambrose was finally thinking of heading his own way to find his grandpa in the Nebraska Territory. |

| Liza: | First thing I'll do when I get settled is ask around 'bout your grandma and let her know where you are. I'll bet she's worried sick. |

| Johnny: | Liza, I know you've got enough sense not to tell anyone about me. Anyway you'll find enough help in town until you find |

your husband, Hamp. And Bennie, if I ever hear you mentioning anything about you knowing a Johnny Reb, you'll see more ghosses than you ever thought there were (shaking his forefinger). Do you understand?

Bennie: My mouth is shut. (Pretending to zip his mouth)

Johnny: (Pats Bennie on the back) That's good.

Bennie: Johnny, you bin so nice to me lately, I went and forgot you were a Confedrut. I'm gonna stay awful still till grandma fetches me.

Johnny: Well, you just make sure of that. If anything ever scares you and Miss Liza, you just holler "ghosses" as loud as you can and anything in it's right mind would be scared away. (Reaches for the blankets) Here, Liza, you and Bennie are gonna be needin' these quilts. It's gonna get mighty cold traveling to West Port.

Liza: No, I would be so ashamed to be seen with those tattered up quilts. Besides, you and Ambrose are gonna be needin' em more than Bennie and me. You two are going to be the ones sleeping outside. Go ahead, divide them between ya.

Johnny: Get along now! Whoever you meet, tell them you've got a Fed soldier husband.

Brose: I'll be leavin' now. Good luck everyone.

Liza: Good-bye, Ambrose. I can't tell you how grateful I am to you. Thank you so much!

Bennie: (Walks over to get snares) Brose, you can have my snares.

Brose: Thank you, Bennie. But you can keep them.

Liza: Well, it's time we left. Good-bye everyone.

Bennie: Bye, Ambrose. Bye, Johnny.

Brose: Bye. (Waves)

Johnny: Bye. Take care. (Turning to speak to Ambrose) Get a move on, Brose. You better take all the corn and spuds you can pack into a couple of quilts.

Brose: What about you?

Johnny: Never mind about me. You've done great, Brose. You took care of four people who really needed you. Did it real cheerful, too. Me and Liza knew how much you wanted to take off.

Brose: Ya think I should have gone part way with Liza and Bennie, just to make sure they start off right?

Johnny: Nope, she'll appear more helpless without ya. There must be someone to help her 'round town. Now get a movin'.

(Ambrose carries hoe to garden to dig yams and potatoes; meanwhile, the Johnny Reb picks up a nearby stone, reaches in his pocket for knife and starts to carve something in the rock. Then he leaves. Ambrose returns shortly.)

(Ambrose walks onto stage)

Brose: Johnny, Johnny! (He looks around and then picks up the rock and begins to read aloud) They ruined your corn crop, sonny, but don't ever forget the crop of friends you made. Thanks, the Johnny Reb.

(Brose smiles and then walks off stage)

11 THE GIFT OF FAIRY TALES, FOLKTALES, AND FANTASY

> Deeper meaning resides in the fairy tales told to me
> in my childhood than in the truth that is taught
> by life.
> — Schiller

Three energetic nymphs oozed through the mud at the bottom of a pond. They explored bubbles, bumped into pebbles, and slid over slippery hummocks. One of the nymphs became aware of a faint light overhead. She was intrigued. What was it? Where did it come from? Keeping her eye on the diffusing light above her, she started inching up a waving stem. Suddenly the stem ended. A flat water lily leaf blocked her way. She edged along its underside until her nose emerged into a breathless new environment. She crawled out on top of the leaf, stunned by the brilliance surrounding her. The warmth caressing her skin stimulated her. She blinked, and perceived a greenery surrounding her which was totally unlike the slime at the bottom of the pond. She looked up at white puffs drifting across the source of light in the new blue above her. As she sat in wonder, her body dried in the warm touch of breeze fingers. Other inhabitants of this world soared and swooped with shimmering wings in the brightness. New colors and fragrances beckoned to her from the pond edge. She felt a brittle "crack" on her backside and slipped out of her shell. Soft, damp wings of her own emerged and unfolded into the warmth. She waved them experimentally as they solidified ... and found herself skyborne. As she joined others sky-sweeping and exploring, she looked down at the little pond. She could barely see the other nymphs at the bottom. She knew that she could never go back to what she was. She hoped they would someday join her in this new world of beauty and freedom.

Try reading aloud this slight fantasy to a group of gifted children, or to a group of teachers of gifted children. Ask them to identify the theme of the selection. Even very bright students will often have difficulty in correctly interpreting an author's theme. Yet is is that which goes beyond the literal meaning of a work which separates truly great literature from books that are forgotten as soon as the last page is read. Every fine author has something important to say and it is an essential role of every teacher of gifted children to create the kind of trusting environment which will allow the children to be divergent in their responses and to discover the author's message.

Fairy tales can create a startling new environment for the mind. Once a child has ventured beyond earthly restrictions, he or she can never crawl back into old mental modes of thought. All nymphs may become dragonflies, but not all inquiring minds are given the freedom to discover that which lies beneath the literature of the folklorist or writer of fantasy—the literature which can change and shape values. Yet this is the subtle power which all great literature can provide. It throws a new light on the outer world through the upheavals it generates in the inner world. One cannot understand light if one has only known darkness. George MacDonald examines this intriguingly in his thought-provoking faily tale, "The Day Boy and the Night Girl." He says that he writes "for the tale," but deeper meanings pervade all of his works.

A mother flew into a school library with her young redhead in tow. "Who gave my son this fairy tale?" she asked, accusation on her tongue and fire in her eye. When the librarian confessed her guilt, the mother started a perfect tirade concluding with "I want my child to read nothing that contradicts the teaching I am giving him at home!" When she blanched at the suggestion of a good biography, for fear an uncensored idea might slip in, the cause appeared hopeless. The librarian asked what kind of book the mother would like to have offered to her child. "A book on mechanics," she said, "Perhaps how to build something."

How tragic that this mother was not aware of the building of character which good fantasy, mythology, folk tales, and legends can and do promote! For humanness does not just happen. It requires nourishment. Will the supreme beauties of life be revealed in a how-to-do-it manual? Pure intellectual knowledge leaves out the essential ingredients for genuine growth.

Albert Einstein, whose humanity matched his intellectual genius states (in *Albert Einstein, the Human Side*):

> Humanity has every reason to place the proclaimers of high moral standards and values above the discoverer of objective truth. What humanity owes to personalities like Buddha, Moses, and Jesus ranks for me higher than all the achievements of the enquiring and constructive mind.

Such insights turn us to the kind of literature that promotes spiritual awakenings. All fairy tales and fables have metaphysical and theological undertones.

Let us not be afraid of affording our children who are gifted with supple and energetic minds the opportunity to use them. Character development does not appear to be high on the priority list in modern American schools. But our world has such a desperate need for men and women of character, who esteem others, who promote excellence in values and morality. Fairy tales and folk tales help children to find themselves—their best selves.

Bruno Bettelheim, in his convincing case for the importance of fairy tales, *The Uses of Enchantment*, tells of a mother who overcame her uneasiness about fairy tales and told her small son "Jack the Giant Killer." At the end of the story the child asked, "But there aren't any such things as giants, are there?" His mother had a reassurance for him on the tip of her tongue, as he continued, "but there are such things as grownups, and they're like giants!" A five-year-old recognized the foe, and also that he would grow up someday to acquire the same powers.

Children need to develop the inner resources to cope with the complex world around them. They must feel a reason for being; they must be assured that they will contribute to life, that they will overcome the giants of fear and uncertainty, and that they will ultimately triumph. Our intellectually talented children must not be relegated to a corner for "misfits." Their clarity of thought can help us all to see through the obstacles and barriers that keep good from being manifested in the contemporary world.

Fairy tales are spiritual explorations. How much of contemporary mass media can make that claim? Astute minds are inseparable from pulsating hearts, and both must join in this exciting search for answers to the meaning of life, which will ultimately liberate humankind.

The great master of literature, Leo Tolstoy, wrote: "To teach and educate a child is impossible and senseless on the simple ground that the child stands nearer than I do, nearer than any adult does, to that ideal of harmony, truth, beauty and goodness to which, in my pride, I wish to lead him." And yet Tolstoy continued to write for children, leaving over 600 folk and fairy tales for their enlightenment. He has been accused of didactic moralizing, yet with humor and honesty, his profoundly simple tales continue to speak to us of the most basic questions. It is not the pedagogue nor the preachers who will help our astute children to cope with this world; it is the artist. The artistic genius of Tolstoy continues to address us, through tales that may indeed occasionally present a moral, but more profoundly through his gem-like folk-master-pieces, which, in truth, *are* morals.

Tolstoy himself, as a child, fell asleep to the fairy tales of an old man who had been purchased for the family because of his knowledge of fairy tales and his masterful telling of them. The happiest moments of Tolstoy's childhood were with his elder brother Nicholas, who could spontaneously and continuously spin out tales and create imaginative play which left an indelible impression on the young Leo. Long after Tolstoy had created his classics, *War and Peace* and *Anna Karenina*, he stated that the folk and fairy tales he was writing in his 80s were his most important works. In these simple tales were the same basic questions that threaded their way through the complexities of his great novels.

The questions he addressed are the ones that make all great fairy tales deathless and ageless; for behind the humorous or magical, the savage or tender, there lurks the struggle between evil and good. The choice is to be made within each reader. Behind the rollicking, the mystical and the implausible lie fresh answers to the age-old questions "Who am I?," "Where am I?," "Why am I?," and "What am I?."

Gifted young thinkers will not use a fairy tale as a drowsy voyage into never-never land, but will feel an awakening, and leap to challenge the suggested answers that come not from the tale, but from one's own deep and intuitive wells of thought.

How clearly Leo Tolstoy saw the beauty of a truth that preoccupied his latter days. He shared it in his brief fable, "The Three Questions." Are we not all faced daily by these same issues?

When is the most important time to undertake anything?

Who are the most important people in our lives?

What is the most important pursuit?

Tolstoy's answers shine lucidly from the tale. The most important time is *now*, the most important person is the one with whom you are, and the most important pursuit is to do good to that person. One young reader, after hearing this tale, wrote to the teller, "This moral lesson has become a part of me, and I think of it often. Thank you for sharing this gift of meaning to my life."

This same young reader was affected by the friendships she encountered in *Tom's Midnight Garden*, by Phillipa Pearce, and *A Wrinkle in Time*, by Madeleine L'Engle, brilliant modern fantasies. This gifted reader and thinker wrote to her teacher, "The effect these books had upon me is very precious. Both books actually changed my feelings about myself and the world. While reading them I felt quite lifted out of this world, from the limits of time and space. I felt something higher and more relevant to life, and yet I did not have a contempt for the little things and concerns which occupy us most of the time. These books took me to wider spheres ... to contemplate something beyond the mere concrete and material world. Having had this glimpse of something higher has changed my perception of this world a little bit. This sort of change feels essential."

All through the ages, inspired poets and philosophers and tellers of tales have caught glorious glimpses of a higher sense of reality, of a divine energy, of life aflame with love. They have communicated these momentary glimpses through their lives, and through their writings. Gifted children will relate to them, when exposed to the heritage they have left in print. From the earliest tales, such as *Gilgamesh* — believed to be the first story ever written, told long before the invention of writing — to *In the Suicide Mountains*, a modern fairy tale by John Gardner, the theme of friendship has been recurrent. We need one another.

What else does literature that has come to us from the beginnings of recorded time have to say to young modern intellectuals? Children listen to the undercurrents behind the minutia of daily humdrum and relate them to their reading. Unseen forces appear to have a magic influence on our lives. Gifted children are able to make that mental leap that ties everything together. They catch the subtle inferences and symbolic innuendos beneath tales and link them to eternal challenges. The soul-powers within astute children are ready to be activated, eager to grow.

The intellectually quick need to wrestle with good and evil as well as with calculus, to contemplate the humanity and inhumanity of man as well as historical facts, to plunge into the deeper meaning of life and death instead of memorizing batting averages. The world needs gifted thinkers to raise the values which appear to govern society.

Fairy and folk tales do relate specifically to the conditions of contemporary society. Consider the Watergate scandal in relation to Hans Christian Anderson's immortal "The Emperor's New Clothes." Ask your bright children if they recognize the regime of a Hitler or an Idi Amin in *Watership Down*. And surely H. C. Anderson's *The Nightingale* is a powerful comment on what technology could be doing to our values as it outraces conservation of nature.

Academically advanced children may well have a say in the direction life takes in the twenty-first century. Do we not owe it to the future to expose them continually to literature that sorts out, shuffles, and explores values? Without leaders of moral fiber, strong character, and high values we tread a precarious road to the future. The world's libraries are full of imaginative fairy and folk tales that stimulate growth in these areas. Teachers must be sure that the classroom vibrates with such books, and that quickened minds are directed to them.

Beauty does not leap out of a bed of flowers spontaneously, nor does it leap from the pages of a book. It must be planted, nurtured, encouraged; distractions must be collared; goodness must be pursued courageously and relentlessly. But seeing gifted children catapulted into an intense inner journey, through mental moments of horror as well as grace, to an awakening which ultimately blesses, is rewarding beyond all else.

It is significant indeed that so many outstanding thinkers of our day tell of a childhood rich with fairy tales and fantasy. When Albert Einstein was asked what children should read that would best help them to become scientists, his response was "fairy tales." If future experts in technology have also a vision of a more compassionate humanity, the uses of science can be directed toward the benefit, not the destruction, of life.

A college student, nourished joyfully throughout her childhood by a story-telling father (an elementary school principal!) recently read *The Dark Is Rising*, by Susan Cooper. "This book made a profound impact on me," she confessed.

> It spoke to the child and the adult in me. As a child, it spoke because of the imaginative stimulus and the strong thread of good versus evil that runs throughout. It left me feeling strong, fulfilled, confident in the power of the good — 'the light.' As an adult it spoke on all of these strengths, and on deeper things. It is pure poetry. I could read it for the sheer beauty of its images and descriptions. The symbolism is striking — giving much food for thought. It changed me. It reopened a lot of mental doors — doors that enabled me to drop a cynical attitude about the miraculous. At this point, I'm not sure any more. Perhaps I, like Will Stanton, am also an 'old one' — a special chosen person whose duty it is to serve 'the light' and preserve all that is good in the world.

This college senior has been awarded a Fulbright Scholarship, and plans to spend the summer, before her year in the recesses of research in German libraries, giving of herself in taking care of a bed-ridden grandmother. This is her thoughtful choice. Her intellect has not outrun her heart. Fairy and folk tales have been a basic part of her past.

Throughout all time, our inspired tellers of tales have reminded us that love and life are inseparable. Their concerns for mankind have been welded to their spaciousness of vision as they have created new worlds for exploration. In these worlds of clarity our gifted children will cavort in disembodied flight, discovering fundamental truths popping up as suddenly as toadstools and comments on contemporary society sneaking in on chicken-feet behind a black cloak. For alert and quick-witted readers these are exciting quests for identity, self-knowledge, and moral stability.

If our gifted children are at home in fairyland, perhaps they can help to make our world home a bit more secure. If they have reached a higher resource beyond pure knowledge and reason, if they have caught a vision from a myth, if they have been touched by inspiration in a fairy tale, their lives will attest their faith. Having spoken freely with their most noble ancestors in folk tales, who have shared eternal convictions in the power of love and freedom, tomorrow's children will be able to direct a new history with less desire for personal power and more awareness of the eternal powers.

Kornei Chukovsky, the most beloved author of books for Russian children, has said about early childhood,

> The young child uses fantasy as a means of learning, and adjusts it to reality in the exact amounts his need demands. The present belongs to the sober, the cautious, the routine-prone, but the future belongs to those who do not rein in their imaginations.

Let us help to unleash our gifted — so that they may lead us all into the light.

APPENDICES

Appendix I

Selection Aids to Assist in the Development of Unit Models

Adventuring with Books: A Booklist for Pre-K to Grade 8, by Patricia Cianciolo. Urbana, IL: National Council of Teachers of English, 1977.

African Asian Reading Guide for Children and Young Adults, compiled by Jeanette Hotchkiss. Metuchen, NJ: Scarecrow Press, 1976.

American Historical Fiction and Biography for Children and Young People, compiled by Jeanette Hotchkiss. Metuchen, NJ: Scarecrow Press, 1973.

The Black Experience in Children's Books, by Barbara Rollock. New York: Public Library, 1974.

The Bookfinder: A Guide to Children's Literature about the Needs and Problems of Youth Aged 2-15, by Sharon Dryer. Circle Pines, MN: American Guidance Service, 1977.

Children's Books of International Interest, by Virginia Haviland. Chicago: American Library Association, 1978.

Children's Books Too Good to Miss, by May Hill Arbuthnot, et al. New York: University Press Book Service, 1971.

Folklore: An Annotated Bibliography and Index to Single Editions, by Elsie B. Ziegler. Westwood, MA: Faxon, 1973.

A Guide to Non-Sexist Children's Books, compiled by Judith Adell and Hilary Klein. Chicago: Academy Chicago, 1976.

Independent Reading Grades One through Three, by Gale S. Jacob. Greensboro, NC: Bro-Dart, 1975.

Juniorplots: A Book Talk Manual, by Diana Lembo and John T. Gillespie. New York: Bowker, 1967.

Literature by and about the American Indian, by Anna Lee Stensland. Urbana, IL: National Council of Teachers of English, 1973.

Reading Ladders for Human Relations, edited by Virginia Reid. Washington, DC: American Council on Education, 1972.

Subject Guide to Children's Books in Print. New York: Bowker, 1979.

FOR ADDITIONAL READING ON GIFTED EDUCATION

Adams, James. *Conceptual Blockbusting.* San Francisco Book Company, 1976.

Ellis, Albert, and Robert A. Harper. *A New Guide to Rational Living.* Englewood Cliffs, NJ: Prentice-Hall, 1975.

Fabun, Don. *Three Roads to Awareness: Motivation, Creativity, Communications.* Beverly Hills, CA: Glencoe Press, 1970.

Freehill, Maurice. *Gifted Children: Their Psychology and Education.* New York: Macmillan Co., 1961.

Gowan, John. *The Academically Talented Student and Guidance.* Boston: Houghton Mifflin, 1971.

Guilford, J. P. *Intelligence, Creativity and Their Educational Implications.* San Diego, CA: Robert Knapp Publisher, 1968.

Hanks, Kurt. *Design Yourself!* Los Altos, CA: Wm. Kaufmann, 1977.

Hauck, Barbara, and Maurice Freehill. *The Gifted Case Studies.* Dubuque, IA: W. C. Brown Co., 1972.

Hildreth, Gertrude. *Introduction to the Gifted.* New York: McGraw Hill, 1966.

Nutt, Grady. *Being Me.* Nashville, TN: Broadman Press, 1971.

Raph, Jane. *Bright Underachievers.* New York: Teachers College Press, 1976.

Thomas, George, and Joseph Creslimbini. *Guiding the Gifted Child.* New York: Random House, 1966.

Torrance, E. Paul. *Rewarding Creative Behavior.* Englewood Cliffs, NJ: Prentice-Hall, 1965.

Vail, Pricilla. *World of the Gifted Child.* New York: Walker & Co., 1979.

Appendix II
UNIT STUDIES

SUGGESTED TOPICS AND TITLES FOR PRIMARY GRADES

Families

Alexander, Martha. *Nobody Asked Me If I Wanted a Baby Sister.* New York: Dial, 1971. (Gr. K-2).

Blaine, Marge. *The Terrible Thing That Happened at Our House.* New York: Parents Magazine Press, 1975. Pictures by John C. Wallner. (ps-3).

Buckley, Helen. *Grandfather & I.* New York: Lothrop, Lee & Shepard Co., 1959. Picture by Paul Galdone. (Gr. K-3).

Buckley, Helen. *Grandmother & I.* New York: Lothrop, Lee & Shephard Co., 1961. Pictures by Paul Galdone. (Gr. K-3).

Carle, Eric. *The Secret Birthday Message.* New York: Crowell, 1972. (ps-3).

Carrick, Carol. *The Accident.* New York: Seabury, 1976. Pictures by Donald Carrick. (ps-3).

Carrick, Carol. *The Foundling.* New YorK: Seabury, 1976. Pictures by Donald Carrick. (ps-4).

Caudill, Rebecca. *A Pocketful of Cricket.* New York: Holt, Rinehart & Winston, 1964. Illustrated by Evaline Nees. (Gr. K-4).

Dubois, William Pene. *Lazy Tommy Pumpkinhead.* New York: Harper and Row, 1966. (Gr. 1-5).

Greenfield, Eloise. *She Come Bringing Me That Little Baby Girl.* Philadelphia, Lippincott, 1974. Illustrated by John Steptoe. (Gr. K-3).

Heide, Florence. *Shrinking of Treehorn.* New York: Holiday House, 1971. Drawings by Edward Gorey. (Gr. K-3).

Hoban, Russell. *A Baby Sister for Frances.* New York: Harper and Row, 1964. Pictures by Lillian Holan. (ps-2).

Shulevitz, Uri. *One Monday Morning.* New York: Scribner's, 1967. (Gr. K-3).

Viorst, Judith. *Alexander & the Terrible, Horrible, No Good, Very Bad Day.* New York: Atheneum, 1972. Illustrated by Ray Cruz. (Gr. K-3).

Waber, Bernard. *Ira Sleeps Over.* Boston: Houghton Mifflin, 1972. (Gr. K-3).

Zolotow, Charlotte. *If It Weren't for You.* New York: Harper and Row, 1966. Pictures by Ben Shecter. (Gr. K-3).

Friendship

Balian, Lorna. *The Aminal.* Nashville, TN: Abingdon, 1973. (ps-2).

Clifton, Lucille. *Everett Anderson's Friend.* New York: Holt, Rinehart & Winston, 1976. Illustrated by Ann Grifalconi. (Gr. K-3).

Clifton, Lucille. *My Brother Fine With Me.* New York: Holt, Rinehart & Winston, 1975. Illustrated by Moneta Barnett. (Gr. K-3).

Cohen, Miriam. *Best Friends.* New York: Macmillan, 1971. Pictures by Lillian Hoban. (ps-1).

Cohen, Miriam. *Will I Have a Friend?* New York: Macmillan, 1967. Pictures by Lillian Hoban. (Gr. K-1).

Ets, Marie Hall. *Play with Me.* New York: Viking, 1955. (ps-1).

Lobel, Arnold. *Frog & Toad Are Friends.* New York: Harper & Row, 1970. (Gr. K-3).

Lobel, Arnold. *Frog & Toad Together.* New York: Harper & Row, 1972. (Gr. K-3).

Ness, Evalene. *Sam, Bangs and Moonshine.* New York: Holt, Rinehart & Winston, 1966. (ps-2).

Burningham, John. *Seasons*. Indianapolis, In: Bobbs-Merrill, 1970. (Gr. 1-4).

Ets, Marie Hall. *Gilberto and the Wind*. New York: Viking, 1963. (ps-1).

Freschet, Berniece. *The Ants Go Marching*. New York: Scribner's, 1973. Illustrated by Stefan Martin. (Gr. K-3).

Freschet, Berniece. *The Old Bullfrog*. New York: Scribner's, 1968. Illustrated by Roger Duvoisin.

Freschet, Berniece. *The Turtle Pond*. New York: Scribner's, 1971. (Gr. K-3).

Freschet, Berniece. *The Web in the Grass*. New York: Scribner's, 1972. Illustrated by Roger Duvoisin. (Gr. K-2).

George, Jean. *All Upon a Stone*. New York: Crowell, 1971. Illustrated by Don Bolognese. (Gr. 2-5).

Schoenherr, John. *The Barn*. Boston: Little, Brown, 1968. (ps-3).

Stone, A. Harris. *The Last Free Bird*. Englewood Cliffs, NJ: Prentice-Hall, 1967. Illustrated by Sheila Heins. (ps-3).

Tresselt, Alvin. *Beaver Pond*. New York: Lothrop, Lee & Shephard, 1970. Illustrated by Roger Duvoisin. (Gr. K-3).

Tresselt, Alvin. *Dead Tree*. New York: Parents Magazine Press, 1972. Illustrated by Charles Robinson. (Gr. K-4).

Tresselt, Alvin. *White Snow Bright Snow*. New York: Lothrop, Lee & Shephard, 1947.

Yashima, Taro. *The Village Tree*. New York: Penguin, 1972. (Gr. K-3).

Zolotow, Charlotte. *The Storm Book*. New York: Harper & Row, 1952. Illustrated by Margaret B. Graham. (Gr. K-3).

Animals Everywhere

Conford, Ellen. *Impossible Possum*. Boston: Little, Brown, 1971. (Gr. 1-3).

Cooney, Barbara, illus. *Chanticleer and the Fox*. New York: Crowell, 1958. (Gr. K-3).

DeBrunhoff, Jean. *Story of Babar*. New York: Random, 1960. (ps).

Fatio, Louise. *The Happy Lion*. New York: McGraw Hill, 1954. Illustrated by Roger Duvoisin. (Gr. K-3).

Kraus, Robert. *Gondolier of Venice*. New York: Windmill, 1976. (Gr. 4-6).

Kraus, Robert. *Pinchpenny Mouse*. New York: Windmill, 1974. Illustrated by Robert Byrd. (ps-3).

Lionni, Leo. *Frederick*. New York: Pantheon, 1966. (Gr. K-3).

Lionni, Leo. *Swimmy*. New York: Pantheon, 1963. (ps).

McClosky, Robert. *Make Way for Ducklings*. New York: Viking, 1941. (Gr. K-3).

Miles, Miska. *Nobody's Cat*. Boston: Little, Brown, 1970. Illustrated by John Schoenherr. (Gr. 1-3).

Miles, Miska. *Wharf Rat*. Boston: Little, Brown, 1972. Illustrated by John Schoenherr. (Gr. 1-3).

Potter, Beatrix. *Tale of Peter Rabbit*. New York: Warne, 1902. (Gr. K-2).

Rayner, Mary. *Mr. & Mrs. Pig's Evening Out*. New York: Atheneum, 1976. (Gr. K-2).

Seuss, Dr. *Thidwick the Big Hearted Moose*. New York: Random House, 1948. (Gr. K-3).

Steig, William. *The Amazing Bone*. New York: Farrar, Straus, & Giroux, 1976. (ps-3).

Ward, Lynd. *The Biggest Bear*. Boston: Houghton Mifflin, 1952. (Gr. K-3).

Folktales

Andersen, Hans C. *Emperor's New Clothes*. New York: Random House, 1971. (Gr. K-3).

Andersen, Hans C. *The Nightingale*. New York: Van Nostrand, 1969. (Gr. 3-up).

Andersen, Hans C. *Princess & the Pea*. New York: Seabury, 1978.

Andersen, Hans C. *Steadfast Tin Soldier*. New York: Atheneum, 1971. (ps-2).

Andersen, Hans C. *Thumbelina*. New York: Van Nostrand, 1973. (Gr. 1-4).

Andersen, Hans C. *Ugly Duckling*. New York: Scribner's, 1965.

Briggs, Raymond. *Jim & the Beanstalk*. New York: Coward, 1970. (Gr. K-3).

Brown, Marcia. *Once a Mouse*. New York: Scribner's, 1961. (Gr. K-2).

Domanska, Janina. *The Turnip*. New York: Macmillan, 1969. (Gr. K-3).

Gag, Wanda. *Nothing at All*. New York: Coward-McCann, 1941. (Gr. 1-3).

LaFontaine, Jeande. *The North Wind & the Sun*. New York: Watts, 1964. Illustrated by Brian Wildsmith.

Ryan, Cheli. *Hildilid's Night*. New York: Macmillan, 1971.

Zemach, Harve. *The Judge*. New York: Farrar, Straus & Giroux, 1969. Illustrated by Arnold Lobel. (Gr. K-3).

Long Ago and Far Away

Bemmelmans, Ludwig. *Madeline*. New York: Viking, 1962. (Gr. K-3).

Bemmelmans, Ludwig. *Madeline's Rescue*. New York: Viking, 1953. (Gr. K-3).

Bryant, Sara. *The Burning Rice Fields*. New York: Holt, Rinehart & Winston, 1963.

DePaola, Tomie. *Helga's Dowry*. New York: Harcourt, Brace, Jovanovich, 1977.

Ets, Marie Hall, and Aurora Labastida. *Nine Days to Christmas*. New York: Viking, 1959. (ps-2).

Hodges, Margaret. *The Wave*. Boston: Houghton Mifflin, 1964. Illustrated by B. Lent. (Gr. K-3).

Leaf, Munro. *Wee Gillis*. New York: Viking, 1938. Illustrated by Robert Lawson. (Gr. K-3).

Lobel, Arnold. *On the Day Peter Stuyvesant Sailed into Town*. New York: Harper & Row, 1971. (ps-3).

Matsuno, Masako. *A Pair of Red Clogs*. Cleveland, OH: Collins-World, 1960. Illustrated by Kazue Mizumura. (Gr. K-3).

Small, Ernest, and Blair Lent. *Baba Yaga*. Boston: Houghton Mifflin, 1966. (Gr. K-3).

Turkle, Brinton. *Obadiah the Bold*. New York: Viking, 1965. (Gr. K-3).

SUGGESTED TOPICS AND TITLES
FOR INTERMEDIATE GRADES

Folktales

Aardema, Verna. *Behind the Back of the Mountain: Black Folktales from Southern Africa.* New York: Dial, 1973. (Gr. 2-6).

Asbjornsen, Peter Christian, and Jorgen E. Moe. *East of the Sun and West of the Moon.* New York: Macmillan, 1953. (Gr. K-3). (Norway).

Bang, Molly. *Wiley and the Hairy Man.* New York: Macmillan, 1976. (Gr. 1-4). (United States).

Berson, Harold. *How the Devil Gets His Due.* New York: Crown, 1972. (Gr. K-2). (France).

Berson, Harold. *The Thief Who Hugged a Moonbeam.* New York: Seabury, 1972. (Gr. K-3). (France).

Bierhorst, John, ed. *The Girl Who Married a Ghost and Other Tales from the North American Indian.* New York: Four Winds, 1978. (Gr. 5-up). (American-Indian).

Bishop, Claire Hutchet. *The Five Chinese Brothers.* New York: Coward-McCann, 1938. (Gr. K-3).

Brown, Marcia. *The Bun: A Tale from Russia.* New York: Harcourt, Brace, and Jovanovich, 1972. (Gr. K-3).

Brown, Marcia, adapt. *The Flying Carpet.* New York: Scribner's, 1956. (Arabia).

Brown, Margaret Wise, adapt. *Brer Rabbit: Stories from Uncle Remus.* New York: Harper and Row, 1941. Illustrated by A. B. Frost. (Gr. 1-5). (Black American).

Carpenter, Frances. *Tales of a Chinese Grandmother.* Rutland, VT: C. E. Tuttle, 1972. Illustrated by Malthe Hasselriie. (Gr. 3-8).

Chase, Richard. *Grandfather Tales.* Boston: Houghton Mifflin, 1948. (Gr. 4-6). (United States).

Courlander, Harold. *The King's Drum and Other African Stories.* New York: Harcourt, Brace, and Jovanovich, 1962. Illustrated by Enrico Arno. (Gr. 3-7).

Courlander, Harold. *The Son of the Leopard.* New York: Crown, 1974. Woodcuts by Rocco Negri. (Africa).

Courlander, Harold, and George Herzog. *The Cow-tail Switch and Other West African Stories*. New York: Holt, Rinehart & Winston, 1962. Illustrated by Madge L. Chastain. (Gr. 4-6).

Daniels, Guy, trans. *Foma the Terrible*. New York: Delacorte, 1970. (Russia).

De la Mare, Walter. *Tales Told Again*. New York: Knopf, 1946 (1927).

Emrich, Duncan. *The Hodgepodge Book: An Almanac of American Folklore*. New York: Four Winds, 1972. Illustrated by Ib Ohlsson. (Gr. 1-up).

Felton, Harold W. *True Tall Tales of Stormalong: Sailor of the Seven Seas*. Englewood Cliffs, NJ: Prentice-Hall, 1968. Illustrated by Joan Sandin. (United States).

Ginsburg, Mirra. *The Lazies: Tales of the Peoples of Russia*. New York: Macmillan, 1973. Illustrated by Marian Parry. (Gr. 3-6).

Grimm Brothers. *About Wise Men and Simpletons: Twelve Tales from Grimm*, translated by Elizabeth Shub. New York: Macmillan, 1971. Illustrated by Nonny Hogrogian. (Gr. 3-6).

Grimm Brothers. *The Donkey Prince*. Retold by M. Jean Craig. New York: Doubleday, 1977. Illustrated by Barbara Cooney.

Grimm Brothers. *The Juniper Tree and Other Tales from Grimm*, translated by Lore Segal and Randall Jarrell. New York: Farrar, Straus, & Giroux, 1973. (Gr. 4-up).

Harris, Christie. *Mouse Woman and the Mischief-Makers*. New York: Atheneum, 1977. Illustrated by Douglas Tait. (Gr. 4-6). (American-Indian).

Heady, Eleanor B. *When the Stones Were Soft, East African Fireside Tales*. New York: Funk & Wagnalls, 1968.

Hoge, Dorothy. *The Black Heart of Indri*. New York: Scribner's, 1966. (China).

Holladay, Virginia. *Bantu Tales*, edited by Louise Crane. New York: Viking, 1970. Woodcuts by Rocco Negri. (Africa).

Jagendorf, Moritz A. *Noodlehead Stories from around the World*. New York: Vanguard, 1957. Illustrated by Shane Miller. (Gr. 4-6).

Lang, Andrew. *The Arabian Nights*. New York: Watts, 1967. Illustrated by Vera Bock.

Leach, Maria. *Noodles, Nitwits and Numskulls.* Cleveland, OH: Collins-World, 1961. Illustrated by Kurt Werth. (Gr. 3-5).

Lester, Julius. *The Knee-High Man and Other Tales.* New York: Dial, 1972. Illustrated by Ralph Pinto. (ps-3). (Black American).

McDermott, Gerald. *Anansi the Spider.* New York: Penguin, 1977. (Gr. K-3). (Africa).

Malcolmson, Anne. *Yankee Doodle's Cousins.* Boston: Houghton Mifflin, 1941. Illustrated by R. McCloskey. (Gr. 4-8). (United States).

Manning-Sanders, Ruth. *A Book of Charms and Changelings.* New York: Dutton, 1972. (Gr. 2-6).

Melzack, Ronald. *Raven, Creator of the World.* Boston: Little, Brown, 1970. Illustrated by Laszlo Gal. (Eskimo).

Merrill, Jean. *The Superlative Horse.* New York: W. R. Scott, 1961. (Gr. 4-7). (China).

Nic Leodhas, Sorche, pseud. (Leclaire Alger). *Gaelic Ghosts.* New York: Holt, Rinehart & Winston, 1963.

Nic Leodhas, Sorche, pseud. (Leclaire Alger). *Ghosts Go Haunting.* New York: Holt, Rinehart & Winston, 1965. Illustrated by Nonny Hogrogian.

Nic Leodhas, Sorche, pseud. (Leclaire Alger). *Twelve Great Black Cats and Other Eerie Scottish Tales.* New York: Dutton, 1971. Illustrated by Vera Bock.

Ransome, Arthur. *The Fool of the World and the Flying Ship.* New York: Farrar, Straus, & Giroux, 1968. Illustrated by Uri Shulevitz. (ps-3). (Russia).

Rees, Ennis. *Brer Rabbit and His Tricks.* New York: Young Scott Books, 1967. Drawings by Edward Gorey. (Gr. K-4). (Black American).

Shapiro, Irwin. *Heroes in American Folklore.* New York: Messner, 1962. Illustrated by Donald McKay and James Daugherty. (Gr. 5-up).

Sherlock, Philip K. *Anansi the Spider Man, Jamaican Folk Tales.* New York: Crowell, 1954. Illustrated by Marcia Brown. (Gr. 3-7).

Singer, Isaac Bashevis. *The Fools of Chelm and Their History.* Translated by Elizabeth Shub. New York: Farrar, Straus, & Giroux, 1973. Illustrated by Uri Shulevitz. (Gr. 4-up). (Jewish).

Singer, Isaac Bashevis. *When Shlemiel Went to Warsaw and Other Stories,* translated by the author and Elizabeth Shub. New York: Farrar, Straus, & Giroux, 1968. Illustrated by Margot Zemach. (Gr. 4-up). (Jewish).

Steel, Flora Annie. *English Fairy Tales.* New York: Macmillan, 1962 (1918). Illustrated by Arthur Rackham.

Uchida, Yoshiko. *The Dancing Kettle and Other Japanese Folk Tales.* New York: Harcourt, Brace, Jovanovich, 1949. Illustrated by Richard C. Jones. (Gr. 4-6).

Van Woerkom, Dorothy. *The Rat, the Ox, and the Zodiac.* New York: Crown, 1976. Illustrated by Errol Le Cain. (Gr. K-3). (China).

Wyndham, Lee. *Tales the People Tell in Russia.* New York: Messner, 1970. Illustrated by Andrew Antal. (Gr. 3-5).

Fantasy

Babbitt, Natalie. *Eyes of the Amaryllis.* New York: Farrar, Straus, & Giroux, 1977. (Gr. 4-up).

Babbitt, Natalie. *Kneeknock Rise.* New York: Farrar, Straus, & Giroux, 1970. (Gr. 4-up).

Babbitt, Natalie. *Tuck Everlasting.* New York: Farrar, Straus, & Giroux, 1975. (Gr. 4-up).

Bond, Nancy. *A String in the Harp.* New York: Atheneum, 1976. (Gr. 5-9).

Boston, Lucy M. *The Children of Green Knowe.* New York: Harcourt, Brace, Jovanovich, 1967. Illustrated by Peter Boston. (Gr. 4-6).

Boston, Lucy M. *The Sea Egg.* New York: Harcourt, Brace, Jovanovich, 1967. Illustrated by Peter Boston. (Gr. 2-5).

Cameron, Eleanor. *The Court of the Stone Children.* New York: Dutton, 1973. (Gr. 5-up).

Carroll, Lewis, pseud. (Charles L. Dodgson). *Alice's Adventures in Wonderland and Through the Looking Glass.* New York: Macmillan, 1963 (1865, 1872).

Christopher, John. *Beyond the Burning Lands.* New York: Macmillan, 1971. (Gr. 5-9).

Christopher, John. *The Pool of Fire.* New York: Macmillan, 1968. (Gr. 5-7).

Collodi, Carlo. *The Adventures of Pinocchio.* New York: Macmillan, 1963 (1892). Illustrated by Naiad Einsel. (Gr. 3-6).

Cooper, Susan. *The Dark Is Rising.* New York: Atheneum, 1973. Illustrated by Alan Cober. (Gr. 4-9).

Cooper, Susan. *The Greenwitch*. New York: Atheneum, 1974. Illustrated by Michael Heslop. (Gr. 4-7).

Cooper, Susan. *The Grey King*. New York: Atheneum, 1975. (Gr. 4-9).

Cooper, Susan. *Over Sea, Under Stone*. New York: Harcourt, Brace, Jovanovich, 1966. Illustrated by Marjorie Gill. (Gr. 4-6).

Cooper, Susan. *Silver on the Tree*. New York: Atheneum, 1977. (Gr. 5-9).

Cunningham, Julia. *Macaroon*. New York: Pantheon, 1962. Illustrated by E. Ness. (Gr. 3-6).

Dahl, Roald. *James and the Giant Peach*. New York: Knopf, 1961. Illustrated by Nancy Burkert. (Gr. 3-up).

Dickinson, Peter. *The Devil's Children*. Boston: Little, Brown, 1970.

Dickinson, Peter. *Emma Tupper's Diary*. Boston: Little, Brown, 1971. Illustrated by David O. White. (Gr. 7-up).

Dickinson, Peter. *Heartsease*. Boston: Little, Brown, 1969.

Dickinson, Peter. *The Weathermonger*. Boston: Little, Brown, 1969.

Du Bois, William Péne. *The Twenty-one Balloons*. New York: Viking, 1947. (Gr. 5-9).

Engdahl, Sylvia Louise. *Beyond the Tomorrow Mountains*. New York: Atheneum, 1973. Illustrated by Richard Cuffari. (Gr. 7-up).

Engdahl, Sylvia Louise. *Enchantress from the Stars*. New York: Atheneum, 1970. (Gr. 6-up).

Engdahl, Sylvia Louise. *The Far Side of Evil*. New York: Atheneum, 1971. Illustrated by Richard Cuffari. (Gr. 7-9).

Engdahl, Sylvia Louise. *This Star Shall Abide*. New York: Atheneum, 1972. Illustrated by Richard Cuffari. (Gr. 5-9).

Garfield, Leon. *The Ghost Downstairs*. New York: Pantheon, 1972. Illustrated by Anthony Maitland. (Gr. 7-up).

Garner, Alan. *Elidor*. Edited by Linda Davis. Cleveland, OH: Collins, 1979. (Gr. 5-up).

Godden, Rumer. *The Dolls' House*. New York: Viking, 1962 (1947). Illustrated by Tasha Tudor.

Grahame, Kenneth. *The Wind in the Willows*. New York: Scribner's, 1940 (1908). Illustrated by Ernest H. Shepard. (Gr. 4-up).

Hoban, Russell. *The Mouse and His Child.* New York: Harper & Row, 1967. Illustrated by Lillian Hoban. (Gr. 1-5).

Hunter, Mollie, pseud. (Maureen McIlwraith). *The Kelpie's Pearls.* New York: Harper & Row, 1976. Illustrated by Steven Gammell. (Gr. 3-7).

Jarrell, Randall. *The Animal Family.* New York: Pantheon, 1965. Illustrated by Maurice Sendak. (Gr. 3-up).

Juster, Norton. *The Phantom Tollbooth.* New York: Random House, 1961. (Gr. 5-up).

Kendall, Carol. *The Gammage Cup.* New York: Harcourt, Brace, Jovanovich, 1959. Illustrated by Eric Blegvad. (Gr. 4-6).

LeGuin, Ursula K. *The Farthest Shore.* New York: Atheneum, 1972. Illustrated by Gail Garraty. (Gr. 5-up).

LeGuin, Ursula K. *The Tombs of Atuan.* New York: Atheneum, 1971. Illustrated by Gail Garraty. (Gr. 5-8).

LeGuin, Ursula K. *A Wizard of Earthsea.* Emeryville, CA: Parnassus, 1968. Illustrated by Ruth Robbins. (Gr. 5-up).

L'Engle, Madeleine. *A Wrinkle in Time.* New York: Farrar, Straus, & Giroux, 1962. (Gr. 7-up).

Lewis, C. S. *The Horse and His Boy.* New York: Macmillan, 1970. (Gr. 5-up).

Lewis, C. S. *The Lion, the Witch, and the Wardrobe.* New York: Macmillan, 1970. (Gr. 5-up).

MacDonald, George. *The Golden Key.* New York: Farrar, Straus, & Giroux, 1976. Illustrated by Maurice Sendak. (Gr. 4-up).

MacDonald, George. *The Light Princess.* New York: Crowell, 1962. Illustrated by William Péne Du Bois. (Gr. 1-5).

Mayne, William. *Earthfasts.* New York: Dutton, 1966. (Gr. 5-up).

Merrill, Jean. *The Pushcart War.* New York: W. R. Scott, 1964. Illustrated by Ronni Solbert. (Gr. 4-8).

O'Brien, Robert C. *Mrs. Frisby and the Rats of Nimh.* New York: Atheneum, 1971. Illustrated by Zena Bernstein. (Gr. 3-7).

Pearce, Ann Philippa. *Tom's Midnight Garden.* Philadelphia: Lippincott, 1959.

Saint-Exupéry, Antoine De. *The Little Prince*. New York: Harcourt, Brace, Jovanovich, 1943. (Gr. 3-7).

Sleator, William. *Blackbriar*. New York: Dutton, 1972. Illustrated by Blair Lent. (Gr. 5-8).

Steig, William. *Abel's Island*. New York: Farrar, Straus, & Giroux, 1976. (Gr. 4-up).

Tolkien, J. R. R. *The Hobbit*. Boston: Houghton Mifflin, 1973.

Wrightson, Patricia. *Down to Earth*. New York: Harcourt, Brace, Jovanovich, 1965. Illustrated by Margaret Horder. (Gr. 4-6).

Realism
(can be divided into specific categories)

Burch, Robert. *Queenie Peavy*. New York: Viking, 1966. Illustrated by Jerry Lazare. (Gr. 4-7).

Byars, Betsy. *After the Goat Man*. New York: Viking, 1974. Illustrated by Ronald Himler. (Gr. 5-9).

Byars, Betsy. *Summer of the Swans*. New York: Viking, 1970. Illustrated by Ted Colonis. (Gr. 7-up).

Cameron, Eleanor. *Julia and the Hand of God*. New York: Dutton, 1977. Illustrated by Gail Owens.

Cleaver, Vera, and Bill Cleaver. *Ellen Grae*. Philadelphia: Lippincott, 1967. Illustrated by Ellen Raskin. (Gr. 4-6).

Cleaver, Vera, and Bill Cleaver. *Grover*. Philadelphia: Lippincott, 1970.

Cleaver, Vera, and Bill Cleaver. *Me, Too*. Philadelphia: Lippincott, 1973. (Gr. 7-9).

Cleaver, Vera, and Bill Cleaver. *Where the Lilies Bloom*. Philadelphia: Lippincott, 1969. (Gr. 4-9).

Cunningham, Julia. *Burnish Me Bright*. New York: Pantheon, 1970. Illustrated by Don Freeman. (Gr. 5-8).

Cunningham, Julia. *Drop Dead*. New York: Pantheon, 1965. Illustrated by J. Spanfeller. (Gr. 5-9).

Dickinson, Peter. *The Gift*. Boston: Little, Brown, 1974. (Gr. 7-12).

Fitzhugh, Louise. *Harriet the Spy*. New York: Harper & Row, 1964. (Gr. 5-up).

Fox, Paula. *Blowfish Live in the Sea.* Englewood Cliffs, NJ: Bradbury, 1970. (Gr. 6-8).

Friis-Baastad, Babbis. *Don't Take Teddy.* Translated by Lise McKinnon. New York: Scribner's, 1967.

Garfield, James B. *Follow My Leader.* New York: Viking, 1957. Illustrated by Robert Greiner. (Gr. 4-7).

George, Jean. *Gull Number 737.* New York: Crowell, 1964. (Gr. 5-10).

George, Jean. *My Side of the Mountain.* New York: Dutton, 1967. (Gr. 4-9).

Greene, Bette. *Philip Hall Likes Me, I Reckon Maybe.* New York: Dial, 1974. Illustrated by Charles Lilly. (Gr. 3-6).

Greene, Constance C. *Beat the Turtle Drum.* New York: Viking, 1976. Illustrated by Donna Diamond. (Gr. 4-6).

Greenfield, Eloise. *Sister.* New York: Crowell, 1974. Illustrated by Moneta Barnett. (Gr. 5-12).

Griffiths, Helen. *The Wild Heart.* New York: Doubleday, 1963. Illustrated by Victor G. Ambrus.

Hamilton, Virginia. *The House of Dies Drear.* New York: Macmillan, 1968. Illustrated by Eros Keith. (Gr. 5-up).

Hamilton, Virginia. *M. C. Higgins, the Great.* New York: Macmillan, 1974. (Gr. 7-up).

Hamilton, Virginia. *The Planet of Junior Brown.* New York: Macmillan, 1971. (Gr. 7-up).

Hamilton, Virginia. *Zeely.* New York: Macmillan, 1967. Illustrated by Symeon Shimin. (Gr. 5-8).

Killilea, Marie. *Wren.* New York: Dodd, Mead, 1954. Illustrated by Bob Riger. (Gr. 3-7).

Klein, Norma. *Confessions of an Only Child.* New York: Pantheon, 1974. Illustrated by Richard Cuffari. (Gr. 3-7).

Konigsburg, E. L. *From the Mixed-Up Files of Mrs. Basil E. Frankweiler.* New York: Atheneum, 1967. (Gr. 3-7).

Konigsburg, E. L. *Jennifer, Hecate, MacBeth, William McKinley and Me, Elizabeth.* New York: Atheneum, 1967. (Gr. 3-8).

Lenski, Lois. *Strawberry Girl.* Philadelphia: Lippincott, 1945. (Gr. 4-6).

Little, Jean. *Kate.* New York: Harper & Row, 1971. (Gr. 5-7).

Little, Jean. *Take Wing.* Boston: Little, Brown, 1968. (Gr. 3-7).

Mann, Peggy. *My Dad Lives in a Downtown Hotel.* New York: Doubleday, 1973. (Gr. 5).

Mathis, Sharon Bell. *The Hundred Penny Box.* New York: Viking, 1975. Illustrated by Leo Dillon and Diane Dillon. (Gr. K-3).

Mathis, Sharon Bell. *Teacup Full of Roses.* New York: Viking, 1972. (Gr. 7).

Miles, Miska. *Annie and the Old One.* Boston: Little, Brown, 1971. Illustrated by Peter Parnall. (Gr. 1-3).

Neville, Emily C. *Berries Goodman.* New York: Harper & Row, 1965. (Gr. 5-9).

O'Dell, Scott. *Island of the Blue Dolphins.* Boston: Houghton Mifflin, 1960. (Gr. 7-up).

Paterson, Katherine. *Bridge to Terabithia.* New York: Crowell, 1977. Illustrated by Donna Diamond. (Gr. 5-up).

Paterson, Katherine. *The Great Gilly Hopkins.* New York: Crowell, 1978. (Gr. 5-up).

Robinson, Barbara. *The Best Christmas Pageant Ever.* New York: Harper & Row, 1972. Illustrated by Judith C. Brown. (Gr. 3-up).

Robinson, Veronica. *David in Silence.* Philadelphia: Lippincott, 1965. Illustrated by Victor Ambrus. (Gr. 5-7).

Rockwell, Thomas. *How to Eat Fried Worms.* New York: F. Watts, 1973. Pictures by Emily McCully. (Gr. 4-6).

Smith, Doris Buchanan. *A Taste of Blackberries.* New York: Crowell, 1973. Illustrated by Charles Robinson. (Gr. 2-5).

Stevenson, William. *The Bushbabies.* Boston: Houghton Mifflin, 1965. Illustrated by Victor Ambrus. (Gr. 4-6).

Taylor, Mildred D. *Roll of Thunder, Hear My Cry.* New York: Dial, 1976. Illustrated by Jerry Pinkney. (Gr. 6-up).

Ullman, James Ramsey. *Banner in the Sky.* Philadelphia: Lippincott, 1954. (Gr. 7-9).

Wier, Ester. *The Loner.* New York: McKay, 1963. Illustrated by Christine Price. (Gr. 7-9).

Wojciechowska, Maia. *Shadow of a Bull.* New York: Atheneum, 1964. Illustrated by Alvin Smith. (Gr. 5-up).

Wrightson, Patricia. *A Racecourse for Andy.* New York: Harcourt, Brace, Jovanovich, 1968. Illustrated by Margaret Horder. (Gr. 4-6).

Yep, Laurence. *Child of the Owl.* New York: Harper & Row, 1977. (Gr. 7-up).

Yep, Laurence. *Dragonwings.* (New York: Harper & Row, 1975. (Gr. 7-up).

Animal Stories

Burnford, Sheila. *The Incredible Journey.* Boston: Little, Brown, 1961. Illustrated by Carl Burger.

DeJong, Meindert. *Hurry Home, Candy.* New York: Harper & Row, 1953. Illustrated by Maurice Sendak. (Gr. 4-6).

Eckert, Allan. *Incident at Hawk's Hill.* Boston: Little, Brown, 1971. Illustrated by John Schoenherr. (Gr. 7-up).

Farley, Walter. *The Black Stallion.* New York: Random House, 1944. Illustrated by Keith Ward. (Gr. 3-7).

George, Jean. *Julie of the Wolves.* New York: Harper & Row, 1972. Illustrated by John Schoenherr. (Gr. 7-up).

Gipson, Fred. *Old Yeller.* New York: Harper & Row, 1964 (c1956).

Henry, Marguerite. *King of the Wind.* Chicago: Rand McNally, 1948. Illustrated by Wesley Dennis. (Gr. 2-9).

Henry, Marguerite. *Mustang, Wild Spirit of the West.* Chicago: Rand McNally, 1966. Illustrated by Robert Lowgheed. (Gr. 4-12).

Johnson, Annabel, and Edgar Johnson. *The Grizzly.* New York: Harper & Row, 1964. Illustrated by Gilbert Riswald. (Gr. 5-9).

Kjelgaard, Jim. *Big Red.* New York: Holiday House, 1956. Illustrated by Bob Kuhn. (Gr. 7-9).

Kjelgaard, Jim. *Snow Dog.* New York: Grosset & Dunlap, 1961. Illustrated by Jacob Landau.

Knight, Eric. *Lassie Come Home.* New York: Holt, Rinehart & Winston, 1971. Illustrated by Don Bolognese.

London, Jack. *The Call of the Wild*. New York: Macmillan, 1963. Illustrated by Karen Kezer. (Gr. 6-up).

Morey, Walt. *Gentle Ben*. New York: Dutton, 1965. Illustrated by John Schoenherr. (Gr. 5-9).

North, Sterling. *Little Rascal*. New York: Dutton, 1965. Illustrated by Carl Burger. (Gr. K-4).

North, Sterling. *Rascal, a Memoir of a Better Era*. New York: Dutton, 1963. Illustrated by John Schoenherr. (Gr. 5-up).

Rawls, Wilson. *Where the Red Fern Grows*. New York: Doubleday, 1961.

Street, James. *Goodbye, My Lady*. Philadelphia: Lippincott, 1954. (Gr. 7-9).

American History

Armstrong, William H. *Sounder*. New York: Harper & Row, 1969. (Gr. 6-up).

Beatty, Patricia. *Billy Bedamned, Long Gone By*. New York: Morrow, 1977. (Gr. 5-9).

Beatty, Patricia. *A Long Way to Whiskey Creek*. New York: Morrow, 1971. Illustrated by Franz Altschuler. (Gr. 5-9).

Brink, Carol R. *Caddie Woodlawn*. New York: Macmillan, 1970. (Gr. 4-6).

Burchard, Peter. *Jed: The Story of a Yankee Soldier & a Southern Boy*. New York: Coward-McCann, 1960.

Byars, Betsy. *Trouble River*. New York: Viking, 1969. Illustrated by Rocco Negri. (Gr. 3-7).

Caudill, Rebecca. *Tree of Freedom*. New York: Viking, 1949.

Clapp, Patricia. *Constance: A Story of Early Plymouth*. New York: Lothrop, Lee and Shephard, 1968. (Gr. 7-12).

Clapp, Patricia. *I'm Deborah Sampson: A Soldier in the War of the Revolution*. New York: Lothrop, Lee and Shephard, 1977. (Gr. 5-up).

Clements, Bruce. *The Face of Abraham Candle*. New York: Farrar, Straus, & Giroux, 1969.

Edmonds, Walter D. *The Matchlock Gun*. New York: Dodd, Mead, 1941. Illustrated by Paul Lantz. (Gr. 4-6).

Field, Rachel. *Calico Bush*. New York: Macmillan, 1966. (Gr. 7-9).

Finlayson, Ann. *Redcoat in Boston.* New York: Warne, 1971. (Gr. 7-12).

Fisher, Aileen. *A Lantern in the Window.* New York: T. Nelson, 1957. Illustrated by Harper Johnson.

Fleischman, Sid. *Mr. Mysterious and Company.* Boston: Little, Brown, 1962. Illustrated by Eric Von Schmidt. (Gr. 3-7).

Forbes, Esther. *Johnny Tremain.* Boston: Houghton Mifflin, 1946. Illustrated by Lynd Ward. (Gr. 7-9).

Graham, Gail. *Cross-Fire: A Vietnam Novel.* New York: Pantheon, 1972. (Gr. 7-up).

Hunt, Irene. *Across Five Aprils.* Chicago: Follett, 1964. (Gr. 7-up).

Keith, Harold. *Rifles for Watie.* New York: Crowell, 1957. (Gr. 7-up).

Lenski, Lois. *Indian Captive, the Story of Mary Jemison.* Philadelphia: Lippincott, 1941. (Gr. 7-9).

Meadowcroft, Enid. *By Secret Railway.* New York: Crowell, 1948. Illustrated by Henry C. Pitz. (Gr. 4-7).

O'Dell, Scott. *Sing Down the Moon.* Boston: Houghton Mifflin, 1970. (Gr. 5-up).

Petry, Ann. *Tituba of Salem Village.* New York: Crowell, 1964. (Gr. 7-11).

Richter, Conrad. *The Light in the Forest.* New York: Knopf, 1966. Illustrated by Warren Chappel. (Gr. 6-up).

Speare, Elizabeth George. *Calico Captive.* Boston: Houghton Mifflin, 1957. Illustrated by W. T. Mars. (Gr. 7-9).

Speare, Elizabeth George. *The Witch of Blackbird Pond.* Boston: Houghton Mifflin, 1958. (Gr. 7-up).

Steele, William O. *The Buffalo Knife.* New York: Harcourt, Brace, Jovanovich, 1968. Illustrated by Paul Galdone. (Gr. 4-6).

Steele, William O. *The Lone Hunt.* New York: Harcourt, Brace, Jovanovich, 1956. Illustrated by Paul Galdone. (Gr. 4-6).

Steele, William O. *The Perilous Road.* New York: Harcourt, Brace, Jovanovich, 1958. Illustrated by Paul Galdone. (Gr. 3-7).

Steele, William O. *The Year of the Bloody Sevens.* New York: Harcourt, Brace, Jovanovich, 1963. Illustrated by Charles Beck. (Gr. 4-6).

Van der Loeff, Anna Rutgers. *Oregon at Last!* New York: Morrow, 1962.

Wilder, Laura Ingalls. *The First Four Years.* New York: Harper & Row, 1971. Illustrated by Garth Williams. (Gr. 4-8).

AUTHOR/TITLE/SUBJECT INDEX

The authors and titles in this index are those of works appearing in the text or in the annotated bibliographies found throughout the book.